Ballet Dancers
in Career Transition

Ballet Dancers in Career Transition

Sixteen Success Stories

NANCY UPPER

Foreword by Kevin McKenzie

McFarland & Company, Inc., Publishers
Jefferson, North Carolina, and London

LIBRARY OF CONGRESS CATALOGUING-IN-PUBLICATION DATA

Upper, Nancy, 1943–
    Ballet dancers in career transition : sixteen success stories /
Nancy Upper ; foreword by Kevin McKenzie.
        p.   cm.
    Includes index.

    ISBN 0-7864-1819-2 (softcover : 50# alkaline paper) ∞

    1. Ballet dancers—Biography.   2. Career changes—Case
studies.   I. Title.
GV1785.A1U66   2004
792.8'092—dc22   2004002927

British Library cataloguing data are available

Cover photograph ©2004 Corbis Images

Manufactured in the United States of America

McFarland & Company, Inc., Publishers
  Box 611, Jefferson, North Carolina 28640
    www.mcfarlandpub.com

To my friend Maxene Mulford,
who planted the seed for this book.

To my agent Sally Brady,
whose deep ballet roots and superb editing
made this book thrive.

To my husband Dennis Upper,
whose steadfast love and support
nourished this book to fruition.

TABLE OF CONTENTS

FOREWORD
BY KEVIN MCKENZIE

The life of a dancer! Ah, what a glorious thing it must be... I'm sure this is what the general public thinks, with special emphasis on the "glorious." Yet every dancer in the real world is busy focusing, instead, on the "must." And no one much likes to dwell on what will happen when all the glory days are past.

I think most dancers would agree that the art of ballet chooses the dancer, not the other way around. I know: I was one of them. Being a dancer is very much like being in love. At first, nothing else much matters. You are helpless in the face of passion, and you can lose yourself within it. Once smitten, you have to give yourself unconditionally. When you settle in, you can't imagine life without it. It evokes your passionate response, completes you, and can be cruel. Yet a dancer's eyes become opened to the world in a way that reflects his or her soul.

In the art form of ballet, there is an ephemeral link between the nature of performing and the presence of love. A performance can capture the very essence of a moment in time and leave both the dancers and the audience awash with emotion. We are left with nothing tangible and yet our spirits are lifted. Like being in love, dancers smile in the embrace of the art form, are grateful as they learn honest, if sometimes hard-won, lessons about how they express themselves and relate to others.

The danger, of course, is to take our profession for granted, or to think that it makes us exempt from the laws of nature. When we can't maintain our level of dance, the frustration can lead us to some pretty strange places until we start to identify our needs and responsibilities in relation to our abilities as dancers.

The average length of a professional dancer's career is ten to fifteen

1

years, and that's after an average of ten years of training! Dancers stop dancing for a bevy of reasons, but as Nancy Upper demonstrates, there is a common trait that all dancers rely on when they face their futures in moments of fear and frustration. That is the ability to commit themselves with intent and focus to an idea or practice and to do so thoroughly.

This ability comes partly from years of physical, intellectual and emotional discipline that ballet requires, partly from the adaptability that one unwittingly acquires from literally thinking on one's feet, and finally from reconciling powerful instinctual responses with the power of observation. Eventually, dancers come to realize that these are fabulous tools with which to redefine themselves and start anew. Altogether, these tools create the ability to grow.

To give up the identity of oneself as a dancer is an awful thing. On the other hand, though, a dancer's ability to find a new identity can be truly awe-inspiring.

The retiring dancer and heartbroken lover are never more alike than when their relationships end. What they had experienced was exciting and, in some cases, glorious. Could anything possibly replace it?

For many, the biggest journey is the search for that answer. For some, it's a clearer path. But there is a universal truth when one finds oneself alone: a support system is all-important, and never do we need one more than in a time of transition. In addition, there is no greater support system than healthy habits. And that system of healthy habits is what dancers have to practice every day in order to succeed: self-motivation, an openness to direction, an awareness of the benefits of discipline, and how to take care of themselves.

It seems that if retiring dancers can hold panic at bay while searching for their next identity, and if they can rely on their own ability to grow, then what replaces ballet often appears to pick them, just as ballet had done years earlier. It can be as surprising as the heartbroken lover discovering that love can indeed be rekindled.

I have watched an entire generation of dancers make their transitions to new lives, and I am now watching another generation discover the magic of the art form for the first time. I have to say that ballet is perhaps the greatest romantic love affair in the world. Nothing can replace this heady state, yet I believe that the lessons learned from the experience become, in some ways, more valuable than the experience itself.

Kevin McKenzie is Artistic Director of American Ballet Theatre

PREFACE

I interviewed these dancers at points in their lives when they were struggling to find new identities, working hard to build new careers, or looking back with different eyes on career changes they made years ago. Thus this book focuses on their career transitions; it does not attempt to give an up-to-the-minute account of what each one is doing *now*.

My long conversations with these dancers profoundly influenced my own career transition, for hearing about the traumas they overcame, achievements they attained, and fulfilling lives they built motivated me to accomplish things I had only dreamed of before writing this book. I hope that you will be as moved and inspired as I was when you enter the lives of these sixteen courageous, remarkable people.

—Nancy Upper

INTRODUCTION

It's a very difficult thing to give up dancing. It's like a little death.
—Robert La Fosse

Dancers die twice, the first time when they realize they are no longer the kind of athletes they were.—Gwen Verdon

In his 1981 book *Growing Young*, anthropologist Ashley Montague cites evidence that children are born with a natural sense of rhythm, developed in the womb, possibly as a consequence of the cradling and rocking of the fetus in co-oscillation with the mother's movements and the syncopated response to the mother's heartbeat. The baby is already in tune with the deepest rhythms of existence. The dance of life has begun. Drs. William S. Condon and Louis W. Sander of Boston University have described this rhythmic interaction between baby and mother as a subtle ballet.

Those babies who grow up and pace their life rhythms to the cadence of ballet training discover that performing on stage lifts their souls to higher planes than normal life usually reaches. With ballet so deeply ingrained, how can dancers ever find other careers as exhilarating?

I spent over thirty-five years trying to find a career that even approached this exhilaration. From my first ballet class in Cincinnati, Ohio, at age six, my greatest dream was to become a ballerina. Although I danced professionally in the Cincinnati Opera Ballet for ten years, I always wanted to be in a *real* ballet company. When I was accepted into the summer program of the School of American Ballet in 1961, my dream seemed attainable.

I loved dancing at SAB, happy to be working toward my goal with the very best teachers. The words of my teacher Melissa Hayden are indelible: "Nancy is the only one who really *dances*." I missed a week of SAB classes when the Cincinnati Opera flew me back from New York to dance solos in *Aida* and *La Traviata*, but I enjoyed my roles, especially being the Egyptian goddess Isis. My best performances were not just about dancing but about the *joy* of dancing.

A week before the SAB summer course ended, I went to the School director to seek help with my quandary of whether to stay in New York to try to become a professional dancer or go back to Cincinnati to college. Timidly, I asked if Mr. Balanchine could watch class to evaluate my potential. Two days later Mr. B appeared in class unannounced to quietly watch. The words the School director returned to me afterwards threw my life asunder for the next thirty-six years. "He thinks you should go back to college."

Back home at the University of Cincinnati, I poured myself into school work, campus activities, sorority life, college musicals, leadership organizations, and honor societies. I became a "big woman on campus" and was elected to Phi Beta Kappa. During college, and for years afterward, I took four ballet classes a week, danced in the Civic Ballet winters and the Opera Ballet summers, still holding onto my distant ballerina dream. I taught, choreographed, managed events, and wrote about ballet to keep every technique honed. My dream finally ended when I married, although I continue to this day a rigorous daily routine of two to three hours of ballet-inspired exercise.

I explored sundry career options after marriage, outwardly trying to find my calling, inwardly still called by ballet. I worked as research coordinator for a medical study on the benefits of exercise, learned to speak fluent French, mastered serigraphy and established my own silk-screen business, earned a Master's degree in education, and worked as a public school curriculum writer. And I still took ballet class.

Driven to achieve even more, because unlike ballet, none of these pursuits was fulfilling, I became a self-employed publications consultant to corporate, educational, and arts organizations, while earning a certificate in business French from the *Chambre de Commerce et d'Industrie de Paris*.

My five happy years on the Board of the Boston Ballet Volunteer Association in the early 1990s steeped me in ballet again for up to thirty hours a week. A full-time communications job at The Massachusetts Institute of Technology forced me to abandon my beloved ballet volunteering, and I spent long hours writing about manufacturing, technology, and corporate operations.

An epiphany came October 9, 1997, when I saw the exhibit *Design, Dance, and Music of the Ballets Russes, 1909–1929*, at the Wadsworth Atheneum in Hartford, Connecticut, with my writer friend Maxene Mulford. I realized how far I'd veered from what I really love. I decided to write a book on career transitions of ballet dancers to speed my own transition back into the fold.

In Paris after the war, Margot Fonteyn went out one night with some friends. "At the Bal Nègre I was entranced as I watched the black dancers. One of them invited me on to the floor. I thought it rude to refuse, and nervously stepped out, trying to follow his rhythm and movement. He steered me once around the hall then returned me to my table, saying, 'You're an attractive girl—it's too bad you can't dance!'"

How awkward Fonteyn felt, how useless her formal ballet training, when confronted with this unfamiliar cadence. Many dancers feel similarly awkward when confronted with the challenge of career transition. Nervously they try to take the right steps to succeed. The dancers in this book did succeed in making transitions into careers that give them each a quite different identity from that of the performing artists they once were.

Not all dancers make successful career transitions, but *Ballet Dancers in Career Transition: Sixteen Success Stories* focuses on dancers who have. Even though the focus in on positive outcomes, some dancers in this book had a harder time with career change than others, and a few are still having a hard time finding their post-ballet career identities.

As unique as each dancer's life is, natural connections link them, giving the book two powerful, unifying themes. The first is transition. The chapters exemplify transition itself by flowing from one life to another just as each dancer's life flows from one career to another and one identity to another and just as transitions link the stages of development in all of our lives. The book thus magnifies the universal transition process by zooming in and linking people for whom career change is an intense experience.

The second theme is ballet. Ballets consist of peak moments linked by steps of transition. *Glissade* (to glide), *pas tombé* (to fall), *pas failli* (to slip), are ballet transition steps charged with universal meaning: sometimes we glide smoothly from one stage of our lives to the next, sometimes we just fall into something new, sometimes we must slip or fail to get to our next life place. The ballet theme goes even deeper, for *enchaînements* built from one step passing into another are but microcosms for the way whole ballets are built from one dancer's knowledge of the steps passing on to another dancer. Career transitions of ballet dancers thus echo the very art from which they come.

Dancers must realize that their rigorous training over the years has given them remarkable skills and personal qualities that are valuable not only to dance, but to any workplace. See Appendix A, "Adaptive Skills and Marketable Personal Qualities," for a list of these valuable competencies. Any employer would be happy to have a worker so well endowed.

Whatever their present careers, wherever they have chosen to place their extraordinary worth, however content they are in their current jobs, all the dancers in the book confided that there is nothing quite as wonderful as dancing on stage. There they found a wholeness, a completion, a glory, that made them celebrate being.

Zeus and Mnemosyne named their daughter and muse of dancing, choral singing, and lyric poetry, Terpsichore, from the Greek words *terpein*, to delight, and *khoros*, dance. But Terpsichore and her sister Muses did not only delight in entertaining the immortals and patrons of the arts, they presided over all intellectual activities. Eloquence, persuasion, wisdom, history, the arts, sciences, and laws of nature all came within their province. They knew the secret of lessening men's anguish and were an inspiration for kings' persuasive orations.

Like the DNA of a mosquito captured in amber, the spirit of the Muses and vitality of dance are preserved within dancers. Their spirit and vitality can spawn new identities when their performing lives end, and can revitalize others wherever their careers take them. As English psychologist and author Havelock Ellis wrote in his 1923 book *The Dance of Life*, "Dancing is the loftiest, the most moving, the most beautiful of all the arts, because it is no mere translation or abstraction from life; it is life itself." Enter these dancers' lives and renew yourself through them.

Part I

Other Careers in Ballet

Poised on the threshold of the stage door like double-faced Janus, a dancer contemplates the world outside after his last performance. He observes the exit, the interior and exterior of the house, himself. He reflects on what he is leaving and thinks, "What do I enter now? Where do I go from here?"

Janus, Roman god of doorways, departures, returns, exits, and entrances, was also the god of beginnings. He presided over the first hour of the day, the first day of the month, and the first month of the year, which in his honor bore his name. His symbols were the key which opens and closes the door, and a doorkeeper's staff to drive away those who had no right to cross the threshold.

When these first six dancers stood on the threshold of career transition and looked back, or inside of themselves, they saw ballet. When they looked forward, they saw ballet. Trained for little else, ballet was the key to their future. Ballet was their staff of life, their means of preservation.

The average age of these six dancers is 62. When their performing careers ended, generally in the 1970s, formal transition programs did not exist and career choices were far more limited than those of dancers today. Most of these dancers preferred studio and stage to books and baccalaureate, so ballet was the only profession they knew. It was natural for them to continue in the field, for it was familiar territory. It was their cultural verity, the logic by which they gave order to the world.

But ballet was not an exterior cultural force controlling them. It is no more outside of these dancers than their thoughts. It permeates their muscles, their minds, their hearts. They and ballet are intertwined: they create it as it creates them.

As these six gradually recovered from performance loss and their respective depressions, injuries, identity crises, or feelings of relief, their driving energies regained momentum and their careers sped forward in exciting new directions. Ingenuity replaced physicality as their means of expression. Fresh inspirations generated new logic to live by and fueled them to produce new ballet verities that enrich and extend our cultural heritage.

EDWARD VILLELLA
Reinvented Himself

"Eddie is the most exciting, incredibly direct dancer. He seduces everyone with his honesty, because the public always senses what is true and what is false." Twenty-seven years after Violette Verdy's affirmation, Villella's honesty still seduces, now as artistic director.

Miami City Ballet is about to create another triumph at Saratoga Springs under his guidance. He ambles up and down the aisles as he gives his pre-performance talk about the physical and intellectual depth of *Prodigal Son*, *Bugaku*, and *Rubies*, the works on this June 12, 1999, matinee program. His presence works like catnip on the audience. A cotton-haired matron coos to her friend, "Isn't he just *mah-velous*."

Villella is an oxygenating presence. He gets the blood running faster, opens wider the windows of the mind.

Thus was his effect on the seventeen dancers before him in Miami City Ballet's first company class that extraordinary day in August, 1986. They danced in plaster dust, without air conditioning, in the partially-renovated store-front building Villella and his board had chosen to house the new company. The room steamed with sweat and the spirit that they were all in this together, starting something fantastic.

Watching the dancers pull up, turn out, and *plié* as he began the class, Villella felt at home, like a refugee returning after the pain of separation. He would build up this company, design every aspect of it, mold it: artistic policy, repertory, marketing, advertising. He didn't have to accept anybody else's problems, personnel, or smile. Before him was the opportunity to pass on Balanchine's legacy, the ballets themselves and the elements necessary to perform them, the approach to technique, to phrasing, and to music.

11

His body tingles and his mind races as the dancers move from the barre to center floor. The thrill of the moment flashes recall of the ecstasy he felt dancing with New York City Ballet in the prime of his career: the fervor of *Prodigal Son*, the elegance of *Rubies*, the spectacle of *Le Corsaire*.

Le Corsaire brings a mental grimace, and fleeting thoughts of Violette Verdy and the White House. The crumbling plaster remaining in this studio recalls the crumbling hip he tried to dance on that fateful night eleven years ago.

It was late spring 1975. President Gerald Ford had invited Verdy and Villella to dance at the White House during a state dinner honoring the prime minister of Singapore. They decided to perform the *pas de deux* from *Le Corsaire*. As Villella took a flying leap off the stage during the coda, a sharp jab in his right hip made him double over with pain in the wings. He finished the performance, but the injury finished his career.

Years of jumping and landing on hard surfaces, the "body-pounding stuff" as Jeff Plourde calls it that ballet demands (see page 116), had worn away the cartilage around Villella's hip bone. Bone on bone pinched raw nerves in between and locked his leg in the socket. Stardom one day, invalid the next.

He became a physical cripple and a mental wreck. Sitting was painful, walking agony, dancing impossible. A simple act like crossing Broadway—a street he once took in eight strides dodging taxis—became a major effort. He had to time his advance into the street, barely making it to the median strip in one light. There he had to stop to regain his energy, strengthen will against pain, then steel every muscle to drag himself to the other side within the next light.

Little did he know (or then care!), that that agonized Broadway crossing, step-by-step, light-by-light, foreshadowed the step-by-step, chance-by-chance transition he made from pain and despair to happiness and international fame again as founding artistic director of Miami City Ballet. He is William Ernest Henley's *Invictus*, lived:

> Out of the night that covers me,
>   Black as the Pit from pole to pole,
> I thank whatever gods may be
>   For my unconquerable soul.

Villella has been fighting through transitions all his life. From working-class Queens street kid to classical ballet dancer in the 1940s and '50s; from dancer to unwilling Maritime College student and back to dancer between 1952 and '57; from technical spitfire to complete artist in the '60s; from America's most celebrated male ballet star to reclusive cripple in the early '70s; from alone and desperate to loved and artistic director in the late '70s and '80s.

By far the toughest fight of all of these transitions was that brought on by his 1975 hip injury. No need to ask, "How did you know it was time to quit?" His hip screamed the answer.

Villella had interpreted life physically since he was a child. Within two years after the scrappy ten-year-old was accepted into the School of American Ballet in 1946, ballet had become his life's passion, his muscle, blood, and soul, and later his sole source of income. But the anatomy that let him leap so high and reap such glory over the years now sunk him abjectly low. Exhausted by pain, frightened by loss, bewildered by what he would do in life, he was at ground zero, an easy target for self pity. But he fought back.

Profile of Edward Villella as Founding Artistic Director of Miami City Ballet. (Photograph by Philip Bermingham, 2001.)

"I fought like crazy not to be depressed," says Villella. "I wouldn't admit that I was depressed. But I certainly think I was for about ten years." In this grim decade of depression, broke and broken, Villella transformed his life.

Plugged with pain killers, he tried a few dancing roles in 1977, desperate to hold on to the sense of himself as a dancer. He finally had to admit three truths:

"My dancing days are over."

"I do not have an immediate position or occupation."

"I still have to look forward to having my hip replaced."

Although Villella couldn't dance, he could talk, teach, choreograph, coach, and direct. "And suddenly I realized I could write. Not extensively, but I could write premises, scenarios, or television productions; this, that, and the other. Suddenly I said, 'Golly, I have some ideas. Oh, isn't that interesting!'" This epiphany made him realize he could use his mind as powerfully as he had used his body, that he had talents other than dancing within him to develop. "You'd be surprised by what's in yourself," he says. "I surprised myself."

He sat down and made a list of ten things he was most interested in, then began to work like crazy to build a career around those, just as he advises his son Roddy to do today. *Invictus* relived.

> It matters not how strait the gate,
>   How charged with punishment the scroll,
> I am the master of my fate:
> I am the captain of my soul.

Villella would not only master his fate, he would reinvent it.

Late in 1977, he accepted a job as choreographer for a television special on ice skating. The job came with the services of an assistant, who turned out to be Linda Carbonetto, his current wife of thirty years. Their immediate mutual attraction led to marriage in 1980. He had found his life companion after spending the majority of his existence alone.

By 1981 Villella could not endure the daily pain of his physical problems any longer and agreed to the hip-replacement surgery he had put off for six years. The operation was successful, and he began to feel like his old self after recovery. He went back to class (against doctor's orders), but a November 1981 performance of *Afternoon of a Faun* with Heather Watts made him realize once and for all that he was, and should be, retired.

Villella's family had now expanded from Linda, his son Roddy by his former wife Janet Greschsler, and Linda's daughter Lauren by her former husband, to include their own daughter Christa Francesca, born April 9, 1981. For the first time, his life was about other people and their needs, not just himself and ballet. Building a new, solid career became essential to him.

What appealed to Villella most was a job that encompassed all of the activities he had been involved in after his injury: lecturing, teaching, choreographing, coaching, directing, and writing. He decided he wanted to become the artistic director of a ballet company. Such a job would allow him to meet the needs of his family while satisfying deep needs of his own: needs for approval and acclaim, for ballet and challenging work to absorb his energy and passion. He set about learning as much as he could about how artistic direction was done, fueled by the creativity of "reinventing" himself to excel in the role.

Villella had a number of offers from large ballet companies, but thought he would learn the most from directing small companies with big problems that needed help. He accepted the directorship of Eglevsky Ballet, and served as artistic advisor to Ballet Oklahoma and New Jersey Ballet.

But the second half of Villella's life—his zero A.D., anno Artistic

Director—began in 1986 at age fifty when he became the artistic director of Miami City Ballet.

A year earlier, Villella had been in Miami giving a lecture demonstration when he was introduced to two residents interested in starting a classical ballet company in southern Florida. They felt the cultural climate was ripe for such a venture and hoped Villella might serve as artistic advisor.

At first he didn't see much future in the idea, but the more he talked with these people, the more he realized how serious they were about the project and the more enthusiastic he became about it himself. They listened attentively and took careful notes as he outlined a precise, comprehensive, eleven-year plan for creating such a company.

When Villella returned to New York, he did considerable research on the cultural demographics of southern Florida and the logistics of building a company there. He became more and more excited about developing what now seemed like a great idea.

Meeting again with the resident advocates convinced him that they would allow him to lead the company on his own terms. A contract was drawn up, which he signed to become Miami City Ballet's Artistic Director. He committed himself fully to the project and moved his family to Miami.

"Family, home, and house are always something I had dreamed for but never had, because I was always bouncing around all over the place," says Villella. "When you find a life partner, and your kids are your pals— I think to have that is wonderful, *wonderful* piece of work." Now he would have an extended family and a life project in Miami City Ballet, and he has done a wonderful, *wonderful* piece of work with those, too.

Villella's success with Miami City Ballet springs from the same source as his success with his family: his deep sense of humanity and his ideology of individuality. "I approach them [family, dancers] as human beings. We're in this together and it's an exploration. Both of us are there. It's not only me exploring, it's they exploring what's available within them. You give potential by that exploration."

Warmed to his convictions, he continues, "I love the process of company class in the morning. When I go down and I see fifty kids there, and they're all giggling and laughing and having a good time, and they're all easy, they are being *themselves*. I want and allow them to be themselves.

"Now within all of that, there's an awful lot they have to adhere to. But I want *them* to apply the discipline, not me. I don't yell and scream, I set an example. I work ten-to-twelve hours a day, six-to-seven days a week. I'm at every performance, I teach company class, I run rehearsals, I run the administration, I do fundraising, I do PR, I do marketing—I mean, I just do the whole thing. So they know I'm never phony with them. I never stay at a fancy hotel, I always stay with the guys, hang out with them. It's you."

Miami City Ballet *is* Edward Villella. Just as he drove himself mercilessly to be a great dancer, he drives himself mercilessly to be a great artistic director. Just as he started from scratch in 1975 putting his life together, he started from scratch in 1985 putting Miami City Ballet together. Just as he felt alive in Balanchine's ballets, he is keeping those ballets alive through Miami City Ballet. Just as he earned worldwide acclaim for his distinctive style, his dancers earn worldwide acclaim for their distinctive styles. Just as his dancing helped to evolve the art form, so does the dancing of this company. Villella's pentimento shows through Miami City Ballet's masterpiece.

In the on-stage company class June 12, 1999 before the Saratoga matinee, the dancers display their individuality warming up in unmatched clothing, from shiny spandex unitards to bulky tee-shirts and leg warmers, from classic black and pink to wild stripes and prints. Enter Villella, lean and trim, in black-rimmed glasses, black Polo shirt, khaki pants, and black jazz shoes, displaying *his* individuality. The pianist opens with a seductive version of *Saint James Infirmary*, followed by *Nowhere Man*, *Let's Get Away From It All*, and *Alexander's Ragtime Band* as the class pace escalates. Villella jazzes his way from barre to barre, a shuffle-ball-change here, a moon-walk there, cut-stepping to switch directions. The music invades him and he's dancing again. He is Miami City Ballet. *Heart and Soul* fills the stage.

Villella corrects little; the dancers know what he wants. He has rooted in them the importance of turnout and musicality so they are second nature in each body. The principle of turnout—the rotation of the feet, legs, and hips outward from the center of the body that is the basis of classical technique, permitting a dancer to initiate and extend movement—is deeply rooted in Villella and subliminally drove his turning out from self-centered focus before injury to focus on others after injury, permitting him to initiate and extend his new career.

"One day I was at the top of the art form, the next day that was gone." He says. "What was the best thing to do once the physical couldn't support what had been the pleasure of my life? Pass it on. Pass on the wealth of information that I had absorbed from George Balanchine, Jerome Robbins, and Stanley Williams, body to body, but specifically mind to mind.

"What's so wonderful about ballet is that it's mind-driven physicality. It's almost a Greek ideal of body, mind, and form.

"With two artificial hips, a bad back, nine broken toes, and stress fractures in both legs, it's just so limiting to how much physicality I can do now. But teaching class in the morning keeps me going. I just love it." Mind trumped body and knowledge became his competitive advantage. Greek ideal with nineties business savvy.

Says economist Peter Drucker, "The only thing that increasingly will matter in national as well as international economics is management's performance in making knowledge productive." Substitute ballet for economics, and you have Villella's Miami City Ballet.

"I've always stayed aware," says Villella. "I didn't bury myself in the world of ballet as a lot of people do. I had many, many other interests—theater, film, music—a formal education [four years at Maritime College], and business interests. I look at myself and say, 'Oh my golly, I'm able to do an awful lot of things.' I think there are so many levels to us as human beings."

Villella looks at his dancers as human beings and encourages them to pursue their interests. He also involves them in all aspects of company operations, holds choreographic workshops if they are interested in that, and invites open communications between administration and dancer. "We encourage our guys to keep their options open. This isn't forever and you're a human being first."

Miami City Ballet moved into a spectacular new building in December 1999, which allowed Villella to dramatically expand the options he can offer his dancers. Sixty-two thousand square feet of innovative architecture house seven sixty-by-forty-foot studios with twenty-foot ceilings to expand repertory, facilities to double the school's enrollment, a physical therapy room, safe storage, and comfortable administrative offices. Villella especially requested huge windows, so the public could watch the dancers at work and the dancers would learn to feel comfortable in front of an audience. A sturdy counterpart to Villella's vulnerable anatomy, this edifice is a legacy to his patient vision of making Miami City Ballet into one of the top three companies in the country, if not the world (see http://www.miamicityballet.org). "But it all takes time," says Villella. "This idea of patience is paramount."

"I'm really not very interested in legacy," he continues modestly. "I just want to make my company the best I possibly can make it, nationally and internationally." What moves him most is the human material he works with, dancers and ballets.

"Balanchine said his ballets were only alive when they were being danced. But are they really alive when they are danced by people who don't understand their inner meanings, their subtleties? We need the essence, the pumping heart, the blood, the vital organs, the intelligence of the ballet, in order to know it. Intimate contact between people and minds is essential for the ballets to be presented in this living, breathing state."

Thus he devotes himself to guiding, developing, and caring for his dancers as compassionately as he cares for the ballets that he knew intimately, that guided and developed him. His humanity embraces artist and art form alike, and he feels deep personal responsibility for both.

"Aside from any other legacy, let me just say that I hope that the people I have worked with would be able to say, number one, it was a pleasant human experience, and number two, they have gained something professionally from it. Number three, I would really like to help change our field in terms of how companies treat their personnel. After all, they are the product, and they should be treated accordingly, as partners."

VIOLETTE VERDY
From Tchaikovsky *to Tenure*

"For the first time in my life I have a solid, decent salary, and the benefits that you get if you are *professeur* in a university. It is so divine not to have to torture myself about how to go." After going "all over the place" for forty years, Verdy is finally free to do what she does best: teach, coach, and choreograph. Since 1996, she has been a fully-tenured Professor of Dance in the Ballet Department of Indiana University, in Bloomington.

Sunlight beams in the small studio window and shines on her blond froth of hair as she conducts class. Her expressive blue eyes connect with each dancer in the room. She rewards the dancers with her friendly smile, and her quick, analytical mind catches each nuance of movement. Demanding but sensitive, strong but kind, Verdy's flawless teaching has been honed by years of experience with the best dancers in the best companies in the world—La Scala, Royal Ballet, Royal Danish Ballet, Paris Opera, Australian Ballet—and companies coast-to-coast in the United States. Her teaching is enriched by her thoughtful, philosophical nature and spiced with wit.

"I was a guest teacher for Jean-Pierre and Patty two or three times," she says of her introduction to Indiana University in the early '90s, when Jean-Pierre Bonnefoux was IU Ballet Department Chairman. "One of the times I choreographed a ballet there, and I realized then that I loved the place."

Jean-Pierre Bonnefoux and Patricia McBride are her best friends and she works with them often. "Jean-Pierre just told me, he said, 'You're not good fighting for money, so I'll do your contract for you at the University.'"

Violette Verdy in one of her signature roles, as Miss Julie in Birgit Cullberg's 1950 ballet of August Strindberg's play *Miss Julie*. (Photograph by Maurice Seymour, courtesy of his son Ronald Seymour. Reprinted with permission of Jerome Robbins Dance Division, The New York Public Library for the Performing Arts, Astor, Lenox and Tilden Foundations.)

Verdy had been Artistic Director of the Paris Opera Ballet and Boston Ballet for three stormy years each, and since 1984, teaching part-time at New York City Ballet and guest teaching worldwide to make ends meet. She was eager for a secure, peaceful environment. The rolling hills of southern Indiana, one of the best music schools in America, and freedom from administrative baggage beckoned her to Bloomington.

Verdy was born Nelly Guillerm in 1933 in Pont-l'Abbé, a small town in Brittany known for its tough-minded artisans and delicate lace. A community of traditional furniture makers, truck farmers, food packers, embroiders, and lace makers seems an unlikely place to spawn a musically-gifted ballerina, but before Nelly was eight, she played the violin and the piano. Her mother realized that her daughter's response to music was not only amazing, but that music deeply affected the child emotionally. When the music was right for dancing Nelly was ecstatic, but when the music was solemn or mournful, she would sulk or cry.

"I have a tremendously high nervous system," says Verdy. "High energy. I was always playing, doing things, being very, *very* active." Active to the point that she was not eating enough or sleeping enough, so her mother took her to the family doctor.

"The doctor told my mother, 'We have to tire her out, but let us do it in a harmonious way: let us tire her out musically *and* physically. Make her dance!'"

Verdy's father had died when she was four months old, so her mother was the dominant influence in her life. Although Jeanne Guillerm had never seen a ballet, she was captivated by photos of dancers at the Paris Opera and decided that her daughter should become a ballerina. In 1942, during the German occupation, she put her house up for rent and bravely took Nelly to Paris.

Ballet felt like something strong, steady, reliable, and important to nine-year-old Nelly. "At first I was a little bit embarrassed. I didn't like to get undressed, I didn't like to my lift my leg, and I was shy about the physical aspect of using my body that much. And then, there was something about it, the music of course, and then the logic of the exercise. I was a good student at school and suddenly realized that I was a good student at ballet, too. Ballet gave me a sense of continuity and achievement. My teacher was happy, my mother was happy, *everybody* seemed to be happy. It was a way of pleasing my important people—it started like that."

By age eleven she was dancing professionally in a series of ballet evenings choreographed by Roland Petit. The series delighted war-ravaged Parisians and led to Petit's forming the Ballets des Champs Elysées. Nelly signed a six-year contract with the fledgling troupe at age twelve in 1945 and began her ascent ballet fame.

When Nelly was seventeen, French film director Ludwig Berger plucked her from Roland Petit's Ballets des Champs Elysées, changed her name to Violette Verdy, and made her star of his film, *Ballerine*, the story of a young dancer who has three dreams. Her first dream is of being a ballerina, her second is of wealth, and her third is of idyllic happiness. The film turned out to be prophetic of Verdy's own life: prima ballerina, now financially secure, and at peace through the harmony of her spirit with her work.

Verdy toured the United States for the first time with Petit's troupe in 1954. In 1955 she accepted London Festival Ballet's invitation to join them for a season and another American tour. Upon her return to Europe, she danced *Cinderella* and *Romeo and Juliet* as a guest ballerina with La Scala Opera Ballet. But Verdy's blossoming career was abruptly halted at age twenty-three in 1956 when a ruptured Achilles tendon required six months of rehabilitation.

Ballet Rambert invited her back to London when she recovered, a crucial engagement for her personally and professionally: she went alone, without her mother for the first time in her life; she experienced her first romance, with Colin Clark, son of famed art historian Sir Kenneth Clark; and she danced her first *Giselle*. The combined voltage of these three powerful currents in Verdy's young womanhood charged ballet with new meaning for her.

"Ballet became my own personal tool to be free," she says. "To be doing something that was *mine*, that I liked, that I was doing well, freed me from other things. Ballet became my trading thing to bring me happiness, to receive acknowledgment, to be good, and to feel good about myself. It was *my* thing, like a fish in the water. And I *loved* the fatigue, the contentment of dancing and soaking in music. It was the music, number one, until the end."

By immersing herself in the flow of music and dance, she found "a happiness that is practically unrelated to anything, the purest form of happiness you can have." Critics marveled that she 'became' the music, inhabited it, breathed it, as have few other dancers.

A contract with American Ballet Theatre brought Verdy to America again, but imposed a long separation from her mother and Colin Clark. Whatever emotional emptiness she felt she quickly filled with an exhausting, exhilarating cycle of daily classes, rehearsals, and performances.

ABT brought stardom in *Miss Julie,* a role created for her by Swedish choreographer Birgit Cullberg. She danced her first Balanchine ballet with ABT, *Theme and Variations,* but put her own stamp on it by adding an impish little kick to a Balanchine *saut de chat,* which he retained, renamed, and reused as "Verdy's step."

When ABT temporarily disbanded in 1958, Balanchine invited her to join New York City Ballet. She had spent her career to that point in the uncertain world of companies that constantly disbanded and regrouped, offering absolutely no security. New York City Ballet had achieved relative stability, and it was there that Verdy found a home for the next eighteen years.

Her debut with City Ballet was in *Divertimento No. 15,* but Balanchine's attraction to her musicality, femininity, and intellect soon inspired him to create more challenging roles for her. The first of these was *Episodes: Part II* in 1959, to the twelve-tone music of Anton Webern. Schoenberg said of Webern's music that it expresses an entire novel in a gesture, a joy in a breath. Verdy's dancing was like that. Each step was a clearly formed artistic statement.

Verdy's Russian training and French qualities—clear, clean technique, articulated feet, and refined pointe work—excited Balanchine to create *Tchaikovsky Pas de Deux* for her in 1960. "I've always especially liked dancing to a violin," she says, "because it gives a sensuous quality to the way you use your muscles. You have to sustain the movement." *Tchaikovsky Pas de Deux* became her signature piece, and she danced it all over the world with different partners throughout her career. She needed only to step onstage in this bravura masterpiece for the applause to roll in.

"My Russian teachers gave me something which helped me very much when I began dancing for Balanchine. They made me aware of a performance as a great drama, almost a question of life and death. Going from the black wing of a curtain into the light of the stage is something incredible. A performance is not something out of normal life. You are alone on the stage, and when I was dancing Balanchine's work, I felt that I was carrying a better solution for the moment. His choreography is the best solution."

Balanchine tapped her artistic and intellectual depth with the four musical solutions he created for her next. *The Figure in the Carpet* (1960) to Handel's music had as its theme the history, construction, and philosophy of the Persian carpet, one of the greatest concepts in the history of world art. *Liebeslieder Walzer* (1960) was set to achingly beautiful love songs of Brahms. Futuristic *Electronics* (1961) had a taped score, and Verdy had silver tinsel hair. *A Midsummer Night's Dream* Act II *Divertissement* (1962) displayed her quicksilver effervescence and inimitable charm.

If an artist is an adventurer exploring new territory as Eugène Ionesco has claimed, then Verdy is an exceptionally well-equipped explorer. Her intellect and philosophical insight are as keen as her dancing. Although her education was not formal in an academic sense, her mother, a former teacher, encouraged her to read and Verdy became an avid reader. Early in her career, when she prepared for roles such as Carmen or the Fiancée in *Le Loup*, she had rich imagery to draw upon. She prepared for her later abstract and classical roles with equal awareness of their musical, cultural, and literary roots.

Colin Clark reappeared in 1961, and after a turbulent courtship he and Verdy married. After two years of living in a state of perpetual conflict between ballet, which has always been the top priority in her life, her mother, and her husband, the marriage ended in 1963.

After the divorce Verdy continued to perform, but a bout of tendinitis became so severe in 1964, she was forced to have an operation which failed to produce a cure. She lost two years of dancing during her painfully slow recovery.

Verdy added three new dimensions to her life during this difficult time: learning Russian, teaching ballet, and Vedanta, a Hindu philosophy that assumes the unity of all reality, and teaches that the believer's goal is to transcend the limitations of self-identity and realize his place within this unity. Verdy met an Indian guru in Austin, Texas, and eventually followed him to his retreat in India where "you are completely away from everything else, completely involved."

Vedanta for her was not something separate from life, but a philosophy that was a clarification of life. It helped to heal her.

Verdy returned to City Ballet in 1966 transformed and mellowed, and in 1967 Balanchine created the Emeralds section of *Jewels* for her. Fauré's music required extended legato dance phrases, which she performed with silken aplomb.

"Divine as it is to dance Balanchine's ballets," she says, "nothing can compare with working with him and seeing him create something in front of you, for you. Seeing how he solves the problems that come up with the music, and how simple and right his solutions are. It happens with no one else in that way." Balanchine was a different kind of guru to her and their shared reality was music.

Verdy continued to dance for the next nine years and Balanchine continued to create roles for her, but the scar tissue that had accumulated from her injuries weakened her feet and ankles and made her prone to further impairments. Recovery meant repeated temporary layoffs, but Verdy philosophically took it all in stride.

"Every dancer wants to lift the body and take it a little higher and further than the body wants to go," she says. "We overdo it and have a little setback here and there." Although she was always able to return to dancing after layoffs, only she and Balanchine knew how deeply her injuries hurt.

During rehearsals for *Pulcinella* in 1973, Balanchine was showing Carol Sumner how she should unveil herself as Pulcinella's bride, a role he originally set on Verdy. As Sumner departed for a break, he said to her, "Be prepared to dance this in Wolf Trap. Violette is still limping. In her foot—and I think," Balanchine put his hand over his heart, "here as well."

Over the years her setbacks and comebacks gradually became more difficult, but she drove herself to stay in top form. Her early ballet training helped. "When you have the kind of very strong, slow schooling that I had, that builds you for life."

Meanwhile, on the other side of the Atlantic in the city where Verdy had made her stellar ballet and film debuts, the Paris Opera was sinking as a result of its knife-in-the-back bureaucracy and poor management. Enter big-time Swiss composer and former Hamburg Opera manager Rolf Liebermann in 1973, as Paris Opera's general manager. Within three years, he miraculously brought the Opera back up to the level where it always should have been.

Liebermann was a great personal friend of Balanchine and familiar with Verdy's considerable intellectual, artistic, and teaching abilities. In 1976 he invited her to become the first female Artistic Director of the Paris Opera Ballet. She accepted.

She was scheduled to perform one more year with New York City Ballet before assuming her Opera post in 1977. She and Peter Martins went on a little tour in the spring of 1976 to Allentown, Pennsylvania, where they did the *Pas de Deux* from *A Midsummer Night's Dream* and the *Tchaikovsky Pas de Deux*. She smiles. "Little did I know it was going to be my last performance."

"Shortly after Allentown, I was so excited about going to Paris and so busy getting myself ready for the move, I broke one of my toes, at home, actually, on the bathroom door! So the end struck me sooner, I went to Paris sooner, and I never performed again, that was it."

It was not such a serious break that she was incapacitated—a cane and a plaster were all she needed to be able to move around. Nonetheless, she had to cancel a number of performances she was scheduled to do, including her season with New York City Ballet.

Then Liebermann called to say that the Paris Opera Ballet was in a big battle with opera management and the unions and asked if there were any chance she could come sooner.

"I said, 'Yes, because I broke one of my toes, so I might just as well go to you now.' And I never came back. Never came back to dance. I came back for moving, but not to dance. That was it. It was one way to go like any other. I felt good." She laughs, "One thing we avoided was the whole sentimental mush of a farewell performance or *anything* like that."

Verdy was glad not to be dancing that first year as Opera Ballet director. She had decided that she would not take away any performances from the dancers there and was much too busy anyway learning the administrative side of running a company. "I had a hundred-and-fifty-five dancers, and some of them were *great* dancers. I wasn't going to administer, and take care of them, and *dance.*"

She had also accumulated an enormous amount of emotional fatigue during her performing career that took a year, in fact five years, to release. That first year after she stopped dancing, 1976-1977, she looks upon as "one year of mission, of study. It gave me a chance to rebalance my life."

She justifies her transition philosophically, with a twinkle in her eye. "I could have danced another seventy-five years, easily, and maybe even a little more. But because of the servicing I needed to do to do to my body— and I was so dedicated to that, I accepted the boring aspect of the daily servicing of everything: slow work, extra exercises, Pilates, everything you have to do to be in complete good shape—it was entirely time consuming. I was willing to do it, but when the Paris Opera offer came along, I realized that rather than repeat my good discipline, it was maybe time to move along."

Had she not had such a time-consuming process in her dancing, she might have felt more deprived. But at this point, she had done it. "I would have loved to do a few more *Giselle*s and a few more *Beauty*s. I would have loved to have one or two more pieces with Mr. Balanchine. But then, how much more do you need? I wasn't greedy anymore, so I could go without. I was ready. Mentally I knew that I could switch without being totally depressed and unprepared. I had done it."

"And it was *lovely* to have a new chance," she continues, "it was a fresh lease. I was going to be using myself differently, have a fresh look at myself. I was going to check on the baggage I had, see what I had discovered, what was left, what I was going to learn, and what I was going to be good at—it was really wonderful.

"Buuuuut—" The reality of less activity took its toll. "After one year, I started picking up a lot of weight, and it really was a problem. At first it was not unpleasant, because I was not so gaunt in the face." But the more she gained, the unhappier she became because her self-image was threatened. "I saw myself in a different way. It was not comfortable."

She had been fascinated with using her brain instead of her body that first year at the Opera, but now she had to include exercising again in her packed schedule, and watch what she ate and drank. Time-consuming disciplines of a new kind.

She has retained some of those extra pounds, but pleasantly so, and she still has the perfect glowing skin and cheerful face of the roseate beauty in Fragonard's painting *The Swing*.

By 1980 Rolf Liebermann felt he had completed his work at the Paris Opera and was ready to move on. Verdy was ready to go, too, drained by Opera bureaucracy and the demands of her job. Of the several offers extended to her, including a tempting invitation to join Baryshnikov in running American Ballet Theatre, she accepted the co-artistic directorship of Boston Ballet in the summer of 1980, a role she would share with founder E. Virginia Williams.

Boston Ballet was a fifth the size of the Paris Opera at that point in number of dancers and budget, but Verdy felt that less-complicated Boston would give her a chance to function at a high level while allowing her to maintain her spiritual center. Glimmers of her third *Ballerine* dream were beginning to flicker already: maintaining serenity was of primary importance to her—but her second dream was still out of reach: struggles for money lurked in her future.

After two years of teaching and choreographing for Boston Ballet, money struggles wrenched her away from these pleasures when she became sole Artistic Director in 1983. Fundraising and administrative responsibilities consumed time she had spent with her dancers. "Directing is so frustrating," she says. "You can't really do what you do best. I'm better in the theatre, you know."

So there she fled. In 1983, her best friend Jean-Pierre Bonnefoux asked if she would like to teach that summer at the Chautauqua Institute where he was summer Artistic Director of the Ballet Department. Chautauqua is a tranquil lakeside community in southwestern New York which their website describes as an "intergenerational haven for renewing family life, for renewing mind and spirit, for renewing intellectual curiosity and interaction ... where stress is relieved ... in an atmosphere open to freedom of individual expression ..." Verdy adored the place and has been teaching and choreographing there every summer since. There she finds her own mental, emotional, and artistic renewal.

When E. Virginia Williams died in 1984, Verdy decided not to advance to her position. After Boston, "I dismissed myself from *any* further directing, *ever,*" she says, even when she was asked to lead the Indiana University Ballet Department. "I learned my lesson being a director in Paris *and* in Boston. I was offered everything that would come up, but I declined because I didn't want to be in that position again."

She contracted with Peter Martins to teach the company part-time at New York City Ballet to earn a living. "He couldn't use me enough, though, so he said, 'Please feel free to do things on the side. We'll give you a slightly smaller salary, but you won't be lost to us and you'll be with freedom.'"

The practicality of this arrangement was deceptive. Verdy loves to travel and was able to guest-teach around the world. She could also maintain an apartment in New York and teach at New York City Ballet when she was home. But her City Ballet salary was far from enough to live on, so she had to travel *constantly.*

"It became too much for me," she says. "It was too exhausting. I was never at home because I would have go teach to get money to pay for the apartment, and I could never *be* in the apartment!

Jean-Pierre was her angel again by bringing her to the serene, secure campus of Indiana University. There her second and third dreams materialized: of not wealth exactly, but financial security, and idyllic happiness.

Verdy is healthy, with TIAA-CREF retirement investments, her own home, her Chautauqua summer income, teaching residencies, and choreographic commissions.

She has also written three books which return small royalties: two for children, *Giselle: or the Willis* (1970) and *Of Swans, sugarplums, and satin slippers: ballet stories for children* (1991), and one for adults, *Giselle: A Role for a Lifetime* (1977). She is happy.

The dominant theme of happiness recurs again and again in Verdy's life, like the recurring dominant theme in a sonata-rondo musical composition. In the sonata-rondo, variant musical episodes in different keys alternate with the main theme through harmonious transitions. The letter formula for this form might read A–B–A–C–A, where A represents the fixed returning element, and B and C the episodic ones.

In Verdy's life to date, her A theme is "the purest happiness you can have" which she found through ballet. Her brief B theme was artistic direction and her strong C theme, teaching. With the dissonant B theme removed from her life forever, she can now develop new, melodious

Violette Verdy as Professor of Dance, Indiana University, Bloomington. (Photograph by David Dercacy.)

elements in the teaching-choreo-graphing-coaching role she loves that will only enhance her happiness.

"I've had time to develop a good little central core from the discipline I had as a dancer," she says, "that's not going to let me down wherever I go."

She instills this same discipline in the dancers she teaches now and guides them to feel the elemental happiness that ballet brings. Or, if they are not right for ballet, she helps them to find something that corresponds to some aspiration or longing that they have.

"If you do something very, very well," she advises, "*anything*—it could be ballet or it could be something else—but if you do it very, very well, you have forever a kind of a central reserve of knowledge, judgment, wisdom, information, resources: you are equipped. You have to have developed that little heart. That *filet mignon*, if you will. If you have that, you have your little compact to go anywhere."

That "little heart" makes transitions from one of life's themes to another consonant, too, like those in music.

"Transition is only that," she says. "It's a continuity, not a break, not an interruption. It is a lovely transformation, a refining process—a reconversion of the same, wonderful energies and knowledge, and a tremendous chance to continue to grow up."

Verdy is fascinated by the whole process of teaching, coaching, choreographing, and caring for dancers at all stages of their development. "That magic relationship that you can have one-on-one—with each one of the dancers—when you have that long enough, you create a relationship where the students really want to be with you and you can be with them. That is just absolutely all it is about!"

Said Verdy's compatriot Edgar Degas, "When all the muses meet together, they dance." Verdy is a multiple muse to her students, deep as the Pierian Spring.

She was in fact Spirit of the Spring in *La Source,* a *pas de deux* Balanchine created for her in 1968 to music Délibes wrote for the original 1866 full-length ballet. The *La Source pas de deux* became one of Verdy's favorites, in which she rediscovered herself through Balanchine's subtle choreography each time she performed it.

Verdy often danced *La Source* with Edward Villella, and although she loved working with him, she admitted frankly in a 1972 interview, "With his manly style, his perfect complement is probably a more modest, gentle dancer. I offer a more competitive presence, because my style is so complex. But we are both intelligent enough to make our styles match. He simplifies me, I refine him." Just as she refines the dancers with whom she works today.

JEAN-PIERRE BONNEFOUX AND PATRICIA McBRIDE
Etoiles

Etoile in French means star, but the word has as many related meanings and idiomatic extensions as *star* in English. One *étoile* meaning is a dancer of international status in the highest echelon of a ballet company's hierarchy.

Jean-Pierre Bonnefoux ascended to *danseur étoile* in the Paris Opéra Ballet at age 21, Patricia McBride to the equivalent in New York City Ballet at age 18. Both Bonnefoux and McBride became international luminaries with all the qualities of their celestial counterparts: radiance, magnetism, sparkle, and their own very human warmth.

A celestial star often is composed of two or more self-luminous bodies in close gravitational association, not unlike the self-luminous pairing of Bonnefoux and McBride, who joined as romantic partners in 1968, professional partners in 1970, and marital partners in 1973. Two such intertwined lives seemed to dictate a single, unified chapter.

Patricia McBride was born August 23, 1942, in Teaneck, New Jersey, a thickly settled metro-suburban town with tree-lined streets and single-family homes. Located across the Hudson River from Manhattan, Teaneck's population is diverse and culturally sophisticated.

Jean-Pierre Bonnefoux was born April 9, 1943 (not April 25 as several ballet reference books state), in Bourg-en-Bresse, France, 414 kilometers southeast of Paris between the Saône River and Jura Mountains. Bourg, the capital of the fertile farming region of Bresse since the Middle Ages, has had periods of great splendor and to this day is an important international marketplace. Bourg-en-Bresse welcomed scholars and literary men in the 18th and 19th centuries, including the painter Gustave Doré (1832–1883) whose work figured into Bonnefoux's career in the 1970s.

Nature, nurture, and environment shape personality, and the vastly different settings in which McBride and Bonnefoux spent their early childhoods—hers in America's model community (proclaimed so in 1949), his in a European cultural crossroads—shaped their different but exquisitely complimentary temperaments. She is calm, single-focused, in-the-moment; he is animated, multi-focused, enterprising.

A humble pair of ballet slippers inspired McBride's career; being relocated to Paris inspired Bonnefoux's. "Someone in the family had given me the slippers," says McBride, "and my mother thought that ballet would be nice for me to do."

An accomplished pianist, McBride's mother sensed that quality in performance would reflect quality in teaching. "My mother and my grandma visited all the dance schools to find the best one, and they went to all the recitals." Although Ruth A. Vernon had been teaching in town for only a year, Mrs. McBride judged her school and recitals to be by far the best. She enrolled her seven-year-old daughter, who loved it from the start. Says McBride, "I was just happier dancing than doing anything else." (Her younger brother Eugene took to the piano and today is a professional pianist and composer.)

Mrs. McBride worked full-time as an executive secretary in a New Jersey bank, obliged to support the family from the time Patricia was three years old when Mr. McBride suddenly left his wife and children. "She had a lot to deal with as a young mother," says McBride. "We lived with my grandparents, and as they grew older she had to take care of them while raising me and my brother and holding a full-time job. I don't know how she did it.

"I just *loved* my Mom. She could do all the dances of the Big Band era [1935–1945] and was especially good at the Jitterbug and Lindy. As much as she liked dancing, though, she wasn't a pushy mother at all; she just wanted me to do what made me happy. I always felt her love and support—she was an amazing woman." McBride speaks in tender, reverent tones when she speaks of her mother, who died in 2002.

"I absolutely adored Miss Vernon, too. I think you always adore your first teacher when you're young. After my Mom, she was the most influential person, and the person that I most wanted to be like. She and my Mom became great friends, and my Mom taught ballroom dance in Miss Vernon's school."

Ruth Vernon had joined the Metropolitan Ballet when she was 14 and retired three years later, at 17. "She was a great character," says

Jean-Pierre Bonnefoux and Patricia McBride as New York City Ballet principal dancers in George Balanchine's *Theme and Variations*. The dancers featured this photo on the cover of their brochure promoting the 1978-79 national tour of Patricia McBride, Jean-Pierre Bonnefous and Company. (Photograph by Martha Swope / *Theme and Variations* choreography by George Balanchine © The George Balanchine Trust.)

McBride, "a fascinating person and a wonderful story-teller. She was in all the operas as a dancer or an extra, often performing the boys' roles because she was tall. She used to tell us the pranks they played.

"She had beautiful legs and feet, like the ideal Balanchine dancer. She was a strict but loving teacher, and always made me feel good about myself which gave me self-confidence."

McBride started with one class a week the first year, then rapidly advanced to five classes a week. "Miss Vernon inspired me to *want* to dance. She would choreograph a recital every year, and I'd do tap, acrobatics, and ballet; I was a gypsy one year, a swan—I always had lots of numbers. My grandmother made my costumes.

"Miss Vernon would sit in a chair beneath the edge of the stage right in front and conduct her dancers like an orchestra. We could see her face, shoulders, and arms flailing. I would smile at her and not think about the audience at all. I *loved* being on stage and performing to please her. She instilled so much happiness and fun into dancing, I had a really positive performing experience." Throughout her career, McBride radiated sheer enjoyment onstage, thanks to Miss Vernon. "I always felt so loved and confident when I danced."

The devoted nurturing of her mother and teacher helped develop McBride into a loving, compassionate woman. Happiness pervades her conversation, optimism guides her spirit. Although outwardly serene, Patricia McBride is emotionally and intellectually complex.

While McBride illuminated Miss Vernon's recitals, Bonnefoux brightened Parisian nightlife, performing in a *brasserie*. Bonnefoux's father, a city government official, moved the family to Paris when Jean-Pierre and his twin sister were seven years old. To fulfill her love of dance through her children, Madame Bonnefoux located a ballet teacher for her daughter.

"I believe that my mother wanted to be a dancer," says Bonnefoux. "She really enjoyed it. She would bring me when she came at the end of class to pick up my sister, and one day the teacher said, 'Why don't you start with your boy too?' so I did.

"It was not very exciting in the beginning because there was no music, just the steps. We couldn't afford to pay that teacher much, and I don't know if she had ever danced professionally—she took some classes I guess—but she gave us a sense of the ballet vocabulary.

"She also must have had some connections, or known somebody who asked her if she had some dancers who could perform, because we started performing in a *brasserie* when we were eight years old. At that time, most of the cafés in Paris had a small orchestra and a stage and would put on *divertissements*. People would go out at night, have a drink, and see the show.

"We performed in the show of a large café with a good stage, famous for its orchestra. Magicians would do tricks, the orchestra would play Viennese waltzes, then my sister and I would dance. It was very festive. We would go to school as normal French children do, and perform on weekends. I choreographed all of our dances."

When they were nine, Bonnefoux and his sister successfully auditioned for the ballet school in the Théâtre du Châtelet, the ornate 1862 theater where Serge Diaghilev's Ballets Russes had made their sensational Paris début in 1909. "There were just girls in that school, and me," says Bonnefoux with a smile.

"We worked with a very famous teacher for about a year, Madame Salomon, but we did not have to pay for classes: we performed every night in exchange for lessons. We performed in operettas, dancing, singing, and acting, in that beautiful theater with its great past."

"There was a piano in the back of our studio at the Châtelet, and one day a few months after I started somebody was there at the piano. When we started to dance it was with music, and the music made it *magic*—suddenly the steps had meaning."

Bonnefoux and his sister also began piano lessons when they were nine, with a private teacher outside of the Châtelet. "At 10 years old we auditioned at the Paris Opéra School. Eight hundred kids auditioned, and they took 20 or 30. My sister and I were chosen."

Dance was not young Bonnefoux's first love, however. "I liked dancing, but to be an actor was really what I wanted to do. I also wanted to be a conductor." Bonnefoux acted in three movies, the first when he was 10 years old. Friends of his mother told her that directors were looking for children for Hervé Bromberger's 1953 film *Les Fruits Sauvages* (*The Wild Fruits*). She sent Jean-Pierre to the audition, and he was picked as one of the three child leads.

"That was my favorite movie," he says. "I played a young boy who wanted to become a priest, because he was deeply involved in spirituality and believed in supernatural things. It was an extraordinary role for me. That's what gave me the idea of becoming an actor, because I love the idea of being somebody else."

His portrayal of the role was so effective, the press called him the best young actor in years. "Playing in that movie was one of the greatest joys of my life, and something that I will never forget," says Bonnefoux. "It was very important to me, because day and night I was focused on that role, and at that young age I realized the power and rewards of total concentration."

Les Fruits Sauvages won the Best of Festival and Best Competing Film awards at the 1953 Berlin International Film Festival. Fifty years later in 2003, Bonnefoux discovered a photography book on great actors of the '50s. On one of the pages was his photograph at 10 years old.

At age 12, he played the role of a music prodigy studying to be a conductor. "I conducted an orchestra in that movie and worked with a conductor who rehearsed me for the gestures I was supposed to do in front of the orchestra, so they could follow me. They didn't really follow—it was a *movie*—but I got very excited about having an entire orchestra under my command and bringing so many musicians into harmony with just my hands and body movements. The conductor who rehearsed me had been the favorite student of the famous French conductor Serge Fournier and became my piano teacher after I finished the movie."

Bonnefoux acted in a third movie at age 13. "I think at one point I could have really become an actor," he says, "but how hard it would have been to find jobs I'll never know." At age 14, he had already arrived at a crossroads in his young career. "At 14 I was supposed to start on a play.

I didn't know whether to do it or to wait, because in six months I had the chance to enter the *corps de ballet* of the Paris Opéra. I had no idea what I wanted to do, acting or dancing—I was really excited about both of them. My parents went to see a Hindu who could see the future. He predicted that I would be a successful dancer, would marry late, and would marry a woman who was not French. He also predicted that I would leave the Paris Opéra when I had accomplished the maximum I could achieve there, and that I would be the one to decide when to leave."

A celestial star is at its maximum when it is most brilliant. Great teachers, such as Pierre Reynal, helped Bonnefoux to achieve that brilliance. Says Bonnefoux, "Reynal is one of the best teachers for actors in Paris, and an actor himself. Much later I worked with him on two ballets: he helped me to develop characterizations for Hippolyte in *Phèdre* and Albrecht in *Giselle*. He was an extraordinary man because he gave me responsibility for the truth of a role and taught me how to achieve depth of interpretation."

Concurrent dancing, singing, stage acting, movie acting, conducting, playing piano, academic school, and childhood mentors developed Bonnefoux into a high-energy, multi-talented man capable of intense focus on one task among the many he can manage at one time. What Barbara Newman wrote of him in her book *Striking a Balance* (Houghton Mifflin, 1982) is as true now as it was when she interviewed him in 1979: "Somewhere behind the façade of Jean-Pierre Bonnefous' face and body lay a series of intricate, interlocking processes, like the works of a Swiss watch, which produced his dancing.... [He] offered you both what he could do and a tantalizing sense of the intelligence powering the body that was doing it. He was simultaneously physical and metaphysical. As a result, he brought a mysterious dimension to ... every ballet I ever saw him dance that captured the eye, the mind, and the imagination." Bonnefoux is as complex as McBride.

The Hindu seer decided Bonnefoux's future in 1957; Ruth Vernon had decided McBride's in 1955. McBride had trained with Miss Vernon since 1949, but when she turned 13, Vernon was boldly honest with her. "I can't teach you any more," she said. "If you want to be a professional you should go to New York." McBride and her girlfriend were the best students in Vernon's top class, and she knew that the girls were ready for more challenge.

"Miss Vernon didn't really know of the School of American Ballet," says McBride. "nor did we. She had seen an advertisement in *Dance Magazine* for the 54th Street Dance Circle in New York, so we went there. I loved it. I studied with Sonya Doubravinskaya, a Russian teacher who was *very* different from Miss Vernon. Tony Bocchino choreographed, and I would work with him on pointe Saturday afternoons after my class with Sonya. I was exposed to good training, and I would also go back to take classes with Miss Vernon.

"One day after I had been at the Dance Circle for six or eight months, an older student said to me, 'You're wasting your time. You should go to Balanchine's school, you look like a Balanchine dancer.'" McBride laughs, "I was really tall and skinny at that point in my life" (she is 5' 3" now).

"I didn't want to leave, but my Mom thought I should try to get into the School of American Ballet. She felt that maybe I wasn't getting enough attention where I was. So I auditioned, took the SAB summer course, and loved it. My destiny, I guess, was in that direction—you know how someone says something and you do it? If that person had never said that, possibly my mother wouldn't have taken me out of that school, and I would've waited until I was 18 to audition for the company."

Lessons at the School of American Ballet were more than Mrs. McBride could afford, but her application for financial aid won Patricia a full scholarship.* Says McBride, "My Mom and I jumped up and down with joy when we received the good news!

"I was placed in the 4:00 P.M. B class, which was possible for that school year, because Teaneck High School was very helpful in letting me get out of certain classes so I could go to New York. The next year my ballet classes were in the morning, so SAB said I would have to go to a professional children's school for my academics."

McBride and one of her friends entered the ninth grade at the Lodge School, run by Mrs. Lodge and her daughter for students training in the performing arts. "It was less expensive," says McBride. "My Mom couldn't afford *the* Professional Children's School, but the Lodge was a good school as well.

"I always liked school. I would get on a bus, go to school early in the morning to get all my correspondence work, then go to my SAB ballet class at 10:30. Then I'd go back to the Lodge for classroom work, return to SAB for my 2:00 pointe class, then go home."

At age 15, McBride made her professional début with the André Eglevsky Petit Ballet Company. Shortly thereafter, Tamara Geva (one of Balanchine's former wives) invited McBride and several other SAB students to perform in the off–Broadway show, *Come Play with Me*. "We sang and danced—it was a totally different experience from dancing ballets and I learned a lot," says McBride. "My SAB friend Gloria Govrin and I would do our homework together backstage."

McBride had planned to finish high school a year early and had taken all the required subjects to graduate. "But," she says, "we were doing pre-

This was years before the days of Ford Foundation funding, which began December 16, 1963, with their announcement of a 10-year grant of $7,756,750 "to strengthen professional ballet in the United States."

views of *Come Play With Me*—it hadn't opened yet—when I found out that I was getting into the company." Her dream of joining New York City Ballet had come true, so she poured the commitment and hard work she had given to her academics into becoming a professional dancer, and in 1959 at age 16 entered the NYCB *corps de ballet.*

"My teachers at the School of American Ballet were great inspirations," she says, because each had a strikingly different personality and teaching style." Anatole Oboukhoff had graduated from St. Petersburg's Imperial School in 1913 and became a soloist with the Maryinsky Theatre in 1917. He joined the School of American Ballet faculty in 1941 and, wrote Jennifer Dunning in her book *"But First A School" The First Fifty Years of The School of American Ballet* (Elisabeth Sifton Books, Viking, 1985), "Oboukhoff is remembered by his students as a disciplinarian who was also a colorful character, a teacher who gave exhausting, very structured, technically demanding classes that managed, at the same time, to be highly inventive."

Felia Doubrovska graduated from the Imperial School in 1913, the year Balanchine entered. She joined the SAB faculty in 1948 and taught there until 1980, a year before her death. Wrote Dunning, "Like Oboukhoff, Doubrovska is remembered as one of the most demanding and yet endearing of teachers." Says McBride, "She would make an entrance into class that was beautiful to see. You could tell from the way she carried herself that she had been an extraordinary dancer. She was very feminine, and always elegantly dressed and perfumed."

"Madame Tumkovsky had a sunny, warm personality," says McBride of former Kiev State Theatre soloist Antonia Tumkovsky. "We could relate to her so easily. She always gave the hardest combinations, but we were grateful for how they developed our technique." McBride expresses deep gratitude for all of her wonderful teachers at SAB, including former Kiev State Theatre soloist Helene Dudin, former leading Maryinsky dancer Pierre Vladimiroff, and British dancer and teacher Muriel Stuart, one of Anna Pavlova's original students.

Her deepest gratitude goes to Balanchine, as does that of every dancer in the New York City Ballet family. "He was the most important man in my life," says McBride, "a father figure and a mentor to me for decades. His talent was overwhelming. You just couldn't imagine where it came from. He continuously did the most amazing things in a completely natural way. He knew he was a great teacher, and as his students I think the relationship we all had with this man was very unusual. He was always there, our light and our hope." Wrote Bernard Taper in *Balanchine: A Biography* (Times Books, 1984), "Developing young dancers to their limits and beyond was [Balanchine's] satisfaction and stimulation. It was this that constantly renewed him."

"He is with me today," says McBride now, "intertwined with my spirit. From when I was a child, Balanchine and Jerome Robbins were my idols, and they are still with me every day."

Bonnefoux entered the Paris Opéra Ballet *corps de ballet* in 1957 at age 14. "The Paris Opéra director called in a friend of mine and me and told us that we were going to have the honor to be part of that extraordinary tradition of the Paris Opéra. I knew that something like that might happen, but at 14 I was not that tall, and I thought he would say, 'I'm sorry, but you're too young and too small.' I tried to get as tall as I could in front of him, although I think it had been decided already."

Bonnefoux brings to mind French singer Mireille (1906–1997) who, from 1955 to 1974, mentored aspiring young French singers in her Petite Conservatoire de la Chanson. Mireille didn't hesitate to reject *"ceux qui n'ont pas dans l'oeil la petite étincelle qui relie l'artiste au public"*—those who don't have that certain sparkle in the eye that links the artist to the audience. Bonnefoux had that sparkle.

The venerable Paris Opéra couldn't quell his pubescent hormones, however. "I don't know how focused I was," he admits. "At that time I was really interested in girls; that's what I was dreaming about all the time. I just wanted to dance, to partner those beautiful older women. It was really a dream."

Luckily his school studies were finished, or surely they would have received little attention. He says, "In France in 1957, you only had to go to school until you were 14 years old, so I was done with my regular schooling and could go into the company if I was ready." He was ready, in technique and stage presence, although the youngest member of the company by several years.

In spite of his fascination with girls, Bonnefoux understood the commitment implicit in joining the Paris Opera, that hallowed ground where ballet was born. "Being in the Opéra Ballet was like becoming part of the great ballet legacy that began with Louis XIV 350 years ago," he says.

Louis XIV (1638–1715) was an accomplished dancer. His popular image as the Sun King arose from his performance in *Le Ballet de la Nuit*, at age 14, as the Rising Sun, accompanied by dancers portraying Honor, Grace, Love, Riches, Victory, Fame, and Peace. He was indeed a brilliant leader who brought honor, grace, riches, and fame to France through his Académie Royale de Musique, which he founded in 1669, and which evolved into l'Opéra de Paris—the Paris Opera.

"It was such a great honor to be part of that legacy," says Bonnefoux. "It's almost like being part of the great family of the circus—people know each other, travel together, meet people, and have a common mission. I felt that I was a part of the great family of the Paris Opéra.

The Opéra's heritage was so special, so rich and deep, I really wanted to be there.

"My teachers in the School were sensational, and after I joined the company I continued to learn from remarkable teachers. Some them were Russian immigrants who had worked with Marius Petipa in the premier of *Sleeping Beauty* in 1890. It was just extraordinary. I always felt that I had a direct link to Petipa and the best of the great masters of the previous century. I loved the idea of being part of that legacy.

He describes the teachers who had the greatest influence on his career. "My first teacher in the School, Suzanne Lorcia, was very powerful, very tall, and had a sense of theater that she could teach. She was a marvelous principal dancer in the company for years before she began teaching, and she used to do the barre with us.

"Some teachers taught the academic steps very strictly and exactly. That was hard, and I learned to be afraid of teachers and not always to trust myself. Sometimes when a teacher is so strict, he or she can make you feel that you're not very good and you lose confidence. They helped to shape my philosophy of teaching now, which is that the most important quality to instill in dancers is self-confidence. You do that by respecting students and giving them a sense of their own talent."

Bonnefoux says that *corps de ballet* dancers often went outside of the Paris Opéra to take class and names a few of his non–POB teachers, particularly Gérard Mulys, his favorite. "He was so strong that his strength would help me to do it whether I was tired or not. He was passionate about teaching and felt it was his duty to pass on the ballet tradition. I worked with him for ten years, three or four times a week, alone for one or one-and-a-half hours with no piano, just him, me, and his stick pounding the rhythm of the music.

"Raymond Franchetti was one of the best teachers for male dancers in Paris because of the atmosphere of friendly competition he created among the male dancers. We were like athletes training hard for the same goal: to be the best. But we had fun doing it. Serge Peretti was the most famous teacher for male dancers in Paris because he could teach *petit allegro* as well as *port de bras*."

At New York City Ballet in 1960, Edward Villella started partnering McBride when Balanchine paired them in the Third Movement of *Symphony in C*." Says McBride, "We had good chemistry together from the first moment. Eddie's charm and charisma made me feel so confident." In the July 1980 *Dance Magazine* transcription of that year's Dance Magazine Awards ceremonies she says, "I was 17 and he was an 'old' 21. We really worked so hard together, and we loved every minute of dancing on the stage." Their partnership grew into one of the most famous in the history of the company, and one of the greatest of their era.

Balanchine created his first role for McBride alone in 1960: the Duchess of L'an L'un in *The Figure In The Carpet*, a ballet he choreographed as a tribute to the April 1960 Fourth International Congress of Iranian Art and Archaeology. Nicholas Magallanes, one of the company's leading dancers and finest dramatic actors, was her partner. According to Anne Murphy in her February 1981 *Ballet News* article, *The McBride Magic*, Magallanes was McBride's first real friend and mentor in the company. Says McBride in the article, "Nicky! I'll never know what he saw in me—this little teen-aged kid." She says now, "He took me and my friends Carol Sumner, Gloria Govrin, and Mimi Paul under his wing and made me feel that I belonged."

She earned that belonging with her congeniality, dependability, and hard work. "I was a *workhorse* in my early days," she says. "I always filled in for people who were absent or injured and was on stage every night." The *fouetté* contests McBride had with her friends at Miss Vernon's school to see who could last the longest were exemplary of her drive. "I enjoyed feeling pushed," she says. "It made me happy."

McBride was promoted to soloist in 1960 after *Figure in the Carpet*. In 1961 at age 18, she became the youngest principal dancer in the company.

In contrast to McBride's nightly on-stage education, Bonnefoux says in *Striking a Balance*, "At Paris Opéra I used to take two one-and-a-half-hour classes every day ... then I had at least four hours of rehearsal—that's seven hours of dancing, six times a week, and I would be dancing onstage only once or twice a week. That way, dancers have no sense of what it is to be onstage.... Older dancers or friends would tell me, 'Take any concert, good or not good, bad stage, slippery stage, twelve persons in the audience, no lights, anything. Do it, because that's where you learn reality.' The reality for a dancer is onstage. The rest doesn't give him any sense of the reality."

Michel Descombey, who came to Paris Opéra as ballet master and director in 1962, encouraged dancers to expand their experiences outside the Opéra. Says Bonnefoux in Olga Maynard's January 1971 *Dance Magazine* article *A New Apollo?*, "[Descombey] helped me very much. He inspired me to work hard, and not be afraid of trying new things in ballets outside the traditional repertoire."

Maynard says that the first work Bonnefoux danced "outside the Opéra (and outside France) was with Descombey, who took him to the Frankfurt Ballet as a guest artist in a modern repertoire." Bonnefoux performed a *Hiroshima pas de deux* with Claire Motte, which Descombey created for them to music by Krysztof Penderecki.

Bonnefoux's first notable Paris Opéra role came in 1962 at age 19 while he was still in the *corps de ballet*. Former New York City Ballet dancer Una Kai came to the Opéra to set Balanchine's *The Four Tempera-ments*, in which Bonnefoux partnered Martine Parmain as the third theme, phlegmatic. His first experience with Balanchine's work, *Four Ts* fascinated him. With his own keen musicality, Bonnefoux admired "the inventive choreography, and the great connection between the music, the choreography, and the dancers."

Maurice Béjart created his *Damnation of Faust* for the Opéra in 1964 with the Faust role as a double persona and cast Bonnefoux as the danc-ing double. Béjart similarly doubled the wedding couple in his 1965 *Les Noces* for the Opéra and again cast Bonnefoux as the double. Bonnefoux had been named an *étoile* in 1965 at age 21, after his brilliant performance with Claude Bessy in George Skibine's *Daphnis and Chloe*.

Marie-Françoise Christout announced Bonnefoux's promotion in the June 1965 *Dance Magazine* in her *News From France* column and described his role in *Les Noces*: "…The thoughts of principal dancers Martine Parmain and M. Ariel (clothed in heavy robes of state) were expressed by Nanon Thibon and Jean-Pierre Bonnefous in severe white tights. Thus while one couple moved with dignity through the traditional ritual, the two "visions" expressed their hidden emotions, using the full range of classical virtuosity."

You may question the two spellings of Jean-Pierre's surname: Bon-nefoux and Bonnefous. Explains Maynard in *A New Apollo?*, "His name is actually Bonnefoux. The spelling Bonnefous came about through a printing error, which he was too modest to make a fuss over when it appeared on a program.

"'It does not so much matter what name you dance under as how you dance' Bonnefoux says in the article. 'What is important to me is to dance well, to be a good artist.'"

As a young dancer, influenced by Eric Bruhn and Rudolph Nureyev, Bonnefoux says in *Striking a Balance* that he tried to get "more and more perfect in the classics," master their pure classical line, and sharpen the geometry of each step. As an *étoile*, he began to tire of the classics and "was dying to work with choreographers, because … it was so much more exciting to have a part in the creation."

Roland Petit staged his *Notre Dame de Paris* for the Opéra in 1965 with Bonnefoux in the lead male role, and "I went on doing a lot of Béjart and Roland Petit," says Bonnefoux in *Striking a Balance*. "As a first dancer, I had everything I wanted. Three principal dancers shared the roles so I could do a whole lot of different things, and I knew that if choreographers would come, most of the time they would try to work with me. To work with a choreographer [is] the ideal situation."

When France and Russia had a cultural exchange in 1966, a member of the Bolshoi wanted Bonnefoux and *étoile* Claire Motte to dance *Giselle* and *Swan Lake* in Moscow. Says Bonnefoux in *Striking a Balance*, "I was not afraid of anything, so I said, 'Sure, fine, I'll go there. But I realized I'd never danced *Giselle* and I'd never danced *Swan Lake.*" At the time Paris Opéra gave precedence to older dancers, and he was one of the youngest *étoiles.* "I went to the director of Paris Opéra and said, 'I'm going to dance with the Bolshoi, so I really have to dance those ballets.' They gave me one *Giselle* and one *Swan Lake* and then I went to the Bolshoi ... when you're so young, you can take all the chances. It's great not being afraid of anything."

Dying to express himself in new ways, Bonnefoux started to choreograph in 1966. "I started to do little things for television, choreographing for actors and dancers." He was positive, however, that to be able to do "something at least not too bad," he needed to see Balanchine. The spark of Balanchine's work in *The Four Temperaments* inflamed his desire for much more.

At New York City Ballet, the spark of the McBride–Villella partnership fired Balanchine's genius to create *Tarantella* for them in 1963, a dazzling display *pas de deux* full of technical feats, tambourines, and high spirits. Explosive applause punctuated *Tarantella* at its premier January 7, 1964 in the New York State Theater, and wherever McBride and Villella performed it thereafter.

The old *commedia dell' arte* story of Harlequin winning Columbine from her rich father Cassandre inspired Balanchine to choreograph a *Harlequin pas de deux* for Maria Tallchief and André Eglevsky in 1950, but someday he hoped to do the whole ballet. When sets became available in 1964, and with McBride and Villella perfect for the leading roles, he set to work. *Harlequinade* premiered February 4, 1965, in the New York State Theater. Says McBride, "I *loved* doing *Harlequinade.* I just *adored* that ballet. It is near and dear to me—as are *all* of the ballets Mr. B made for me."

Balanchine paired McBride and Villella in the *Rubies* section of *Jewels*, which premiered April 13, 1967, in the New York State Theater. "'Rubies' was a very different role from the ballets he had made for me before," Says McBride, "because it was full of jazzy movements, turns, jumping, and moving through space. When we were learning it, Mr. Balanchine danced every step, Eddie's *and* mine, and beautifully showed us exactly what he wanted. Mr. B was a natural partner. What he did with Stravinsky's music was amazing, although we had to count every step. I felt very secure dancing with Eddie, though, because I could throw myself into his arms with great abandon and he would be *there.*"

Jewels is pure dance with no literary content at all. Yet Balanchine says in *Balanchine's New Complete Stories of the Great Ballets* (Francis Mason, editor, Doubleday & Company, 1968), "I suppose if [the *Emer-*

alds part] of the ballet can be said to represent anything at all, it is perhaps an evocation of France, the France of elegance, comfort, dress, perfume.

"Others seem to have found "Rubies" representative of America. I did not have that in mind at all. It is simply Stravinsky's music, which I have always liked...."

Balanchine's juxtaposition of France and America, and his mention of music as a choreographic muse, foretell events to come in the lives of McBride and Bonnefoux.

Feeling unchallenged and bored at the Paris Opéra "dancing everywhere the same old ballets over and over again," Bonnefoux says in *Striking a Balance*, "I was going nowhere and wasn't growing. I couldn't get excited anymore."

In 1967 he asked for a guest artist contract that didn't oblige him to perform at the Paris Opéra the whole year. Only one dancer, Yvette Chauviré, had had the courage to ask for a guest contract before. "That was *very* hard to get," he says, "but eventually they gave it to me, because they needed me and wanted to keep me."

In 1968, André Eglevsky invited Bonnefoux to come to America to guest star with his company in a series of gala performances in Newark, New Jersey, with New York City Ballet dancers Patricia McBride, Edward Villella, Marnee Morris, John Prinz, and Violette Verdy. Bonnefoux danced with Verdy.

Before the first show, he knocked on McBride's dressing room door. In her article *Living an Encore* in the Winter 2002 newsletter of the North Carolina Dance Alliance, *Dance Voice*, Miriam Durkin quotes McBride, "I knew the first moment I saw him. We fell in love immediately." Says Bonnefoux, "She was beautiful. There was a radiance about her, something calm and touching."

"A dear friend of mine," says McBride, "Christopher Allen, sponsored Jean-Pierre's trip here, so he was staying at Chris's place. Chris invited a group of us to dinner at his home. It was just great—Jean-Pierre and I really connected."

When Bonnefoux returned to Paris, they bridged the Atlantic with romantic letters. McBride went to Paris to see Bonnefoux dance at the Paris Opéra Ballet, and to Toronto when he guested with the National Ballet of Canada. Says McBride, "We kept the correspondence going for two years, and lo and behold, he joined the company [New York City Ballet] in 1970."

John Taras, ballet master with New York City Ballet since 1959, came to Paris Opéra to serve as ballet master from 1969 to 1970. He liked Bonnefoux's clean dancing, quick intelligence, and desire to learn.

When Balanchine accepted Berlin Opera Ballet's 1969 invitation to send some of his dancers to perform in Germany, Jacques D'Amboise was supposed to have danced *Apollo*. "Somehow Jacques could not dance," says Bonnefoux, "so Balanchine asked John Taras who could replace him. John said, 'I met that young fellow in the Paris Opéra, and I think he would do very well.'"

Bonnefoux learned *Apollo* from Taras in Paris, then had just four days with Balanchine before the last dress rehearsal. "Working with him I realized how much I had to learn and how *exciting* it was to work with that great master," says Bonnefoux. In *Striking a Balance* in says, "Balanchine emphasized certain movements—it was absolutely incredible how forward we were going in one direction. In four days I don't know what I learned, but it gave me the strength to go through ten more years in dancing. When you know that somebody like that exists somewhere, even if you're not working with him, it gives you a goal."

Back in Paris, his four days with Balanchine simmered in his mind. One day they came to a boil. In 1969 Boston Ballet had invited him to dance *Les Sylphides* with Italian ballerina Carla Fracci. "I had danced with Carla at La Scala in Milan, La Fenice in Venice, and San Carlos in Naples, and just loved working with her," he says. "One or two months before we were supposed to go to Boston, the Paris Opéra informed me that they had changed their program because one of the singers was ill— the singers were always more important than the dancers. They had to put in a ballet instead of the opera and told me that I would have to stay to dance.

"I said, 'I've already signed a contract to do *Les Sylphides* in Boston with Carla Fracci.' The director said, 'I'm sorry, you cannot go there, you have to do this ballet in Paris.' I said, 'No, I cannot accept that—' He was not very interested in what I was telling him, so eventually I said, 'If you do that, I will just have to leave.' He said, 'Where will you go?' I said, 'I will go to America.'

"As soon as I left his office, I met a friend of mine and explained what I had done. I asked her, 'Whom do I know in America now?' She said, 'You just worked with Balanchine.' I said, 'Ah, that's right! That would be *extraordinary!*'

"Those two things pushed me to leave: I couldn't stand the way I was working at Paris Opéra anymore, and I wanted to work with Balanchine.

"Then I thought, 'Leave Paris? My country?' Even though I knew that I had to make the move, I needed that little push. That really forced me.

"I called Balanchine and said, 'I would like to go to your company.' He said, 'Oh, that's not possible. You want to come for one season. You'd be the guest. When I give the roles to you, my dancers wouldn't do them.

Then you would leave. It's not fair to my dancers. It's not going to happen, it wouldn't work.'

"I said, 'Okay, fine.' Then two days later, I called back again—which was not like me at all. I had so much respect for him, that I don't know where I found the nerve to call him a second time. But the second time I called back and said, 'What about if I would come for two seasons?' He said, 'Okay.' He was making a commitment of two seasons already.

"I said 'Then I will come now.' He said, 'You cannot come right now. Maybe in a few weeks.' He explained that he was in a difficult situation because the company was somehow on strike; there were some problems with the musicians. I said, 'Oh, that's okay—'"

Bonnefoux reflected that he had been doing better than "all right" in Paris; at times it had been great. He had his guest artist contract, was a coveted *étoile*, and had also been starring in a Parisian television show. He had rejected all that with his resignation, and now Balanchine told him not to come yet.

Bonnefoux had three choices. "Carla Fracci asked me to join American Ballet Theatre to dance with her, so I could have danced at ABT. I also could have stayed at the Paris Opéra. But I had committed myself to Balanchine, so I got on a plane, flew to New York, and waited for the strike to be over.

"When the strike was over I joined New York City Ballet—but because of the strike, I could not be paid. I was without money. It was a hard time."

Bonnefoux took class at New York City Ballet, striving "like a *workhorse*" to adapt to the speed and style of the company. And he and McBride continued their grand *pas de deux*.

Says McBride, "The first time we danced together was when Mr. Balanchine partnered us in *Tchaikovsky Pas de Deux* in May 1970. Dancing with Jean-Pierre was wonderful! He made me feel like a woman."

Balanchine cast Bonnefoux in Tchaikovsky's *Swan Lake* in the May 23, 1970, matinee. "I didn't like dancing it at all," he says in *Striking a Balance*. "It was the second act only, but I didn't come to do that and I was not very happy.... I came not to be recognized, not to stand outside of the company, but to be a part of it. And not only to be a part, but to dance like everybody and to dance a lot, a little bit of everything."

Bonnefoux continues in *Striking a Balance* that he was trained to become the best dancer he could as a respectful duty to the choreographer and to the company. Ballet "was not supposed to be fun. There [was] something more important than having a good time. When I came here, Patricia and different dancers asked me, 'Did you have fun doing it?' I said, 'What is that? I tried to do my best, that's all. It has nothing to do with enjoying it.' I thought I was doing the ballets right, I thought I was doing my best, but they didn't look right. I could feel that Balanchine wanted different things." McBride taught him to let go of his worries and take pleasure in the sheer joy of dancing.

Maynard wrote in her article that after the 1970 spring and summer seasons, already Bonnefoux showed remarkable affinity with the repertoire and rapport with the dancers. She quotes Violette Verdy who says, "Jean-Pierre's adaptation to a large part of our repertoire gives proof of his intelligence and taste ... perspicacity seems to be his means of evaluating a role and adapting himself to it. Rare for a male dancer (and especially for a French one) is his attitude towards Balanchine and the company. Jean-Pierre has humility.

"He is consistently very open, receptive, and patient, behaving always as a listener, an observer, rather than acting eager to prove himself." Verdy goes on to praise his beautiful technique, extraordinary sense of line, plastique, and flair for both dramatic and contemporary choreography.

Beyond his technical virtuosity and versatility, Maynard concludes that he has "a warmth and sweetness as uncommon in an *étoile* as Jean-Pierre Bonnefous is uncommon among dancers."

McBride's unique gifts inspired Jerome Robbins when he returned to New York City Ballet in 1969 as ballet master (he had been associate artistic director of the company from 1949–1959). Says Anne Murphy in *The McBride Magic*, "almost immediately [Robbins] began making a *pas de deux* for McBride and Villella that grew into *Dances at a Gathering*." Says Robbins in the article, "She has complete sensitivity to and trust in her partner, but actually she immediately connects with whoever else is onstage—it's almost an actor's connection.... That's why she's so good in *Dances at a Gathering*: she instinctively understands the subtleties of those relationships."

Balanchine's 1971 *Who Cares?* to music of George Gershwin was a complete change of pace. He created "The Man I Love," "Fascinatin' Rhythm," and "Clap Yo' Hands" for McBride, whose smile made three-part harmony with song and step.

Murphy limns McBride's exquisite dancing in a few eloquent words. "Though she has performed *Agon* and *Episodes*, the eccentric arcs and angles of such ballets are not her natural forte. She is most at home in Balanchine's long, complex, high-density allegro line, which she seems to traverse at the speed of thought, a speed that allows for no hint of transition or preparation. Her swiftness is the key to her virtuosity, which comes less from the discrete elements of jumps, turns, or footwork than from the whole calligraphic line of the phrase, which, like calligraphy, is always legible; there are no blurred details.

"...Perhaps McBride's most pervasive quality, in every role she dances, is an inviolable feminine reserve: she can flirt, vamp, or be passionate, but never vulgar ... McBride remains womanly, chaste, incorruptible."

Offstage, casual in midi-skirt and boots, McBride introduced Bonnefoux to O'Neal's Baloon, a former Lincoln Center restaurant then popular with New York City Ballet dancers. McBride and Bonnefoux are in fact immortalized in that setting with 31 other people, mostly ballet dancers, in the mural *Dancers at the Bar* painted by artist Robert Crowl in the late '60s-to-early-'70s. The mural hung over O'Neal's bar, but when the old place changed hands it was moved to the present site of O'Neal's Restaurant.

On June 29, 1973, McBride and Bonnefoux were together in a far different setting: the Teatro Nuovo in Spoleto, Italy. Jerome Robbins and the 16th Festival of Two Worlds presented *Celebration: The art of the pas de deux.*

The McBride–Bonnefoux *pas de deux* culminated in marriage September 8, 1973. Says McBride, "We were married in the same church where Jean-Pierre's mother was married in La Clayette, France, a little village in the Saône-et-Loire region of Burgundy." Although Balanchine disapproved of the marriage, he continued to create roles for McBride and to star Bonnefoux in important works.

Balanchine created a lavish *Coppélia* in the spring of 1974 as a special evening-long story ballet for the Saratoga Springs audience. He invited Alexandra Danilova to collaborate with him on staging the ballet, for in the 1930s and '40s she had been the West's reigning Swanilda. *Coppélia* became one of McBride's signature roles, for she, too, personified the charm, energy, and wit of Délibes' score with the right balance of feeling and humor.

In 1975 Bonnefoux took the initiative to speak with Balanchine and Lincoln Kirstein about starting a class for 10-year-old boys at the School of American Ballet. Traditionally the boys took class with the girls, and Bonnefoux felt that the boys should have a class of their own. Says McBride, "Although he was busy dancing, he took the teaching very seriously—that was his background." Says Bonnefoux in *Striking a Balance,* "If you want to improve a school, or to give a better chance to youngsters ... what's most important is that they have one or two teachers that they really respect and admire and follow. Those teachers can show them things that they will never forget."

"He loved teaching," says McBride, "and he was good at it. He could always work at two or three things at a time and rather liked doing several things at once. I could really only focus on my dancing. I just couldn't manage to do anything else.

"It was a full life. I didn't really have time for much, rehearsing every day and dancing every night. When the seasons were off, I would guest appear with Eddie Villella and have guest appearances with Jean-Pierre. I got to do *Sleeping Beauty* and *Giselle* and other ballets that were not in our repertoire. That it was *stimulating*, what I did on the outside. I was very busy."

In the mid–1970s Balanchine cast Bonnefoux as Phlegmatic in *The Four Temperaments*. This pure dance role became one of Bonnefoux's favorites. He says, "There is no character but the quality of the movement. When you think about something purely abstract, you think of its essence and it feels so full. That ballet is the closest I came in my whole career to that essence of dance. You think of taking off all the extra, planing it away, making less and less."

Acting was always very important to Bonnefoux. He says in *Striking a Balance*, "I [try] to imagine a text ... to make everything clear ... to make a walk true." He studied Alberto Giacometti's 1947 statues *Man Walking* and *Man Pointing* before *The Four Temperaments* to project their string-thin verticality and electrifying presence. He examined Gustav Doré's drawings of *Don Quixote* to emulate their noble frenzy.

"Dancers bring their work home and constantly think about it," says McBride. "You have to do that as a dancer. You can't be a dancer and not do your homework; it has to stay with you." McBride herself seems not so much to dance her roles as to become them. She and Bonnefoux always arrived on stage with more than 100 percent of themselves.

When Mikhail Baryshnikov joined New York City Ballet in 1978, McBride became his partner because "after our first performance Mr. B told me we looked good together," she says. "Misha had an enormous repertoire to learn in a very short time, but he was a quick study and worked hard. It was amazing how fast he could learn with so little instruction and rehearsal. Dancing with him was an interesting experience."

For the 1978 SAB Workshop, Bonnefoux choreographed *Quadrille* to excerpts from Johann Strauss's *Die Fledermaus* for eight of SAB's younger pupils. Wrote Tobi Tobias in her September 1978 *Dance Magazine* review of NYCB's '77-'78 season, "I hope that *Quadrille* will last in the SAB repertory long after its original cast has grown up, because tact and wit are evident everywhere in Bonnefous' choreography."

Balanchine thought of creating a second company in 1978, New York City Ballet II, that would tour. "It came *that close* to happening," says McBride, "but never happened. Jean-Pierre was one of the first people who wanted to do complete Balanchine ballets with students from SAB, so Mr. Balanchine let us form our own company with SAB and NYCB dancers. We couldn't use the New York City Ballet name, so we used our names." They called their troupe Patricia McBride, Jean-Pierre Bonnefoux and Company.

An agent helped them to book the company for a tour of California,

Las Vegas, and Florida. "It was a wonderful tour," says McBride, "and Jean-Pierre managed the whole thing. I just danced; he rehearsed, directed, and danced. It was a lot of work for him, but he was very good at it.

"I thought he was a natural for directing. He is very good with people and very understanding with dancers. He's a warm person, and people relate to him well. He has a good ear for dancers and can sympathize and help. And he *loves* teaching."

Says Bonnefoux, "Since I was 18 years old, I always thought that I would work with dancers, and that I would choreograph and teach. They are things that I love to do. I love the idea of developing young dancers and building a company."

In 1979 McBride was in the prime of her career and happily dancing injury-free. Bonnefoux had had knee surgery and a seriously-injured right foot earlier in his career, and as 1979 progressed his right ankle began to bother him more and more.

A nightmare disturbed his sleep one night before a particularly demanding day of matinee and evening performances. He dreamed that he would have an accident, be taken to the hospital, and have surgery. He thought little of the dream in the morning as he prepared for his full day. He was particularly looking forward to dancing with Patricia that evening in *Scotch Symphony.*

The first and second movements of *Scotch Symphony* went well, with magical partnering and characterization. In the third movement *pas de deux* before the finale, Bonnefoux fell during a difficult step in his solo variation. He tried to get up but couldn't. "I couldn't move," he says. "My left foot was disjointed from the ankle. It was pretty bad. Eventually some dancers came to pick me up and took me offstage, but they made it look like that lift was part of the ballet. Pat finished the ballet alone."

Bonnefoux *was* taken to the hospital. Anticipating surgery, grimly he awaited the diagnosis, but the doctors opted for a cast instead. As Lincoln Kirstein once said, "Surgery is not an injury, it's a tragedy."

Bonnefoux couldn't dance for two months. Physically handicapped, yet emotionally resilient, he says poignantly, "There are always other things that I'm interested in usually, so it was okay." Still, he cycled through all of the four temperaments: melancholic despondency, sanguinic optimism, phlegmatic equanimity, choleric anger.

He says, "Like a car in a race coming around, hitting that speed and getting very fast, I had the feeling that I used to be that car coming around at extraordinary speed. All of a sudden I was in the sideway and not going anywhere. *They* were going somewhere and I was going nowhere. It becomes very hard.

"It was one of the grand times for Patricia as a dancer. She was dancing with Baryshnikov, beautiful, and having a great time. I was at home on crutches. I envied her being able to express herself and be herself. It's very hard when you cannot spend your energy, especially when you're used to feeling the thrill of using your body fully. My body had been like a fine-tuned engine that performed best revving at high RPMs. Now I was idling."

After two months "in the sideway" recuperating, Bonnefoux began the tedious process of reconditioning his body, hoping to do one last show dancing well. "I didn't want a big gala performance," he says, "but I wanted to dance again being *proud* of my work and to receive recognition for that work. I wanted people to appreciate how important it was to me to dance well."

He made his comeback in a television performance with McBride. "Right after the taping I felt terrible. It was so hard to dance. I'm a perfectionist and couldn't dance up to my high standards. When we looked at the results of the day's shoot and I saw myself, I hated it. I said 'If that person on the screen is me, forget it. I don't want to be that person. That's enough. That's it.'" In 1980 he stopped dancing at age 36.

"I knew that even without injury I would have stopped one year later. That whole last year [1979-1980] was pretty hard and difficult. I felt that I had danced badly. I realized that I couldn't really go back and be in good shape, so I just stopped dancing. I was ready.

"The one hard thing was that I *wished* I could have done one last show dancing really well before I said goodbye. I was so *deeply* rooted in that wish, it took me years to get over."

Burning with unspent energy, Bonnefoux was eager to work. "I thought that when I stopped dancing I would get employed all the time. But people knew me as a dancer and didn't know me as a choreographer or teacher. So it was hard to find jobs. One job here, one job there—I stayed like that for three years."

Bonnefoux and McBride had longed to have children, but each hopeful start had resulted in miscarriage. "I was getting older," says McBride, "so we decided to adopt." Melanie, born in Korea in 1978, was two years ten months old when Bonnefoux and McBride received her. "What was great," she says happily, "is that I was five months pregnant with my son when Melanie arrived in 1981.

"Mr. Balanchine was very happy when I told him we wanted to adopt, and when I took Melanie to see him he was amused by the fact that I was five months pregnant and nobody knew.

"I didn't want anybody to know because I wasn't sure, but I told people that we were adopting. I danced until I was three months, then it was in the summer and everybody was off. Mr. Balanchine was the first person I wanted to tell.

"He was quite wonderful, which took me by surprise. I remember telling him that I couldn't be dancing because I was pregnant, and he was great. He said, 'Oh, do you want to be?' I said, 'Yes.' I got teary-eyed. He said, 'Oh, but you'll be back. You can do it when the company's at home.' He was *completely* opposite of what I thought. When I got married, it was a shock to him. He was *not* happy about that. So I thought, 'Well, he's not going to be happy about the children,' but he was supportive."

Pregnant and not dancing, McBride spent her days and nights joyfully mothering Melanie. "It was hard at first because she was so needy. She arrived without speaking English and had nightmares. But I had a little Korean word guide and she learned English in four months. By the time Chris was born she was speaking English. It was a very busy time, but having children was just a revelation." Christopher was born early in 1982.

Bonnefoux continued to teach at the School of American Ballet while accepting choreography and ballet master jobs around the country. Says career transition executive Jim Borland, Ph.D., "The transition process may be seen as going from a known 'solid' place to another solid place which then becomes known. The time in between some have likened to being on a high wire or trapeze." Bonnefoux was struggling between solid places in his career, but poetically viewed, according to playwright Eugène Ionesco, "An artist is an adventurer exploring new territory." Combining Borland and Ionesco, Bonnefoux's transition was a tightrope adventure in quest of a new solid place on which to build his artistic home.

The small company of New York City Ballet dancers that he and McBride had toured in 1978-79 had been good basic training for his adventure. His engagements over the next three years muscled his fitness for it.

His triumphant *Othello* world premiered at Louisville Ballet February 20, 1981, in which McBride starred as Desdemona to Bonnefoux's Othello. In the May 1981 *Dance Magazine* William Como praised Bonnefoux's "...divertissements which immediately [showed] the dancers of the Louisville Ballet to advantage.... The final confrontation between Othello and Desdemona flowed dramatically from beginning to end in a dance vocabulary that showed Bonnefous at his most moving." *Othello* was Bonnefoux's last appearance as a performer.

The Metropolitan Opera Ballet hired him to stage *Le Sacre du Printemps* for their December 3 Stravinsky program. To prepare, he went to the performing arts library in Lincoln Center to study the score. "I found a score that was annotated by Stravinsky to help the choreographer Nijinsky," he says. "There were Stravinsky's music phrases then he showed the phrases that Nijinsky should use, because he felt the choreographic phrases were different from the music phrases. That score was just amazing.

"I took the example of Balanchine. When I saw Balanchine working always with the score, I figured that even if I was not very good [a modest understatement], that would help me a lot. And it really benefited me, for my classes and for staging that Stravinsky ballet." Bonnefoux choreographed *Three Overtures* for the Metropolitan in February 1982 to music of Hector Berlioz.

"It was quite a busy time for him," says McBride. "The injury had cut his career short and he was looking everywhere for work." Of her own career she says, "I think I would have been happy staying home and being a wife and mother. I was so happy at home with the children there. I was very fulfilled. I didn't really want to go back, but Jean-Pierre kind of pushed out to be a dancer."

In 1982 after 10 months of blissful mothering, McBride returned to New York City Ballet. Balanchine was hospitalized then, and ballet masters Peter Martins, Jerome Robbins, and John Taras were guiding the company. McBride visited Balanchine in the hospital with her babies. He welcomed her back saying, "You are looking a little better." "I was like, *fat*," laughs McBride, "but he was very supportive."

A call from Ruth Page brought McBride back to performing. Page had choreographed a ballet version of *The Merry Widow* operetta, which was videotaped in the fall of 1982 by Chicago's WTTW and PBS for a spring 1983 broadcast. McBride danced Sonia, the widow; Peter Martins, Prince Danilo.

"My first performance with the company [NYCB] was *Coppélia—hard!*," laughs McBride. "It takes time to get back in shape. Peter [Martins, designated successor to Balanchine] was supportive and everyone was happy to see me, but I felt pulled and guilty about not being able to give my children as much time as I had before. My mother helped a lot, and a babysitter who was quite wonderful. I was with them a lot, too, because Peter was very kind to give me a schedule where I would rehearse early then be free to pick up my children in school after dancing when they got older. When the ballet season was off, I would have lots of time. I took class every day, but I was always there for them."

Bonnefoux continued to search for his next solid place. A particularly divergent project was the *Snow White* he choreographed with ice skater John Curry, aired over PBS December 10, 1982.

The shoals of their respective transitions away from dancing and back again made rough sailing for their marriage. "I think every couple goes through good times and bad," says McBride. "For a year-and-a-half, almost two years, we were separated. It a was difficult time; the marriage wasn't working. The children were with me in New York, and Jean-Pierre was freelancing a lot." She was dancing well again, too, which made those years even harder for him.

In the summer of 1983 a project developed that grew into a solid, wonderful summer home for both of them. Bonnefoux and McBride had guest-performed during NYCB's 1974 summer break at the Chautauqua Institution, a tranquil lakeside community in southwestern New York State where visitors retreat for intellectual, spiritual, and artistic renewal. "The place is magic," says Bonnefoux. "The lake, the beauty, people learning—it's a very special place."

Captivated by the Chautauqua atmosphere and Chautauqua School of Dance, Bonnefoux returned the following year with a group of dancers from the School of American Ballet. "We did a whole evening which was very successful.

"In 1983 the school was looking for a new director. I felt I needed a base and was really interested in education, so they asked me to spend the summer there. There were only a few dancers spending their summers in Chautauqua and taking classes, and at the end of the summer they would do a small recital. I can't believe I saw the possibilities, but I was very clear in my mind about what could happen there—there are some moments in life when you can see clearly the future. I could see that that place could be important for me, dancers, and choreographers, and that we could do important work there together. I felt that I could really make this program go forward and could sense that the people in Chautauqua were ready for that."

Bonnefoux became the school's director in 1983. He and McBride resolved their marital discord, and she has joined him in Chautauqua every summer thereafter as a teacher and coach. So has gifted teacher Violette Verdy, one of their dearest friends.

In the fall of 1983, Bonnefoux accepted a two-year engagement as ballet master, teacher, and resident choreographer of Pittsburgh Ballet. His Pittsburgh residency did not preclude his accepting other assignments, so when Louisville Ballet commissioned him to create a ballet for the company in 1984, Bonnefoux welcomed the opportunity to continue building his reputation as a choreographer.

Music is as much of a muse for Bonnefoux as it was for Balanchine, and a piece that particularly inspired him was Pulitzer Prize-winning Charles Wuorinen's composition called *The Magic Art.* Bonnefoux had first heard about Wuorinen from McBride's brother Eugene, who had worked with the composer as a pianist. Gene introduced Bonnefoux to Wuorinen's music, and to *The Magic Art.*

Wuorinen happened to be in residence with the Louisville Orchestra at the time, creating a direct link to the musical source. Fascinated with Wuorinen's contemporary recontextualization of Purcell's music in the piece, Bonnefoux called him to ask if he could create a ballet to it for the Louisville dancers. Wuorinen arranged excerpts from *The Magic Art* to

Jean-Pierre Bonnefoux, Executive and Artistic Director, North Carolina Dance Theatre, with his wife, Patricia McBride, Associate Artistic Director, North Carolina Dance Theatre. (Photograph by Rolland Elliot, 2003.)

which Bonnefoux choreographed *Courtly Dances*. "I love to work with composers," he says. "It brings me into a different and very satisfying world."

Bonnefoux and Wuorinen met again early in 1985 in New York City. Mary Sharp Cronson had initiated a series of "Works in Progress" programs at New York's Guggenheim Museum that examined the creative process by allowing audiences to hear artists talk about what they do, then see examples of work. On February 3 and 4, 1985, the composer and choreographer discussed *The Magic Art* and Wuorinen's *String Trio*, which Bonnefoux had choreographed for Pennsylvania Ballet. Dancers performing excerpts of Bonnefoux's ballets to these works included students from the School of American Ballet, NYCB principals Patricia McBride and Alexandre Proia, and three Pennsylvania Ballet dancers.

United States rock musician Frank Zappa once said, "Music, in performance, is a type of sculpture. The air in the performance is sculpted into something." Wuorinen, Bonnefoux, and dancers sculpted the Guggenheim air those two February nights.

Shortly after his Guggenheim gig, Bonnefoux received a call from Indiana University Professor of Music Marina Svetlova, former dancer in the Ballet Russe de Monte Carlo, prima ballerina with the Metropolitan Opera, and chairman of the Ballet Department at Indiana University's renowned School of Music since 1969. Svetlova was ready to step down and the Department was looking for a new chairman.

"She had heard about me and asked me if I was interested," says Bonnefoux. "I went to see the situation and, again [as in Chautauqua], I felt that the place had great possibilities. At the time there were not that many good university programs in ballet. The dance department was a part of one of the best schools of music in the country, and that, plus my love of music and working with musicians, convinced me it was the right place to move.

I just could not wait in New York for jobs to come and do a few things here and there—that just was not for me. I like the idea of getting people to believe in what I can do for them. The idea of building is always exciting for me, and it's something that I hope I can do well. I like being busy and working hard, so it was very satisfying to start building somewhere again, and to try to convince people there how far we could go."

McBride remained in New York with Melanie and Christopher. With her usual positive outlook on life she says, "The schedule Peter arranged for me gave me the best of both worlds—ballet and motherhood." She and Bonnefoux commuted back and forth between Bloomington and New York City, although hardly the ideal family situation for the children. They welcomed their Chautauqua summers together.

Hard at work building the IU ballet program, in 1987 Bonnefoux nonetheless accepted New York City Ballet's invitation to choreograph a ballet for their 1988 American Music Festival. He asked the company to commission Charles Wuorinen to compose a new piece for him.

Wuorinen composed *FIVE* in New York, then sent the score to Bonnefoux in Bloomington. "The piece had not been *played* yet," says Wuorinen, "so he had to work from the score. There was no recording, no crutch for him, which was a challenge, but Jean-Pierre is much more musically literate than most choreographers. He did pretty well with it, I thought. He is a very cultivated, intelligent person."

The resulting ballet, *FIVE,* premiered April 28, 1988, in the New York State Theater with Michael Byars in one of lead roles. After the premier and a loving good-bye to his wife and children, Bonnefoux returned to Indiana University.

McBride's situation at New York City Ballet was hardly ideal, in spite of her external sanguinity about it. Although her rehearsal and performance schedule allowed her more time with her children, she admits, "It was hard performing only once or twice a week. It's hard to get into shape that way. Also, when I came back after my pregnancy most of my ballets had been cut, and the ballets I did dance were rather strenuous. I remember how nervous I was having to dance a full-length *Coppélia,* and that was my one performance that week, or having to do *Rubies.* I'd have one *Rubies* one week, then I had to train like a *workhorse* to be in shape for my performance the next week. I really felt that I did my best when I danced *a lot,* so I had to make up for that by working out on my own.

"You maintain yourself, but as you get older, your barres get longer. I felt good physically, but I wasn't a young dancer anymore and there were young people coming up, as is natural, who shared everything I danced, all of my old roles. Peter wasn't giving me the opportunities to dance.

"I was used to having new ballets staged for me, and that part I really missed. I had my repertoire, but I didn't have any new works that were done for me. It felt like a great hardship to be there and not to dance that much. Mr. Balanchine wasn't there, and my career was very different. It was a struggle to hold on."

Her innate optimism immediately intervenes, "It wasn't a struggle, because I had a repertoire of ballets that I still loved to dance. Dancing these and Jerry Robbins sustained me, and Peter made two new ballets for me, *Valse Triste* and *Tea Rose*," which Martins named after her distinctive perfume.

One day early in 1989 while walking down the street, McBride felt an inner voice say, "It's time to stop." "I am a feeling person," she says, "and I just knew in my heart that I didn't want to do it anymore. Like when you know you love someone, you just *know*.

"I went to Peter and said 'Peter, I really would like to stop dancing. I don't want to do this anymore.' I had had a very full and fulfilling career as a dancer, had gone places I never dreamed of going, and had danced the whole repertoire. There was nothing, really, that I wanted to reach out to do anymore. I had done it all.

"Although I was 46 years old, I felt physically fit and was injury-free, so I could've stayed with NYCB. But I felt that I had lost my place. It was hard. I got to a point toward the end where I had to switch my mental attitude in order to dance.

"It was a new decade for me coming back as a mother and having to deal with not dancing as much and trying to keep my technique. I guess I am not a very aggressive person, because it all had fallen into my lap. I never *asked* to do a ballet. I never asked Mr. Balanchine, I never asked Jerry Robbins, 'Could I dance this ballet?' I never demanded to be cast for anything in my life. So when I came back to dancing, I realized, 'Gee, Peter isn't going to cast me. How am I going to deal with this?' He had a lot of people that he had to take care of in the company, and personal relationships to take care of.

"I felt good about ending my career. I had a husband and two fascinating children whom I adored and was very fortunate to have. I felt very happy, like I had come full circle, and I didn't want to linger too long as I've seen others do. I felt very fortunate that it was my decision to stop, and, frankly, I really wanted to join my husband at Indiana University to bring our family together."

McBride ended her career with a spectacular retirement performance in the New York State Theater June 4, 1989. "It was wonderful," she says. "Peter Martins made my retirement. He created an evening of most of the ballets that were choreographed for me, but I told him, 'I'd like everybody on'—so all the ballerinas danced my roles. I did five pieces on the program—*Valse Triste* that Peter Martins had choreographed for me, *Coppélia pas de deux* from Act III and *coda*, "The Man I Love" from *Who Cares?*, the last waltz from *Liebeslieder Walzer*, and I finished the program with my solo from *Harlequinade*, the second act solo, which is a beautiful variation. It was just the most wonderful last way of leaving, a dream ending of a long career. I had 30 years with the New York City Ballet, and it was just a most wonderful way to go. It was a very happy, happy performance for me. I was so happy to be retired."

Jerome Robbins stopped by before the performance to give her flowers, then went on to the opening night of his *Jerome Robbins Broadway*. In her *Dance Voice* article, Miriam Durkin describes Martins's surprise for McBride at the end of the performance. "In the finale, she is alone onstage in a blue tutu, dancing a solo from *Harlequinade*. The dance ends, she bows and blows kisses. When she looks up, Villella surprises her with a bouquet of roses. Suddenly, there is a line of men in tuxedos— men she'd danced with throughout her career. They step up one by one to offer more roses. The last one is Bonnefoux, her husband. They embrace—the longest hug of all. They will be living together again in Indiana soon.... For 30 minutes, 13,000 [thornless] roses rain down on the stage as the audience applauds and cheers, and McBride bows."

She danced once more in July 1989: her farewell to New York City Ballet's summer home in Saratoga Springs. She says, "I did *Valse Triste pas de deux* for one last time."

With the family reunited at Indiana University, McBride immediately changed her identity with her enviable talent for living in-the-moment. Writes Durkin, "She embraced her new role as dance faculty and homemaker. She learned to drive. And she reveled in ordinary life."

Says McBride of her life, "I just put all my energy into dancing, and when I stopped dancing, I put it into teaching, staging ballets at the University, and being a mother. I think you're only happy in whatever you do if you give it your all."

Without a break, she went from retiring in July to teaching in August. "It was very exciting getting used to my new, second career, but teaching and dancing are two *entirely* different things. You don't just go from being a dancer to being a teacher. It takes time and transition. With teaching, you have so many different personalities who need your help, and you need to find out what's right for each of them. Dancing was a lot easier because you just have yourself to worry about.

"Teaching well is a learning process; it doesn't happen overnight. And just because you were a good dancer doesn't mean that you're a good teacher. You never stop learning when you're a dancer, and it's the same thing with teaching. You learn and you grow." Wrote Editor Joseph Epstein in the Spring 1987 issue of *The American Scholar*, "A few years after I began teaching, it occurred to me that being a teacher—not being a student—provides the best education. To teach is to learn twice."

The University was a perfect learning environment. "Because it was a very fine school of music," says McBride, "we had a beautiful theater, an orchestra, and lovely studios. I learned to teach there, and I staged many Balanchine ballets that I had danced in my career.

"It was a very different responsibility to be on the other side—teaching and coaching people instead of spending time on my own dancing. What I had learned as a dancer transferred, though. It surprises you, the knowledge you have that you don't realize is there. I didn't have confidence when I first started. It takes years to feel confident in staging works; it takes lots of experience.

"But I just *love* coaching and working one-on-one with dancers. There is nothing greater than passing on knowledge that you have stored up from working with Mr. Balanchine, and there is nothing as rewarding as seeing others perform his ballets the way he would have wanted them performed. When I coach and stage his works I feel his presence guiding me, and I feel a great responsibility to be true to his ideals."

A special joy was working side by side with her husband. "I'm always learning a lot from him," she says. "He is very inspiring, and he amazes me with what he can do. I believe in him *completely*. He made the Ballet Department into one of the most wonderful university dance programs in America."

Still going through his own transition in 1985, Bonnefoux says one of the facets of the University job that appealed to him the most "was to prepare dancers to go to other transitions. After dancing in a company for a few years, maybe some of them would feel that the life of a dancer was not for them—some dancers discover this. Going into a University program was a nice way to still dance while starting to get an education that will prepare you for something else. I wanted to see what that program could do for dancers"—for students as well as professionals returning to school.

Bonnefoux had another reason for accepting the University job: to get more education for himself. He says, "I thought I would have time, not to get a degree, necessarily, but at least to take some classes. He laughs at recalling his inquiry about a lithograph class. "I have always been interested in lithograph, so I wanted to take some classes in that. They asked me to fill out a paper and said, 'What about your education, Professor Bonnefoux? What degrees do you have, or what university did you go to?'

"I was Professor of Dance there full-time, with tenure, but when they asked me, 'What degrees do you have?' I didn't say much. 'What university did you go to?' I told them I never went to university. They said,

'What about high school?' I said, 'I didn't go to high school.' It was hysterical, the way that man looked at me. He was having fun realizing that somebody without that education was a university professor of dance."

Bonnefoux never took the lithograph class, not for lack of credentials but because of his real priorities. "The idea of growing the department and getting it to be better and better, plus teaching and choreographing, *those* were what was really important to me." Ironically, in the process of being a professor instead of a student he gained an education every bit as rich as an academic degree could provide. As Mark Twain said, "I never let my schooling interfere with my education."

One thing Bonnefoux *did* take during his 11 years at Indiana University (1985–1996) was a sabbatical. "I did not think I was ready to direct a company," he says of his ultimate goal. "I thought that I needed to learn more, to look around more, so I took one year off on sabbatical leave. It was just marvelous to be able to go to Europe and teach. I went to the Royal Danish Ballet and Paris Opéra, I worked with Jiri Kylián in the Netherlands, I went to Munich. I also continued the work I had been doing with the National Endowment for the Arts since about 1987. I visited dance companies around the United States to see if they were putting their grant money to good use, or to see if they had worthwhile new programs to fund. All these things during that sabbatical were really interesting." Not only that, they fed his passions for education, helping to develop dancers, and building programs.

As news spread of Bonnefoux's and McBride's second-career successes, enticing offers from other universities and ballet companies came in. "Three opportunities just fell into our laps," says McBride, "although we weren't really looking for them." The timing was right when their friend Jerri Kumery called.

After nine-years' dancing with New York City Ballet, Kumery had joined North Carolina Dance Theatre as ballet mistress to Salvatore Aiello, then NCDT's Artistic Director (1985–1995). When Aiello died in 1995, Kumery became acting Artistic Director while the Board searched for a new AD. "Jerri told Jean-Pierre that she thought he'd be a great director," says McBride, "so he applied."

Bonnefoux clearly had distinguished himself during his 12 years in Chautauqua and 10 in Bloomington. Since his first Chautauqua summer in 1983, he had built the modest dance school into a thriving summer program for 11-year-olds through professional levels that emphasized performance, teaching excellence, and instilling self-confidence in students. Wrote Nicole Dekel in her February 1994 *Dance Magazine* article *Summer Secret: Chautauqua Movement,* "As a teacher-director, Bonnefoux is at once gentle, authoritative, approachable, and demanding; he stewards his program with full confidence in the vitality of classical dance and a limitless belief in its capacity for new expression. In part because of his own optimism, Chautauqua impressed me with an overwhelming sense of promise...."

Of McBride she writes, "A summer at Chautauqua is ... an extraordinary opportunity to learn some of the ballets of George Balanchine under the expert, watchful, and caring coaching [and teaching] of McBride.... [She] is strikingly welcoming and attentive, and her pleasure in the progress of students and young professionals seems genuine and undiminishable. She offers by her presence an example for the aspiring ballerinas around her."

By 1996, after 11 years as chairman of the Indiana University Ballet Department, "it was just not a challenge anymore," says Bonnefoux. "I felt that I knew what directing was, and felt that I was doing sort of routine work. It was not stimulating, and I wanted to do something else." Thus when North Carolina Dance Theatre called to offer him the artistic directorship he accepted, excited about building the company.

He called his dear friend Violette Verdy, one of the world's preeminent teachers, who welcomed the opportunity. Verdy joined the ballet faculty as Professor of Music and added her human warmth, extraordinary talent, and deep intelligence to the IU staff.

Bonnefoux, McBride, Melanie, and Christopher moved to Charlotte, North Carolina in the summer of 1996 and have lived there ever since.

Says McBride of her switch from the world-renowned Indiana University School of Music to a mid-sized Southern city, "I'm a chameleon. I just follow Jean-Pierre wherever he goes. I believe in what he can do. Although we come from different backgrounds, we feel very similar about what we think is important. I feel very fortunate that he has been so encouraging and helpful in shaping my destiny as a teacher and a coach."

As in the School of American Ballet, Chautauqua, and Indiana, the North Carolina Dance Theatre gave Bonnefoux the opportunity to build through collaboration. "I love the idea of building a place where people meet and exchange ideas," he says. "I *love* building something that will be, how do they say in business, 'one plus one makes three?', something that is more than the sum of its parts. I *love* working with many different types of people—you get so much pleasure and learn so much.

"Sometimes I think that dancers are too much on their own. We should not be on the side or work alone. We need to work with other people. You can do your best *only* when you are inspired by other people."

His ordeal of being "in the sideway" and "going nowhere" in 1980 continues to spur his desire to help students, dancers, choreographers, and colleagues wherever he goes—and to learn from them in return.

But, warns Artistic Director of Boston's American Repertory Theatre Robert Woodruff, "Collaboration by itself is meaningless unless there's a very strong spine to what's being made. A strong idea of what we are doing in this room, the statement we're pursuing, and the ideas we're investigating. Because without that muscle I think you just have a lot of agreement."

The muscle in North Carolina Dance Theatre is robust, built by the hard work, perspicacity, and creativity of Bonnefoux, McBride, and their artistic team. NCDT tours nationally, appears at major arts festivals, and performs in New York. Repertoire ranges from Balanchine to Bluegrass, classics to comedy, *Feast of Ashes* to *TV Dinner.* NCDT's website proudly quotes company kudos:

> "...if they decided to settle in Britain they would be among our top ballet companies." *The London Times*
>
> "Superb ... sufficiently armed to conquer the world." *Le Figaro (Italy)*
>
> Dance Theatre has "...produced performers of stunning versatility and dramatic power." *Dance Magazine*
>
> "Unstinting in range and thunder ... a pleasure to behold." *The New York Times*

Artistic importance begins in the studio, where, as in Chautauqua, Bonnefoux, McBride, and their superb teachers and choreographers inspire self-confidence and trust. They emphasize musicality, coloration, and understanding of the roles their dancers dance, guiding them beyond technique to expressive artistry. From studio to stage to life, they teach their dancers to think, thereby empowering them to learn anything.

At the end of 2000, Bonnefoux expanded his role to executive and artistic director of North Carolina Dance Theatre; interim executive director Carl Powell became managing director. Although his workload doubled, Bonnefoux still took responsibility for artistic programming. The company's performances were brilliant. Wrote Sybil Huskey in her January 2000 *Dance Magazine* review of NCDT's 30th anniversary season opener in Charlotte, NC, "...with artistic director Jean-Pierre Bonnefoux and co-artistic directors Patricia McBride and Jerri Kumery, the company is proving to be the artistic jewel in the crown of this Queen City."

Since 1997, the NCDT company has spent a month-long residency at Chautauqua. In July 2001, Bonnefoux was choreographing a new *Cinderella* with his dancers there for their fall opening in Charlotte. He felt tired during the rehearsal, understandable given the 10-to-12-hour-day-six-day-a-week schedule he had maintained for the past 15 years, but exhilarated about his concepts for the ballet and the *pas de deux* he was setting at the moment. Breathing became difficult and painful near the end of the rehearsal, but he ignored the discomfort and finished, pleased with the day's work. He was painfully gasping on the way home, and by evening his chest pain was so intense McBride drove him to the local hospital in Westfield, New York. "It was frightening," she says. "His condition was so serious the hospital helicoptered him to a hospital in Erie, Pennsylvania, where they saved his life.

"They put in a stint right away and a week later performed five bypass surgeries. They couldn't wait—*five* of them. They needed lots of veins because they did so many bypasses, so they took veins from both of his legs. In the left leg they took all the way from the thigh to the ankle, and half way up the right leg.

"We had the most extraordinary surgeon, a French-Canadian. Jean-Pierre liked him and trusted him. He reminded him of his father."

Phlebitis developed in both legs which prolonged Bonnefoux's recovery, but his strong dancer constitution prevailed. "It took a *long* time," says McBride, "especially for that one leg. But he was amazing. It's just amazing how the body recovers. Jean-Pierre also had a goal: he was determined to open the North Carolina Dance Theatre season with his *Cinderella*."

McBride had just performed her greatest role: savior of a life. Her enormous love, constant nurturing, and out-of-character boldness brought Jean Pierre Bonnefoux from the brink of mortality back to vitality.

Says Bonnefoux, "In my heart, I don't believe I would have made it without her. Those five weeks at the hospital she stayed with me. She slept there in a chair that you could convert into a cot. Without her being there day and night, I really don't think in my heart that I would have made it. I really needed her. I needed that love and that stability. It didn't make sense, that was the worst, I think. It didn't make sense that I was lying down. It was very hard emotionally.

"I can't believe how some people are there in the hospital all alone. I don't know how they do it, how they go on without that support."

Friends, family, and colleagues from Chautauqua, Charlotte, and beyond visited Bonnefoux in the hospital. Each unwittingly hastened the healing process with their expressions of love, loyalty, and belief in his return to full health. "It was a great feeling," he says, "to know that people cared and worked a lot for me, to know that you need other people. Sometimes you're fortunate and you get that attention."

Professionally, Bonnefoux has always surrounded himself with capable, caring people who inspire and energize him. When his angina occurred during the *Cinderella* rehearsal in Chautauqua, he was working with choreographers Mark Diamond and Michael Vernon, who finished the ballet during his hospitalization.

"Jean-Pierre was so disappointed to have missed the premier of his *Cinderella* in Chautauqua," says McBride, "but he was back working in Charlotte in early September. I was a wreck." Feeling fit and rejuvenated with both legs completely healed, Bonnefoux was eager to return to full-time work by the end of September. "He went back earlier than I thought was healthy for him to do," she says, "but he was really determined to do this. When he sets his mind to do something, he *does* it."

"I cannot imagine my life if I stopped working," he says. "Apart from my family, what's really most important is to work with people. To find what is the potential in these people, then find a way to help them reach that potential. To teach them that they are unique and special. To help them feel the growth, to imagine it, and then to help that potential happen. To nurture that person. *That's* what's important: to see people be happy with what they do and proud of what they do. *That* is really what I like.

"When you have people who believe in themselves and their work, then everybody works as a team and is proud of the result they create together. They feel that their company is the most important thing and every individual feels responsible for the whole. When you trust people and trust in their potential, what they give is amazing. That's why when I decide to work with somebody, I don't wait for them to give me their trust, I usually trust them first. Trust brings out the best in people.

"It's natural for me. Young choreographers and young dancers have so much to offer, and the most important thing for me is to see them grow into the best they can be."

McBride's passion for developing dancers is as ardent as Bonnefoux's. "I feel such profound rewards when I teach and coach," she says. "It's thrilling for me to see the dancers grow and blossom into new areas of expression and develop the confidence to believe in themselves, so each feels good about his or her individual artistry. The repertoire a dancer dances is key to the dancer's artistic growth.

"Teaching the young students is exciting because they have their whole careers in front of them. Working with the professionals in our company is a different level of passion, but equally as strong. Our NCDT company dancers are extraordinary. They are intelligent and fearless artists who can master the many different styles we do, including the familiar classics, the Balanchine repertoire, modern dance, and leading-edge contemporary works.

"I feel very fortunate to be able to do what I love doing, continuing the tradition of passing on the ballets of Mr. Balanchine, and feel a deep responsibility to the students and professionals alike."

Says Bonnefoux, "Pat said that when she danced she used to receive the accolade and the applause of the audience, and that now, as a teacher, it's time for her to *give*. I think that's great."

Says McBride, "I am constantly learning and growing all the time, through my dancers and my children. The children have exposed me to so many things that I would not have experienced otherwise, and I am so proud of them. Melanie graduated from Fordham University with a double major in English and Theater, and she published her first novel in August 2003. Chris is in the University of North Carolina in Charlotte exploring his many interests. Being a mother, teaching, and staging ballets help me to understand my life in exciting a new ways.

"You should be an eternal student, because there is always something more to discover in dance and in life. You should keep looking for that other level in everything you dance and in every day you live."

Says Bonnefoux, "When you're not challenging yourself with new learning and you stop wanting to grow, this is when your life stops. As long as you say, 'I'm going to find a teacher, I'm going to find some great people whom I can look up to, great masters—that's what's going to guide my life,' as long as you do that, then your life goes on in an exciting way."

Bonnefoux and McBride are great teachers, warm stars as bright as suns. May their enlightening lives guide and empower yours.

BEN STEVENSON
"Sort of Just Happened"

"Ben is America's secret weapon, choreographically," says eminent photographer Jack Mitchell. "He just keeps creating masterpieces." Decades of awards, rave reviews, and filled theaters confirm that Stevenson is a "major, major choreographer."

With choreographic alchemy, Stevenson deftly blends vision, performance, and pragmatism in the right proportions. The studio is his laboratory, his stage, magnetic territory. His ballets grip your imagination, draw you in, and make you hunger for more. Money pours into the box office in the bewitching process.

Ben Stevenson, born April 4, 1936, in Portsmouth, England, had pragmatism instilled as a child by his bus driver father and flower shop owner mother. The theater sharpened his artistic vision. "I've got an older sister who loved ballet," he says, "and she and my mother both loved opera. Whenever an opera or ballet came to town we always went to see it, and they had quite an influence on me." His flair for performance blossomed early in his droll mimicry of Carmen Miranda with his mother's flower baskets on his head.

Stevenson's only hindrance as a youngster was a bad knock-knee that caused his left foot to roll in when he walked. His mother took him to the doctor, who prescribed orthotic inserts for his shoes to raise his instep. The doctor also recommended ballet class: "My daughter had the same problem and took up ballet. All the turnout exercises and dancing movements cured it."

Stevenson's mother followed the doctor's advice and took her seven-year-old son to ballet school, which Stevenson says he "wasn't particularly thrilled about."

Ben Stevenson at 19 years old, as he appeared in Laon Maybanke's delightful photograph album *First Faces* published by Constable & Company Ltd., in 1962. (Photograph by Laon Maybanke, circa 1960.)

"But at the same time, I *loved* anything musical. I was always jumping around to music, so ballet was not something that was going to be tough for me to get into, once I'd decided I'd found the right place. My mother took me to several schools, but I refused to get up and do anything until she took me to the Mary Tonkin School that had some other little boys in the class. "I didn't feel so the odd man out, I suppose, because then I really started. By the time that I was 10 or 11, I was hooked on dancing, and that's what I wanted to do."

The creative ballet energy in England and Europe after World War II fueled Stevenson's passion. On February 20, 1946, when he was nine years old, the Vic-Wells Ballet premiered Nicholas Sergeyev's lavish new production of *The Sleeping Beauty* in London's Covent Garden, starring Margot Fonteyn as Aurora, Robert Helpmann as the Prince, and Beryl Grey as the Lilac Fairy. *The Sleeping Beauty* became a milestone in Stevenson's own career twenty-one years later.

On December 23, 1948, at the Royal Opera House, the Sadler's Wells Ballet premiered Frederick Ashton's historic *Cinderella* to Sergei Prokofiev's new score. Ashton and Helpmann *en travesti* played Cinderella's stepsisters, roles Stevenson would play hilariously in his own *Cinderella* masterpieces for the National Ballet and Houston Ballet.

When Anton Dolin and Alicia Markova returned from touring America in 1949, they reformed their pre-war Markova–Dolin Ballet, now called Festival Ballet for the approaching Festival of Britain, and opened in London on October 24, 1950. With Dolin as Artistic Director and impresario Dr. Julian Braunsweg as Administrative Director, Festival Ballet aimed from the beginning for popular appeal, based on a repertoire of box-office hits and guest stars.

When the company toured through Portsmouth during the 1950 holiday season, Braunsweg phoned Stevenson's ballet school to ask for extras to travel with the company. Wrote Victoria Huckenphaler in the May 1972 *Dance Magazine* on page 84, "Stevenson, then 14 years old, was one of one of the students chosen. When the company reached Brighton, Anton Dolin noticed Stevenson's persistent appearance at the stage entrance after each night's performance. Dolin, in his *Autobiography*, recalls the incident this way: 'I remember the week [in Brighton] for one reason. A small, rather dreadful boy that each night was outside the stage door. By Thursday, he had plucked up enough courage to ask me for a dance audition.' Dolin watched Stevenson in class, and thereupon maneuvered a grant for the boy to attend the Arts Educational School [in London]."

Dolin had an "impeccable eye for dance talent," according to *Dance Magazine* Senior Editor Clive Barnes.

Stevenson stopped his formal education at age 14. "The government grant paid for me do the dance course and the theater course at Arts Educational," he says, "but not to do anything else. The fees were too high to go into the full-time academic and the vocational as well.

"But I was terribly lucky to go to that school, rather than the Royal Ballet or some other strictly ballet school. Arts Educational had strong programs in acting and modern dance as well as ballet, and they encouraged you to teach and choreograph—I did some little bit on the students there for the School. The drama classes are important particularly later on, because as you start to choreograph you want to tell a story."

He had to earn his living in London so started to look for work as soon as he settled into the Arts Educational School. His first job was "washing up and doing all sorts of restaurant things" at a big London Lyons Corner House. In 1953 he found work in his proper calling, as a dancer in the Theatre Arts Ballet company. In 1955 at age 18, he danced with 44-year-old Alicia Markova in *Where the Rainbow Ends*, John Taras's entr'acte ballet in the Christmas play by Clifford Mills and John Ramsay. He also joined the musical *Wedding in Paris*.

By good fortune, the ballet mistress for *Wedding in Paris* was married to the manager of the Sadler's Wells Theatre. "She encouraged me to audition for the Theatre Ballet," says Stevenson, "but as there were no vacancies, I went to the Opera Ballet." The Sadler's Wells Opera Ballet was Sadler's Wells Theatre Ballet's sister company, established in 1946 to nurture young dancers and new choreographers.

Meanwhile in 1955, far away in Houston, Texas, a milestone ballet event occurred that foreshadowed Stevenson's destiny. Wrote Ann Holmes in the September 1979 *Ballet News* on pages 20–21, "The Houston Ballet Foundation was formed in 1955—a classic case of six balletomanes in search of a first-class company. These were balletomanes who had become friends over the years as they attended Houston performances of the Ballet Russe de Monte Carlo in the '30s and '40s and later the young Ballet Theatre. They knew and loved the dancers and when Ballet Theatre ended, they moved to end the emptiness." They formed the Foundation with three objectives: to support local and imported dance, form an academy, and establish a company. They brought in Russian-born former ballerina Tatiana Semenova to launch the academy.

Stevenson, in London, joined the Opera Ballet in 1956, the same year he took his final examination (Solo Seal) for the Royal Academy of Dancing. By unanimous consent of the judges, he was awarded the coveted Adeline Genée Gold Medal. Former ballerina Genée (1878–1970) helped to found the Royal Academy of Dancing in 1920 to monitor and further the standards of classical ballet training in Great Britain and the Commonwealth. Genée became the R.A.D.'s first president in 1936, succeeded by Margot Fonteyn in 1954. Dame Margot presented Stevenson with his medal.

If anyone had told him then that one day he would set a ballet on Margot Fonteyn in America, he would have thought that person daft. When he did create *The Sleeping Beauty* for Fonteyn in 1971, he was still so in awe of her he admits that when he was around her he "felt like a little boy in the *corps de ballet*."

Sadler's Wells Opera Ballet, Sadler's Wells Theatre Ballet, and Sadler's Wells Ballet School were collectively named the Royal Ballet by Royal Charter on 31 October 1956 and it was for the Royal Ballet that Frederick Ashton choreographed *Ondine*, which has been called "a concerto for Fonteyn." *Ondine* premiered at the Royal Opera House on October 27, 1958, with most of the attention riveted on the dazzling prima ballerina. Twenty-two-year-old Stevenson, then in the corps, had his moments of reflected glory dancing solo divertissements.

He remained with the Royal Ballet (Sadler's Wells) until 1959, returning frequently to the Arts Education School to teach. "I started teaching when I was about 16," he says, "They kept asking me to teach the young children, so I always had a job there. It was a way to earn extra money, and I also very much enjoyed it." Stevenson also taught in Portsmouth.

He began to grow weary of dancing in the Royal Ballet with its "nine-to-five sort of regularity," so when Anton Dolin invited him to join London's Festival Ballet as soloist in 1959 he accepted. He relished the opportunity to learn from Dolin and Festival Ballet's brilliant principal dancer John Gilpin. During his first year with Festival, he danced the mazurka in *Les Sylphides*, and Gilpin's roles in *Variations for Four*, *Etudes*, and *Concerti*.

In 1960, Dolin retired as Artistic Director and Gilpin left the company to dance guest appearances around the world. "With Dolin and Gilpin out," says Stevenson, "I thought, 'This is going to be a hideous place to work now,' so I decided to go off to see what I could do on my own." Former U.S. Army General Douglas MacArthur said, "There is no security on this earth; there is only opportunity." Stevenson's career developed from his keen ability to sense opportunity.

"I was approached about doing the role of Tommy Djilas in *The Music Man*, but I had not spoken on stage before so thought that might be a problem. Anyway, I went to the audition and got the part. Van Johnson was doing the Music Man."

An article in London's August 1960 *Dance and Dancers* entitled "Dancer you will know: Ben Stevenson" helped to establish his growing reputation as a talent to watch. He danced in *Half a Sixpence* with Tommy Steele, performed on television for three months in Rome with Caterina Valente, and his portrait, along with those of Brendan Behan, Ann Bancroft, Victor Spinetti, Vivien Leigh, et al. appeared in Laon Maybanke's photograph album *First Faces* (Constable & Company Ltd., 1962).

Every week in 1962 and 1963, Stevenson danced in musical numbers for British television's "Sunday Night at the Palladium." Fellow performers included Judy Garland, Ella Fitzgerald, Shirley Bassey, Gillian Lynne, and Cleo Laine. Said Stevenson's long-time Houston Ballet assistant Patsy Ross in 1999, "Ben is just amazing, the *people* he knows and has danced with—Lynn Seymour, Shirley MacLaine, Chita Rivera, [the above]. He doesn't just *know* these people, they are good friends, and he maintains strong contact with them. He has so much to offer and gives his all to building solid relationships with people, just as he gives his all to his art."

Theatre Royal mounted a revival of *The Boys from Syracuse* at Drury Lane in 1963, with choreography by New York director-choreographer Bob Herget (George Balanchine choreographed the 1938 original). Herget chose Stevenson as one of his lead dancers.

"I stayed in musicals for about four or five years [1960–64]," says Stevenson, "so became very interested in the theater as well as dance, and also in the actual directing of plays and musical productions." Herget became his mentor and friend.

Festival Ballet's administrative director Julian Braunsweg attended the last performance of *The Boys from Syracuse* and sought out Stevenson after the show. "Dr. Braunsweg said to me, 'We really need you to come back to Festival Ballet. All our principal male dancers are off, so we have *no* one, and we're going on tour. Would you come back for a few months?' I did *Boys from Syracuse* on Saturday, and on Monday I was dancing *Les Sylphides* somewhere in Brighton."

Stevenson had been taking class to keep in shape for his musical theater performances, "but I wasn't in the sort of shape I was in when I was in the ballet company. Still, I had spent a lot of time training as a ballet dancer and spent years in ballet companies, so it wasn't so difficult to go back. Also, I thought the Festival tour of the provinces was just something I would do before the next musical. But then I sort of got drawn back into it, and I remained with the company for another six years [1964–1969]."

Stevenson's budding choreographic talent blossomed at Festival Ballet. G.B.L. Wilson reviewed a February 5, 1967, program in the March '67 *The Dancing Times* on page 295. Wilson begins, "Although envisaged as a 'private experimental evening' Festival Ballet's Sunday performance turned out to be a successful public entertainment—hats off to them, and thanks to Donald Albery for putting his New Theatre at their disposal. So all-pervading is the ballet grapevine that it was filled without the need for any other publicity."

Wrote Wilson in his second paragraph, "Ben Stevenson confirmed that he understands the craft of choreography and is worthy of greater encouragement. His comic pas de trios (to Bach)—a skit on the classical style—was witty and did not over-play its hand. His *Cast Out*—an insect ballet—was familiar from the Arts Educational School performance at the Sunshine Matinee, and showed that the choreographer can sustain a particular style without running out of ideas." Stevenson's inventive ballets were a sure sign of creative confidence.

Stevenson's choreographic skill inspired Festival Ballet Artistic Director (1965–68) Donald Albery to ask him to create the company's first-ever performance of *The Sleeping Beauty*. Says Stevenson, "It had been advertised, but no one wanted to do *The Sleeping Beauty* for the company because the Royal Ballet was so famous for its *Sleeping Beauty* with Margaret Fonteyn. Since we were the sort of the underdog company then in London, no one wanted to put their hand in the fire and do our own production.

"Albery basically told me, 'We've *got* to get someone to do it, so *you're* going to have to do it, because it's been advertised and they've sold tickets.' With about a four-week rehearsal period, I did this production of *The Sleeping Beauty* which, much to my surprise, went very well." Parisian ballerina Noella Pontois and John Gilpin danced the leads.

An accident while horse riding in Oxford, England during a 1967 Festival Ballet tour changed the direction of Stevenson's career at age 31. "I broke my ankle," he says. "When I was younger, my thing was to be a dancer. That's what I really wanted to be. After the accident, every time I tried to come back to dancing it would swell up, so I had a lot of trouble proceeding with the ankle. Eventually, I had to stop dancing."

Beryl Grey assumed Festival Ballet's directorship in 1968 ['68–'79]. Stevenson was then ballet master of the company, "but she wanted her *own* ballet master; she didn't want me. She said she thought I had some talent, but she wanted to build her own team so thought it would be better for me to go somewhere else.

"I understood: she didn't know me and wanted to give the job to someone she did. I would have done the same thing, I think. Anyway, I left, but I wasn't quite sure what to do."

Stevenson called Bob Herget in New York, with whom he had stayed in touch since *The Boys from Syracuse.* "What's going on?" asked Herget. "I was just fired from Festival Ballet and I'm not sure what to do," replied Stevenson. "Come here for a vacation," said Herget.

Stevenson packed up and went to New York for a two-week holiday. He started working in the first week and got a job in the second.

Herget knew people, one of whom was Dr. Rachel Dunaven Yocum, Chairman of the Dance Department of the School of Performing Arts. "Bob was a great friend of hers," says Stevenson, " so I was invited to teach two classes there. A student named Keith Lee was in one of the classes; he was also a scholarship student at the Harkness Ballet School, the school of the Harkness Ballet." Lee was thrilled with the class and took word of Stevenson's exciting teaching back to the Harkness School.

"I received a telephone call inviting me to teach a class *there,* so I started off my second week by going to teach a couple of classes at Harkness House. Then Rebekah Harkness asked if I would teach her a private class which was just hysterical, but I did.

"At the end of the week, she told me she wanted to start a second company of talented young dancers from the Harkness School, called the Harkness Youth Dancers, as a stepping stone to the big company, Harkness Ballet. She wanted me to direct the new company.

"I thought it was ideal in a way, because it meant that I could teach and choreograph, and it wasn't a big responsibility, like directing in a big company. Also, it would be a very positive stepping stone for the dancers to the main company."

Stevenson's teaching, dancing, and choreography launched the young company with verve. Reports Jack Mitchell, "I first met Ben Stevenson backstage at the Delacort Theater in NYC's Central Park in September 1969. He had just performed with The Harkness Youth Dancers in *Percussion for Six,* a fast-paced athletic piece for six men. I had photographed the performance for Mrs. Harkness and Joe Papp. Ben's dancing, along with that of Zane Wilson and Vicente Nebrada [*Percussion for Six* choreographer], was fast and sensational."

"It turned out to be a special time for me," says Stevenson. "I did small ballets for the students, not choreographing beyond their ability or range."

Stevenson was enjoying his work with the Harkness Youth Dancers when Mrs. Harkness decided that she no longer liked the first company.

"So she got rid of that." Reported the July 1970 *Dance Magazine* Press-time News:

"The Rebekah Harkness Foundation has announced the merger of the Harkness Youth Dancers with the Harkness Ballet. Rebekah Harkness, producer and founder of the Harkness Ballet, will assume artistic direction of the company.

"Ben Stevenson, director of the Harkness Youth Dancers, has been named resident choreographer of the newly reorganized company for which José de Udaeta and Walter Gore will also stage new works."

Stevenson created several masterpieces in his new role, including *Bartók Concerto* (to Bartók's Piano Concerto #3) which the Harkness Ballet first performed October 4, 1970, at the Teatro Liceo in Barcelona, Spain, and *Three Preludes* (to music of Rachmaninov) which premiered in 1969 in the Bob Hope Theatre in Dallas and won first prize for contemporary choreography at the 1972 Varna International Ballet Competition.

Stevenson says, "There was *a lot* of turmoil and stress in working for the Harkness Ballet. Mrs. Harkness became very involved, and she wanted to be able to say what ballets you could do and what you couldn't do. At one point, she wanted people to do a ballet class playing castanets at the same time, on *pointe*. She liked the Spanish better, really, than ballet, so she engaged a Spanish teacher to teach castanets. Then, to the rhythm of that, the dancers were to do a ballet exercise so the two things would go together. It was *impossible*.

"I didn't really dislike Mrs. Harkness. I thought she was a very generous woman, and she did a lot as far as giving people scholarships and trying to get something going. But the more she became involved, the less and less prolific the company became. She began to write the music for the ballets, then when she was in her fifties, danced in a new Spanish ballet."

Stevenson maintains that Mrs. Harkness was always good to him and didn't interfere with his work. However when Ralph Black, General Manager of the National Ballet in Washington DC called him to say they were looking for someone to stage a production of *Cinderella* and would he do it, Stevenson accepted the offer. "I think it was Clive Barnes who told them, 'Ben Stevenson just did quite a good production of *The Sleeping Beauty* in London, and he is now at Harkness,' so that's how they found me.

"The National had a small company of about 30 dancers to do a full-length ballet, but after I thought about it, I realized that it might be quite nice to do and would get me away from the Harkness for awhile. So I took a bit of time off to do this production for the National, and it went quite well."

He had only two weeks of rehearsal with the National Ballet in which to choreograph *Cinderella*, then one more week after the company returned from a brief tour to rehearse, stage, and premier the production. "I actually created the *pas de deux* for Cinderella and the prince on a Harkness dancer, Jane Miller, in the studios in New York," he says, "and I worked on the prince role myself. When I had the National Ballet dancers in rehearsal in Washington, I wanted to spend my time with them staging the scenes requiring the full company, not focus on the time-consuming *pas de deux.*"

His *Cinderella* for the National premiered April 24, 1970, in the 1,400-seat Lisner Auditorium on the George Washington University campus, the first full-length ballet he choreographed in America. Wrote Kay Rinfrette in London's July-August 1970 *Ballet Today* on page 25, "The choreography, especially effective in solos and group work, and character development are Stevenson's exciting, original conceptions. The choreographic structure of the ballet—Stevenson's use of thematic materials—is magnificent."

During his absence, rivals who worked close to Mrs. Harkness influenced her against him. The resulting situation was tense, and seeing its inevitable outcome, Stevenson resigned. Twelve dancers immediately left in protest. Their loyalty touched him deeply. "That was why the Harkness experience was special," he says. "Those kids leaving with me rather than touring Europe with Harkness, even though I couldn't offer them work for six months."

His *Cinderella* was so successful, Ralph Black invited him to become National Ballet's co-director with Frederic Franklin, enticing him with the opportunity the position offered to choreograph more ballets. Thirty-four-year-old Stevenson had had an offer from the Berlin Opera, but he chose the National, bringing the Harkness defectors with him.

Stevenson could produce more lavish productions of the classics with the larger group. He had learned well from London Festival Ballet's success formula of popular appeal, box-office hits, and guest stars, and the perfect opportunity to apply that formula arose when the Kennedy Center for the Performing Arts opened to the public on September 8, 1971. For its inaugural season, Stevenson staged a magnificent production of *The Sleeping Beauty*, based on Petipa's choreography, Ashton's styling, and starring his idol Dame Margot Fonteyn.

Fonteyn enjoyed working with Stevenson. Victoria Huckenphaler quotes her on page 86 of her May 1972 *Dance Magazine* article on the National Ballet. "Dancers are always wanting to work well with a good person leading them [says Fonteyn]. Ben is a very good ballet master and the company works well for him. The fact that he was a dancer makes him a more understanding choreographer."

Stevenson reciprocates, "All great artists have temperament, but [Fonteyn] is probably the easiest of the big stars. She has a fantastic brain. She always gives you credit, too. After *Sleeping Beauty* I was in her dressing room. When her friends came in—Red Skelton and the like—they were all over her, but she pointed to me and said, '*This* is the man who really put it on.'"

Stevenson in turn enjoyed working with Franklin. Although Franklin was 20 years his senior (born June 13, 1914), they had had similar backgrounds: Anton Dolin first saw the promise of young Freddie as he had of Stevenson, both Franklin and Stevenson had been good dancers, and both were dramatically gifted. Continues Stevenson in Huckenphaler's article, "The marvelous thing about sharing the directorship with Freddie Franklin [is that] he can take over when I'm choreographing. He has had so much experience at putting things on quickly. You think you'll never get something on, then Freddie can take one rehearsal and the whole thing is together. I'm sort of left panting in the background."

Cinderella and *The Sleeping Beauty* won many new fans for the National Ballet, and Stevenson's crowd-pleasing *The Nutcracker* for National's Christmas season won more. Nonetheless, the Kennedy Center began to bring in big-name companies to perform there, like American Ballet Theatre and the Bolshoi Ballet. "They could perform there for free," says Stevenson, "and *we* had to pay, which hurt our subscription. They wanted the Kennedy Center to be like the Washington Metropolitan Opera House—a very nice touring base rather than a place for the local arts. All that was very difficult for *us*, so our company closed."

Big, bold letters headlined George Jackson's front page article in the September 1974 *Dance News*: "National Ballet Folds: Impecunious." Jackson begins, "The capital's classical repertory company has disbanded because it could not foresee paying its debts." He continues in his fifth paragraph, "Ben Stevenson, one of the National Ballet's co-directors, wants to form a chamber troupe (capacity 12 dancers) that could be expanded for special runs such as a Christmastime *Nutcracker*. The group would not perform at Kennedy Center but at less expensive theaters like Lisner Auditorium."

"I hoped to get a small company going," says Stevenson, "because I had a nucleus of dancers that I liked working with, and I had sort of grown into the Washington scene by that time. I liked Washington, I liked the dancers, and it seemed horrible to lose all this."

Having his own troupe would have allowed Stevenson to be where he most enjoys being: in the studio—teaching, coaching, and creating ballets. His chamber company didn't materialize. "I hung around Washington," he says, "but it was impossible to get something going."

His growing reputation had reached Chicago, where Ruth Page had assembled a Board of Directors to fund a ballet company. A Board member called Stevenson to offer him the artistic directorship of the Chicago Ballet.

"I took some of the dancers from Washington that I was trying to get this company together with," he says. "It was a good place to give *them* work and at the same time give *me* an opportunity to continue working somewhere. But when I got to Chicago and met Ruth Page, she seemed very much like a busy bee, humming around there. Then the Board said, 'We don't want to continue doing Ruth's ballets. We'll do one or two a season, but if we're going to raise a lot of money, we want other choreographers to come in—it can't all be Ruth Page.' So I was in the horrible position of having to say to Ruth, 'I'm sorry, Ruth, but we are just doing *two* of your ballets this year.'

"She had worked very hard and given her life's blood to get this company going and make it something of a showcase for herself as a choreographer. Then I came in, someone whom no one had ever heard of saying to her, 'Ruth, we're not going to do your ballets.' The Board did not stand behind me, so I decided, 'That's it. I'm going to go somewhere else.' There was no future there." Stevenson calls his two years in Chicago (1974–75), "the disaster period of my life."

His Chicago years had their rewards, however, including a deepened friendship with Jack Mitchell who came to photograph the dancers, and his first encounter with people from Houston Ballet. "A search committee from Houston came to Chicago to watch company class during my last days there. They had called critics, I think they called Margot Fonteyn, Freddie Ashton—a lot of people—asking who could direct Houston Ballet. They were considering British people, and I was the first Brit.

"I suppose the people they called said, '*He's* been working in America, *he's* been doing stuff,' so they watched class and invited me to Houston to interview.

"People told me, 'Don't go to Houston. It will be *horrible* in Texas because they just want to *buy* things—they're just going to want Baryshnikov and Rent-a-corps.' So I was a bit worried about that and thought, 'How awful. They just pay dancers double to get them to go there.' I felt a little mortified.

"I had never interviewed for a job before so was a bit nervous. I thought, 'It's not going to amount to much.' In the interview I said, 'I don't want guest artists. I want the school to be the most important thing about the company, because *that's* the only way you're going to get good dancers in Houston—train them. People aren't going to want to come from different cities and move to Houston'—it seemed to be in the middle of nowhere to me at the time. 'People might consider going to San Francisco, but they'd never consider going to Houston.'

"I said, 'When we've built the dancers, and our *own* dancers are guest artists, that's the time to be proud of. We have to grow something.' They just sort of sat there silently, so I left and thought, 'That's the end of that.'"

Back in Chicago on the verge of leaving Chicago Ballet, Stevenson was pondering his next move when he was invited to become the Artistic Director of International Ballet, based in London but funded by the South African city of Bloemfontein. "They were going to give $8,000,000 a year," he says, "which was a lot of money at that time. South African dance companies could not tour to one another's territories, so this company was to be based somewhere else but tour to South Africa and other places every year. That was the idea.

"I started to work on a production of *The Sleeping Beauty*, but then sensed that this was going to be very, very strange. It seemed to be something that I wasn't totally at home with. Then Mr. Balanchine called me."

Balanchine has seen Stevenson's *Cinderella* when the National Ballet performed it in New York in the early 1970s. "He liked the work," says Stevenson, "and invited me to set it on a company he directed in Geneva, Geneva Ballet [Ballet du Grand Théâtre de Genève]. New York City Ballet dancer Patricia Neary was resident director of the Geneva company for Mr. Balanchine.

"So I said 'No thank you' to this international company that was going to tour South Africa—which folded about three months after I left—and went to Geneva. I was putting on *Cinderella* there when the phone rang. It was Louisa Sarofim, head of the Houston Ballet search committee. She said that by unanimous decision, I would be the new director of Houston Ballet."

Stevenson weighed the gravity of the decision. When he was dancing he had thought of directing as "something that would be awful" so never actively pursued directing jobs—he had interviewed in Houston because he was invited. "I was never very thrilled with the idea of directing," he says, "the ogre of the company sort of thing. It's a hard role to play. If you're going to be any good at it, you've got to impose some sort of discipline, and you've got to let people know you're the boss.

"Much of the anguish of being a director is having to say to people, 'I'm sorry you're fired, you were late for class,' or 'You were horrible last night in the performance.' There's a lot of negative stuff that's built into being a director, the hiring and firing role and that sort of thing.

"Also, many directors spend very little time in the studio. They have five-year plans to set up and follow, and they work with the administration. Some artistic directors are great fund-raisers, and they're out there trying to raise money. It's inevitable that for artistic directors, teaching and choreographing become a much smaller part of their job."

He reflects back. "After the horse riding accident, I had gotten so into teaching and choreographing that I thought, 'Probably I'm going to be better at doing this, or going after this, than I am at dancing. How long can you go on dancing anyway? Eventually I'm going to have to give it up and do something like teaching and choreographing anyway.'

"Opportunities seemed to be there. People were asking me to do things. They weren't saying, 'Come and dance *Swan Lake*,' they were saying, 'Could you do a ballet?' or 'Could you teach?'

"So I decided, with the ankle problems, that I would go into teaching and choreographing, and those became more of my career than the dancing prospect. I never went after directing jobs, that sort of just happened. I suppose there are people who *want* to be artistic directors, who go after that, but I became that through teaching. From teaching, as I got dancers that I really liked in my class, I thought, 'I'd love to choreograph some little thing for them.' So the choreography came second, after the teaching. Then from *that*, people said to me, 'Will you be the director?'"

Stevenson became director of the Harkness Youth Dancers through teaching, director of the National Ballet and Chicago Ballet through choreographing, and the International Ballet in hopes of doing both. In spite of his trepidation about directing, his intuition moved him to go to the Houston interview. Now that he had been offered the position, he thought, 'I'm going to have to go down there and get on a horse again'—but he sensed the tremendous opportunity Houston offered and accepted the job.

His intuition proved right. He had told the Board during the interview that he would want to start from scratch, have no stars, build his strength from within, and bring some dancers with him. The Board had agreed, and now their unanimous choice of him as Houston Ballet's director told him that he would have their emotional and financial support as he developed the company. Even better, he would be able to spend most of his time in the studio where he loved to be, doing what he loved to do, teaching and choreographing.

As he adjusted to the city, he says, "It was different than I thought. I realized that Houston is a very *green* city, and that Texas is famous for its wild flowers." He accepted Houston's heat optimistically. "It's hot, but I'd rather live in a hot place than a cold place, and I think it's much better for dancers' muscles." Stevenson devoted the next 27 years (1976–2003) to growing Houston Ballet from the seeds of teaching and choreographing that he sowed in the studio. He says with deep feeling, "I've lived there all this time, so it's really my home now."

His first production for the company was *Cinderella*, symbolic of the transformation he envisioned for Houston Ballet from regional mediocrity to international celebrity. Norman King uses the fairy tale in his book

The First Five Minutes [see Resources] as an allegory for the vital business skill of knowing how to inspire others. King writes [italics are his], "...Once the uglies have left the house, suddenly a fairy godmother appears, touches Ella with a magic wand, and lo! she is transformed into a beautiful woman. At that moment, Ella of the Cinders becomes *someone*. Until that magic second, she was *no one*. Now she is an entity, now she is important.

"It is the fairy godmother who makes her feel important, who brings Ella to life by telling her that she is believed in, that she is beautiful, that she is a person of repute and honor. The wand is the storyteller's symbol of psychological metamorphosis, of efflorescence.

"And so, because Ella *believes* she is beautiful and important, she shines at the ball.... The point is, she becomes radiant and lovely because she has been touched by someone else."

Stevenson had the same magic wand effect on Houston Ballet. By the power of his own conviction, he involved others in his vision and inspired them to be visionaries, too, to believe that they and the company would one day shine. He bestowed his first transformational touch in the studio. "I adore teaching," he says, "that is what makes me happy." Wrote Ann Holmes in her September 1979 *Ballet News* article on page 20, "He is universally admired as a great teacher and one can see why. Class with Stevenson is clear, tough, fascinatingly original in a stream of imaginative combinations, and often hilarious." She quotes former Houston Ballet soloist Jeanne Doornbos, who joined the company in 1973, "My dancing today is vastly different and improved. Ben is the best teacher I've ever had. He knows exactly what he wants; he doesn't vacillate. He's just English enough to keep you from throwing yourself around." Though Stevenson has a sarcastic tongue, "he's no ogre," Doornbos reports. In fact, class is usually a howl."

Stevenson based his curriculum on classical technique but also trained the dancers in modern dance and jazz, and added other dance styles as the Houston Ballet Academy progressed. "It is a classical ballet company," he says, "but at the same time, I think new works are very important for the future of a company and the future of ballet in general—to go forward and not keep looking back." The dancers' diverse training prepares them for HB's classical-contemporary repertoire.

From the start, Stevenson's performances were multiple bills. He presented full-length story ballets, acquired works by world-respected choreographers, commissioned new works, and created original works. His desire to choreograph has flowed naturally from his love of teaching ever since he began to teach at the Arts Educational School. Choreography holds double rewards he says, "because you're giving what you do to the dancers who, in turn, give it to the audience."

Stevenson's choice of repertoire launched the company on a rapid ascent. By 1979, he had presented seven full-length ballets—his own stagings of *Cinderella, The Nutcracker, Swan Lake, The Sleeping Beauty*, and *Coppélia*; Ronald Hynd's *Papillon*, and Alicia Alonso's *Giselle*. He had acquired works such as Rudi van Dantzig's *Ramifications* and Frederick Ashton's *Façade*, for which Stevenson brought in Gwen Verdon to do a wild comic take-off on the tango sequence. He had commissioned Norman Walker's *Archaic Moon* and Choo San Goh's *Varaciones Concertantes*, and added his own *Bartók Concerto* and award-winning *Three Preludes* to the repertoire. He created a charming *Alice in Wonderland* in 1998 for the Houston Ballet Academy.

Stevenson brought Houston Ballet into the international limelight in 1978 when the government chose him to travel to China as part of a cultural exchange program. The Chinese government has invited him to return almost annually to teach at the Beijng Dance Academy.

Houston Ballet's international glow intensified in the 1980s when dancers Rachel Beard, Li Cunxin, Janie Parker, and William Pizzuto entered the 1982 International Ballet Competition in Jackson, Mississippi. Janie Parker, whom Stevenson first met in Geneva when he had staged his *Cinderella* there, won the senior division Gold Medal. Stevenson won the choreography Gold Medal for the five outstanding works he brought to the competition: contemporary *Zheng Ban Qiao, Just for Fun*, and *Three Preludes*, classical *Romance* and *Esmeralda pas de deux*.

Houston Ballet renovated its dance facility in 1984 to further the excellence of its ballet training and accommodate the growing company and academy. In 1987, the company moved into its new performance space, the magnificent, state-of-the-art Wortham Theater Center.

Stevenson's career advanced in step with the company. In 1985 he was instrumental in creating the Beijing Dance Academy's Choreographic Department, and he is the only foreigner to have been made Honorary Faculty Member of the Beijing Dance Academy and the Shenyang Conservatory of Music.

In 1986 he won another choreography Gold Medal, this time at the Nagoya, Japan International Ballet Competition for *The End of Time*.

September 2–13, 1987, Houston Ballet premiered Stevenson's newest story ballet, *Romeo and Juliet*, a colorful, humorous, emotional version of the classic that showed off the company's theatrical vitality and filled the theater. Stevenson had danced the classics in England—*Swan Lake, The Sleeping Beauty, Giselle, Ondine*—with *Swan Lake* being one of his favorites "because it has drama, the prince is on from the beginning, and it's very romantic. But I never danced Romeo," he says, "because there weren't any productions in England at the time I was dancing." He created his own Romeo 20 years later to compensate.

In 1989, Stevenson named Sir Kenneth MacMillan as artistic associate and associate choreographer and Christopher Bruce as resident choreographer. MacMillan (born 1929) began his career as one of the original members of Sadler's Wells Theatre Ballet; Bruce (born 1945) made his debut with Walter Gore's London Ballet. Their combined career achievements richly fertilized Houston Ballet's thriving growth.

The 1990 International Ballet Competition in Jackson, Mississippi honored Stevenson again with a special choreography award, since he had already won the Jackson choreography Gold Medal in 1982. Houston Ballet's Martha Butler, 1990 Gold Medal winner, danced Stevensons' award-winning *The End of Time*.

In 1994, his *Cinderella* opened Houston Ballet's 25th anniversary season. *Dance Magazine*'s November 1994 issue featured a five-page article by Valerie Gladstone on the company to celebrate the occasion, with superb photographs by Jack Mitchell that capture the company's vitality. J. Donald Walters wrote in *The Art of Leadership* on page 136 [see Resources], "the true success of an undertaking depends more than anything else on the spirit of the people involved in it. And the spirit of those people is a reflection, always, of the spirit of its leader." The dancers' quotes in Gladstone's article reveal Houston Ballet's spirit, and thus Stevenson's.

Gladstone introduces the company by saying, "Hustonians and those fortunate enough to have seen the 55-member company on tour know that Houston Ballet has some of the best dancers performing some of the most interesting choreography in the country. The combination of Texas-style exuberance and British classicism is dynamite."

She quotes ballerina Lauren Anderson, "The great thing about dancing here is that Ben allows us great freedom and nourishes it. We get such a wide variety of choreography to dance—*Swan Lake, Giselle,* and then also works by James Kudelka, Paul Taylor, and Toni Lander. Because Ben has such good contacts, he also brings in amazing people to coach us. We had Dame Margot Fonteyn for *Swan Lake,* Paul Taylor for *Company B,* Sir Kenneth MacMillan for *Song of the Earth.* Imagine getting the chance to work with people like that."

Eighty percent of the company dancers come through the Houston Ballet Academy, their loyalty and love of the company a reflection of Stevenson's careful attention to each one's anatomy, needs, and temperament. "I deal with them individually," he says, "try to find their strengths, and let them work on those.

"My dancers have to know themselves. They have to understand the quality of the music they dance to and they have to know how to use their eyes. I want them to learn the drama of dance at the same time they are learning technique. If there isn't anything going on in the mind, there won't be anything going on in the dance. My purpose is to make artists."

Then Houston Ballet Artistic Director Ben Stevenson spending a laugh-ing moment with the legendary Bolshoi ballerina Nina Ananiashvili for her appearances in Stevenson's production of *The Sleeping Beauty* in March 1999. Houston Ballet principal dancer Sean Kelly looks on. (Photograph by Jann Whaley, 1999.)

Says Ballerina Dawn Scannell in Gladstone's article, "The reason I'm here is Ben. Nowhere else could I get the variety of pieces. I started out with the *Giselles*, then found I could do neoclassic. I could see my whole sense of movement broaden by doing Paul Taylor's *Company B* and Christopher Bruce's *Cruel Garden*. Christopher Bruce has one of the wildest imaginations in ballet. When we first did *Cruel Garden* he fed it to us verbally, in little tidbits. In the process I learned how to put death, life, and love in the movement."

Stevenson followed the 25th anniversary season with a number of block-buster full-length ballets with big scores, big budgets, big casts. In 1997 he created a million-dollar staging of *Dracula* to coincide with the centenary of the publication of Bram Stoker's novel—the budget was lit-erally $1 million. Ticket sales doubled original projections and extra per-formances had to be added.

Stevenson's *Snow Maiden* premiered at the Wortham Center on

March 12, 1998, with Bolshoi ballerina Nina Ananiashvili in the title role. Margaret Willis reports in her March 1998 *Dance Magazine* article entitled, *Houston's Snow Maiden*, that Stevenson had been thinking of creating a ballet of the famous Russian fairy tale for some time. While visiting Oslo in February 1996 to observe Norwegian Ballet before casting his *Cinderella* there, he saw Ananiashvili dance and realized how right she would be for the role.

Says Ananiashvili in the article, "I went to Houston to see the company, and I was very impressed by Ben's class. He is so thorough that every part of the body gets warmed and exercised. And he is very attentive and has a kindly rapport with all the dancers. To my mind, it was the best class outside Russia."

Grand jeté from the sweat of the studio where ordinary barre exercises bring him Edenic happiness, to Buckingham Palace, December 1999, where the Queen of England placed the gilt Order of the British Empire Sash Badge around his neck. "Having lived in America for 30 years, it was very unexpected," he said in the March 2000 *Dance Magazine* Hotline announcement on page 40. The gilt imperial crown that surmounts the O.B.E. medallion symbolizes not only Stevenson's tremendous contributions to the international dance world, but also his then 24-year reign as Artistic Director of Houston Ballet, a company which has likewise enriched dance, dancers, and audiences worldwide.

Back in Houston, Houston Ballet crowned its 1999-2000 season with Stevenson's $1.2 million *Cleopatra* which premiered at the Wortham Theatre Center on March 9, 2000. Clive Barnes wrote in his June 2000 *Dance Magazine* review that "Stevenson's hot-tub-steamy ballet spectacular had definite Hollywood glitter," and, "Stevenson has given terrific value for [the] money." Barnes correctly predicts in his last paragraph that now that this *Cleopatra* has been launched, "It floats with a certain stately majesty and will doubtless turn out to be a big audience pleaser wherever it plays." Alchemist Stevenson mixes sex, power, and mystique with vision, performance, and pragmatism to create a potent ballet potion.

Dance Magazine honored him with the prestigious Dance Magazine Award for the year 2000 for his "uncommon talent" and "gift for creating and perpetuating dances of great popular appeal." His culturally relevant, classically timeless story ballets demonstrate both adherence to tradition and his independence from it. His imaginative contemporary works touch vibrant cords with ordinary steps.

He says, "I've been very lucky to do what I've done without really having any background in anything except dance." Recall that he stopped his formal education at age 14. "I was never out there sort of beating the bushes trying to find a job. Somehow I found work, lasting work that I could do for a long, long time."

Houston Ballet has a career transition fund to help dancers train for new careers when they stop performing, because Stevenson feels strongly that "it's important to find a job that you really like doing." He cautions, "Choose what you want to do very carefully so you don't have to go through transition after transition throughout your life.

"Talk to your friends, explore what they are doing. Find something that flows off of you easily, as opposed to something you've got to struggle with and will continue to struggle with for the rest of your life. Try to think of what you excelled in at school, or what is going to be the most natural thing for you to do—it's quite difficult to be a neurosurgeon when you're 40 years old."

Stevenson surprised many when he announced his own transition from Artistic Director to Co-artistic Director, effective June 30, 2001. Maureen Gustin wrote in *Dance Magazine*'s May 2001 Presstime News that he had asked the Houston Ballet executive committee for a role that "would keep him in the studio and out of the boardroom. The 65-year-old Stevenson said he'd simply grown tired of 'the stuff that makes the clock go round.' In his new role, he'll continue to teach and choreograph without the interruption of administrative duties and fund-raising." Stevenson's 27 years of Houston Ballet leadership distinguish him as the longest-tenured head of a major American ballet company, to date.

He says, "I'm a sort of go-and-get-it person in a way. Particularly, I've become more so as I've gotten older. I've choreographed a number of *very big* ballets that have big scores, big budgets—*big* things. It's a lot of stress, and much anguish goes into [gasps] 'Will I ever be able to do this?' So I've had to become a little stronger in my way of doing things. I say, 'This is what I want. No, I don't want that. No, I don't want this. I want *that*,' because if I can't feel I can get the things I want, then I can't do the ballet. Making decisions is something dancers don't always do very easily. But I believe that your instinct at the beginning of things is what's important. It's what usually ends up as something you're reasonably proud of. You say, 'I want to do this,' then you *go* for that. It's important to stand by what you want."

He approached his career transition with the same go-and-get-it attitude and went for what he wanted: a life in the studio, his place of bliss, teaching, coaching, and creating ballets.

He became Artistic Director Emeritus of Houston Ballet at the end of the 2002-2003 season to concentrate on teaching, coaching, and choreographing for the new Houston Ballet Youth Dancers. He also became Artistic Director of the nearby Fort Worth Dallas Ballet, for whom he had served as artistic advisor during the previous two seasons. He will grow FWDB from the studio, however, where he can be his artistic best, just as he did Houston Ballet in 1976.

"I always felt inside that I would teach, that that was something I really wanted to do," says Stevenson, again with deep feeling. "I like working with the dancers; I like the studio work *very* much. If you work with people day after day, you can subtly see that they are improving, that they are learning through you. This is very rewarding. You feel that you're really giving something."

When asked what he would like his legacy to be he says, "I don't know how to put this in words, but each body is an individual body—like fingerprints. I would like dancers to feel that they got to know their body and how it works. When someone is not loose-limbed, for instance, and they see someone with their leg up on their ear who's been born with that ability, and they start extorting *their* body trying to do something they've seen someone else do—instead of making their extension perfect, or their amount of turnout perfect, think, 'I'm going to make what I have, *my* body, be as correct as I can. I've got this much turnout and can get my leg that high, but that foot is going to be beautifully stretched.'

"Lightness is very important in dancing. If you are straining to do stuff your body can't do, then you don't have any lightness. Then you stop dancing and you start doing sort of weight lifting or something. I work with dancers who want to be Sylvie Guillem or someone but can't get their leg up above hip level. By distorting every fiber in their body, they sort of do a split *penché* or something—you can imagine what position they're in. They're thrilled at the height of their leg, but they're not looking at the upper body or whatever. So I work with them to help them get to know their own body and perfect what they have, rather than copy other people.

"It's very difficult to put it into words, into one short sentence." He tries, "I feel that my message when I teach is to try and make the dancer aware of their body's limitations so that they can make their limitations work for them." His teaching makes better artists and thus the ballets they dance better works of art.

As renowned opera diva Leontyne Price said, "Once in the studio, you get down to, not the work, but the focus and the *thrill* to be the best you can be."

While in his transition role of Co-artistic Director, Stevenson entrusted Houston Ballet's new story ballet, *Peter Pan*, to choreographic associate and former dancer Trey McIntyre—a symbolic move. In the classic fantasy, Peter Pan chooses to remain forever in childhood, his happiest place of life. As Stevenson returns to his beloved teaching, he, too, chooses his happiest place of life: the studio.

NANCY RAFFA
Journey from the Heart

American girl wins Lausanne gold medal announced the April 1980 *Dance Magazine* headline on page 5. The news clip beneath opened, "Nancy Raffa's victory at the Prix de Lausanne this year was particularly extraordinary: not only was the fifteen-year-old Brooklyn, NY girl the first female in the history of the competition to win the gold Medal, but she was also the first American ever to win this award."

French publications *Les Saisons de la Danse* and *Pour la Danse* had splashed the news to Europe in their March issues. James Monahan admitted on page 403 of London's March 1980 *The Dancing Times* that the little American's participation "brought with it more than a touch of the show-bizz razz-ma-tazz which is not in the unflashy Lausanne spirit. An American TV network was making a feature about the girl and mikes and cameras stalked her everywhere."

Says Raffa with her characteristic humility, "I did not think I had won anything, because they had called all the best dancers onto the stage and had awarded them. The gold medal is very rare to receive, so I assumed I did not have a prize."

When her name was called, she didn't hear it. Thoughts of home filled her head—images of her sick father in one of his Parkinson attacks, her mother and brothers so full of hope when she said goodbye, their family in poverty. "My eyes filled with huge tears, then Wim Broeck, the Belgian dancer who had befriended me during the competition, gave me a nudge and said, 'Nancy *go*, they called you.'

"I entered the stage rather unballerina-like: sobbing and walking like a truck driver. I was so emotional, I could not believe what was happening. All I could think of were my dad and family."

85

She stood there, sobbing in the little blue seafoam dress that Haydée Morales had made for her *Spring Waters* variation—a freestyle delight choreographed by her teacher and mentor Gabriela Taub-Darvash—while Prix de Lausanne President Philippe Braunschweig announced that Nancy Raffa had won the top prize. He hung the Gold Medal gently around her neck.

One of the missions of the Prix de Lausanne is to serve as a professional springboard for talented young dancers. In keeping with this mission, the competition awards prizes of study and apprentice scholarships with the finest schools and companies.

"Already an accomplished virtuoso (indeed alarmingly so)," wrote Monahan, "Raffa was eligible for a scholarship to any of six prestigious ballet schools, including the School of American Ballet and School of American Ballet Theatre. But Madame Darvash would not part with her on any condition whatever."

So Raffa took home $2000.00 in U.S. dollars, which she gave to her family to use for her father's medicine, and the gold medal for her mother, who treasures it to this day.

Nancy Raffa was born September 5, 1964, in rural Poughkeepsie, New York, but her family moved to Brooklyn when she was three months old. In New York, opportunity beckoned for all of them. Her mother, who had graduated from the High School of the Performing Arts, was a pianist, her father, a pharmacist by profession, was a jazz saxophone player. Her older brother Louis was already a budding jazz musician and composer. (Raffa has another older brother, John, a film editor, and two younger brothers: George, a physical education teacher, and Alfonse, a licensed customhouse broker).

"From birth I was exposed to music and art," says Raffa, "and of course being the only girl, my Mom took me to ballet class."

She started in a tiny school in the basement of a Brooklyn church in 1971 and immediately fell in love with ballet. "Even at seven years old, I knew that's what I wanted to do." Her teachers recognized the little girl's talent and urged her mother to bring her into Manhattan.

In 1972 Raffa auditioned at the School of American Ballet, but SAB rejected her. They told Mrs. Raffa, "Your daughter is very gifted but does not have the physical attributes we are looking for—long legs, enough turnout, enough extension. She should try some other kind of entertainment, but not ballet."

"My mom is stubborn," says Raffa. "She wouldn't take that as the final answer. *I* didn't accept their response either. I felt I had done very well in the audition and didn't understand, at eight years old, why they wouldn't take me. Their response actually made me very angry, and it pushed me to want to do the ballet even more. I knew in my heart that this was my path, what I wanted to do, and what I love to do. 'No' just wasn't an option for me."

Mrs. Raffa marched her daughter over to Carnegie Hall where the Neubert Ballet School for Children gave her a scholarship. Ballet Arts welcomed Raffa, too, and put her into adult classes right away. "It was bizarre," she says. "Here was this little girl in classes with professional dancers." She alternated taking classes at Neubert and Ballet Arts and advanced rapidly.

A tragic blow hit in 1972 when Nancy was almost nine that essentially launched her career. Her father had been diagnosed with Parkinson's Disease in 1969, but in '72, he

Nancy Raffa as Kirti in *Don Quixote,* a ballet in which she starred with Fernando Bujones at Wolf Trap Park, Washington, D.C. (Photograph by Jorge E. Gallardo, 1981.)

lost his ability to work and consequently his pharmacy. "My family went on welfare, and that had a huge influence on my dancing. Ballet started out to be something that I loved to do, then turned into something that I took upon myself as a way I could help my family get out of the financial dilemma we were in. I just made it my goal that I wanted to do this.

"I realized that I had capability in what I was doing, and people were giving me opportunities. I thought that if I could be the best I could at ballet, then maybe I could help my family out of our difficult situation. It was a lot for a little kid to handle, but that's the way I was.

"I felt the same way about school. I felt like I *could not* be anything but the best—and worked at being a straight-A student. I exceeded myself to be the best in school and the best I could in dance."

Raffa's mother had been building her career as a classical concert pianist, but her husband's hospitalization in 1973 forced her to look for extra work. One day she was watching one of Nancy's Ballet Arts classes, and the pianist didn't show up. The teacher knew of Mrs. Raffa's talent and asked if she would play for class that day.

"My Mom actually had a gift for it," says Raffa. "She became a ballet pianist like *that* and began to play for classes to support the family."

While looking for more classes to increase her income, Mrs. Raffa happened upon Madame Gabriela Taub-Darvash. Kirov-trained Darvash had moved from Europe in 1972 and established her own studio on 8th Avenue and 56th Street. She had been artistic director and resident choreographer for the State Opera Ballet in Cluj, Romania for 14 years and became renowned in New York for her ability to create strong, artistically-expressive dancers. Mikhail Baryshnikov called her "one of the finest ballet pedagogues in America."

When Mrs. Raffa saw how Madame Darvash taught, she knew her daughter had not had a teacher of her caliber and brought Nancy to the studio for a class. Immediately after class Madame Darvash came over to Mrs. Raffa, "Your daughter is very, very gifted," she said, "and needs better training than she has had. She needs to relearn everything all over again, correctly. I would like to work with her."

Thus began Raffa's long relationship with Madame Darvash. Darvash generously gave her a full scholarship and "was one of the most powerful mentors in my life," says Raffa. "Aside from being my ballet teacher, she taught me about music, art, theater, acting, and the history of Europe. Growing up with her as my guide was an incredible experience."

One of the teachers in Madame Darvash's studio was Geta Constantinescu, also born and educated in Romania. Constantinescu had graduated from the State School of Ballet in Cluj in 1961 and rose from the *corps* to principal dancer in the State Opera and Ballet Company of Timisoara, her native city. She defected to the West in 1970, arriving in the U.S. in the late 1970s with her partner Julio Horvath.

Constantinescu retired from the stage in 1973 to devote herself to teaching and coaching. When injuries brought Horvath's career to a halt in the mid–1970s, he turned to intensive yoga study and began to develop a system of Yoga for Dancers. Gradually he evolved Yoga for Dancers into the Gyrotonics Expansion System™ (also known as "White Cloud") based on exercises he drew from dance, swimming, gymnastics, yoga, and Tai Chi. He later added custom-built machines to help the body move in a systematic way. Constantinescu became a certified Gyrotonics instructor.

Constantinescu and Horvath brought Gyrotonics to Madame Darvash's studio, where they introduced it to 11-year-old Nancy Raffa.

"I took private lessons from Julio and Geta," says Raffa. "He designed the machines while working with me, because I had such a difficult body. He wanted to help my body, and others', do what he knew they had the potential to do. The exercises enabled me to do classical dance, and I continued with them throughout my career. The yoga they taught me began my exploration of Eastern philosophy."

After three years with Darvash, Horvath, Constantinescu, and the coaching of Nora Kovach, Raffa entered and won the 1980 Prix de Lausanne. When she returned to New York from Lausanne in February 1980, arts patron Eugenia Doll (who had also helped Natalia Makarova) offered to pay her tuition at the Professional Children's School. Another lucky break came two months later. Raffa auditioned for Makarova and Company, and Makarova accepted her into the *corps*. A week later Raffa was elevated to soloist. She was 16.

Makarova and Company opened on Broadway in October 1980 with *Paquita*. Raffa danced the first *pas de trois* with Antonia Francesci and Fernando Bujones; Makarova danced the lead. In true star-is-born fashion, when Makarova injured her knee and canceled, she chose Raffa as her replacement. Bujones readily agreed.

Rave reviews verified Raffa's stardom. Clive Barnes wrote in the *New York Post*, "Raffa made a dazzling debut. The girl is the real thing." In *The New York Times*, Anna Kisselgoff called her "a teen-age Alexandra Danilova. She has the perfect line of a true classical ballerina. More important, the dance is in her."

Bujones devoted himself to coaching Raffa and engaged his own teacher, his cousin Zeida Mendez, to work with her. "We think Nancy has a special talent," said Mendez, "not only to become a great partner for Fernando but a sensational dancer in her own right. In three years she'll be able to do every role in the repertory."

Mikhail Baryshnikov had seen Raffa's *Paquita* and invited her to take class at American Ballet Theatre, which he then directed. Six months later he took her into the Company. "I signed my contract in June 1981," she says. "I danced everything in the repertoire, from *corps de ballet* to demi-solo, solo, and principal roles. But my career took a twist in 1985."

Ivan Nagy, who was a close friend of Madame Darvash and an ABT principal, was directing the Ballet de Santiago in Chile. He had taught in Madame's school and remembered Raffa from the Prix de Lausanne. He invited her to come to Chile to work with him for six months as a principal dancer, then return to ABT. Raffa asked Misha for a leave of absence, which he gave to her on the promise that she would return to the company.

"After four years with American Ballet Theatre I felt I needed to get experience dancing elsewhere," she says, "but the main reason I left ABT was to get experience for my life. I went through a very difficult time emotionally coming out of my baby ballerina period. I needed to find myself and some place for true happiness." Raffa had been one of the young dancers featured in *Dance Magazine*'s November 1982 article entitled, The Baby Ballerina Boom, which cautioned against lionizing younger and younger ballet dancers for their powerful box office appeal.

"When I got to Chile my life made an about-face. Chile was under the dictatorship of Augusto Pinochet, and the day I arrived there was a blackout with riots in the streets. Helicopters circled overhead, people threw tear gas bombs, and soldiers beat civilians. I stayed at the Plaza de Armas with my friend Anthony Basile, a dancer from New York, and we watched from our balcony in the pitch black. We were quickly warned to go inside or risk being shot. The protected life I had been living in New York City was completely different from what I was seeing here, and the culture-shock affected me deeply."

As Raffa began to work in the government-controlled theater, she met local people, students, and families, and learned about the Santiago way of life. She met her husband, Chilean native Jorge Gallardo, a set and costume designer who had earned his Master of Fine Arts degree from the University of Chile in Santiago. Her six months leave of absence became two years. Raffa and Gallardo were married November 3, 1986, and she has been speaking fluent Spanish ever since.

"In early 1987 I was negotiating going back to New York when I received a phone call from the director of the Ballet National Français de Nancy, France. The director had seen me at the Prix de Lausanne, was in New York looking for a principal dancer, and met with Madame Darvash to ask about me. Madame told her I was in Chile. The director called to invite me to join her company."

Raffa had a choice: go to Europe or go back to New York. "My intuition told me to go to Europe, so I joined the Ballet Français de Nancy as a principal and ended up staying there for six years." Her husband followed her and became the Ballet de Nancy's set and costume designer.

They lived in Nancy two months a year and toured Japan, Canada, Africa, and throughout Europe the rest. "That was the most fabulous time of my career," says Raffa. "Patrick Dupond was our director, and he chose me to be his partner. Although classically trained at the Paris Opera he loved new work, and that gave me a great breadth of experience." Jirí Kylián, Thierry Malandain, Lionel Hoche, Pierre Darde, and Ulysses Dove were among the avant-garde choreographers Dupond hired to create new work for the company.

"Dove made the biggest impact on the company," says Raffa, "and on my internal life. Two of his works, both very intense, are my favorites, *Bad Blood* and *Faites et Gestes*. Working with this genius was an amazing experience." Raffa gained considerable renown in France for her Dove roles, thanks to *Le Figaro*'s and *Le Monde*'s 1989 laudatory reviews of her performances. Dupond invited Birgit Cullberg to coach Raffa in the title role of *Miss Julie*, her interpretation of which heightened her celebrity.

In 1990, Dupond accepted directorship of the Paris Opera, and Pierre Lacotte took over the Ballet de Nancy. Lacotte retreated from Dupond's avant-garde into the 19th century, restoring *Sylphides* and *Giselles* and ousting the Dove crowd. He chose lyrical, young dancers he could mold to the Romantic style, and Raffa's dynamic artistry was incompatible with his plans for the company. She decided it was time to move on.

Baryshnikov had hired Ulysses Dove to create a new piece for American Ballet Theatre, and Dove hired Gallardo to design the sets and costumes. Raffa seized the opportunity to re-establish contact with ABT.

In 1992 ABT invited her to take company class for a month, optimistic that a principal position would open for her. The position never materialized—management disputes froze funding and contracts.

Raffa forwarded her impressive credentials to Miami City Ballet and Boston Ballet. Edward Villella called her in Europe to tell her they had a place for a principal dancer. She flew to Miami, auditioned, and Villella offered her a principal contract. "I liked Edward right away," she says, "and accepted."

In the fall of 1992 she established residence in Miami and started to learn the repertoire. "Two weeks into the work process," she says with a touch of pain in her voice, "I tore my right hip flexor rehearsing Dew Drop for Balanchine's *The Nutcracker*. I kicked my leg to the side and the whole thing tore." Prophetically, in Chicago's 1981 International Dance Festival Raffa had danced Gabriela Darvash's *One Day I Will Come Back*, a ballet of quiet anguish in which a rehearsing dancer reacts to an injury.

Raffa was ripe for injury in November of '92. She was exhausted from the previous season, stressed from the insecurity of being unemployed when her ABT position didn't develop, fatigued from her move to Miami, worried about the uncertainty of auditioning, and frantic to be prepared when Edward and the company returned from tour. Her husband was still in France, she had no doctor, and one to turn to for advice when her hip flexor tore. Her intuition told her this injury was much worse than the minor aches and pains she had suffered earlier in her career, and that this one would take a long time to heal. She denied its plea for rest and kept on rehearsing.

When MCB returned from their tour the company doctor, an orthopedic specialist, examined her. "If you're lucky," he said, "you'll get 30 percent mobility back in your hips."

This alarming news went up to Villella. He called Raffa into his office, "The doctor tells me this injury is much more serious than what you said." Raffa still denied it and tried to work harder. "I felt an enormous amount of pressure," she says, "having been contracted as a principal and not being able to fulfill my obligations. I felt extremely guilty that the injury had occurred."

Villella told her to take the time she needed to heal properly, then come back. "I would take three-to-four weeks off, my hip would feel better, I'd try to train myself, then the pain would come back within a week. This went on for seven months—then the season was over."

Villella called her into his office again. "This happened and it's unfortunate," he said. "I really liked you when you auditioned. We have three months break, and I'll leave the door open for you when we come back. If you're okay and in shape, I'll give you another try at it. I've done everything I can for you. This is all I can do."

"He was incredibly understanding," says Raffa, "and I was incredibly stressed-out." She went back to New York and met with Geta Constantinescu. "Come work with me," said Geta. "I have special yoga exercises that I know will restore your body."

After two weeks of intensive yoga, breathing, and Gyrotonics, Raffa felt less pain and conditioned enough to re-audition for Villella when he returned from MCB's break. She prepared two variations, he came to New York to see her and said, "Nancy, you look fabulous! Wonderful. We start in three weeks, here's your contract."

Back in company, she danced as though reborn, and her body did not resist the work. Then rehearsals started for the Balanchine repertoire, *Allegro Brillante, Concerto Barocco, Raymonda Variations*. "Balanchine's repertoire is very, very hard on the body," explains Raffa, "and between six, seven hours a day of dancing plus class, my body just did not hold out. I felt weak. I was in pain. I became very depressed because I wasn't able to dance to the caliber I expected of myself and the company expected of me.

"It was the worst moment of my life. I felt like I had failed myself and failed everything and everybody around me. Ballet was my reality up to that point. Now I was losing my career, didn't know if I would ever be able to dance again, and had nothing to fall back on. Dance is all I knew my whole life. My identity was always Nancy, the dancer. I didn't know who Nancy, the person, was. Without dance, I had no way to measure myself, no way to value who I was. At that moment, I felt I had *no* value. I went through a deep, clinical depression."

Villella felt genuine empathy for Raffa and spoke with her at length. "Nancy, sometimes life doesn't turn out the way we want," he said. "I would have loved to work with you. I would have loved to have your ability, your talent, and your person amongst us. But right now I think you need to take some time for yourself."

"I knew he was right," says Raffa. "I knew he was right in saying, 'Look, I can't do this, and I'm sorry.' I resigned from Miami City Ballet in August 1993 without ever performing with the company. They were so understanding, and I felt so embarrassed and terrible about what had happened. I didn't even walk near the building."

Out of the cloistered ballet world, a fallen star, her identity lost, she felt emotionally and physically unbalanced. She had suicidal thoughts. She tried therapists who didn't help. She cried and cried and cried "for centuries of people." A tremendous sense of loss overwhelmed her.

"My husband had a hard time dealing with me. He said that he didn't want to continue life with someone so miserable and sad. He said he wanted to continue to grow as a person and wanted to be peaceful, and that if I didn't find a way to be happy, he wouldn't be able to stay with me.

"What he said is the best thing in the world that could have happened to me. It was the last straw. He was the last link I had to any kind of identity and security, and when that was being jeopardized, I knew I had to go through a definite rebirth."

She completely avoided the dance world, for it re-opened the wound of failure. "I didn't see myself as a victim of circumstance," she says. "I felt like I had failed.

"But I still thought that somehow, some way, I could get better and dance again. I couldn't give up on life. It cost me a lot of energy and effort to do the things that I did, and just to let them go without trying or without fighting back seemed like a waste to me."

Raffa consulted a friend in Miami in her quest for a therapist. The friend found her a job instead. Ironically, the job was in BodyWorks, one of the biggest fitness centers in Miami, cleaning exercise machines. She went from being an international prima ballerina to a machine-cleaner at BodyWorks. While cleaning machines designed to make bodies better, hers just got worse.

"I gained 30 pounds," she admits. "I ate to abuse myself. I was so sad, I punished myself by eating. I ate things I never touched as a dancer—Burger Kings, milk shakes—and I would say, 'Good. You're gonna eat this and you *deserve* it.' Mentally, I was not in a good way."

Raffa had to learn to drive, because the fitness center was an hour-and-a-half away from her apartment. But a week after she got her license, she wrecked the car. "I was in one of my negative, depressed moods, and eating an ice cream cone while I was driving. The wheel got stuck, I panicked, and pressed the accelerator instead of the brake. I hit four cars in the parking lot and nearly killed myself."

The impact of the air bag was a metaphorical slap in the face. "I thought I had lost my life when I lost my career, but that blow paled when I almost *really* lost my life."

She found a network chiropractic healer, Mr. Paul Canali. "Network chiropractic is a type of therapy that works with the innate intelligence of the spine," she explains. "The therapist adjusts subluxations in the spine through contact points that trigger the memory in the spinal cord. The manipulation makes your whole body react physically, chemically, and emotionally. That treatment, together with Mr. Canali's personal support, saved my life."

She ponders the intensity of the therapy. "That was like a going through ten million times over psychotherapy, but it was through a physical way of learning about myself. The therapy puts you into a meditative state where the body reveals and 'clears out' stored traumas from its memory.

"I would have moments where I would start sweating, get feverish, and tremble, then have emotional releases. Memories came back from childhood—things that were psychological stresses from my father being sick, scenes from the hospital, moments of emotional trauma from things I saw in my house when I was younger, fights, abuse, all kinds of things like that. All of that was coming out, coming out, coming out—"

Raffa went through intense network chiropractic therapy for a year-and-a-half, twice a week then once a week. She began to understand herself and to accept herself for who she was rather than for what she did. She began to get happier, to heal.

She studied to become certified as a personal trainer at BodyWorks and was promoted from cleaning machines to personal training. She had put dance away "on the back shelf," but like a beloved treasure began to miss it. She thought, "Maybe I would like to teach."

She had gone from $1,000 a week as a principal dancer to $4.00 an hour as a machine-cleaner so had to work 14 hours a day to pay bills and rent. But her BodyWorks schedule was flexible, and she could choose her hours.

"I decided I would like to give a shot at trying to teach. I didn't know Miami very well—I had only been there for a little over a year—so I opened the Yellow Pages and wrote a letter to every ballet school in the book."

In late spring 1994 she got her first response, from the tiny Pat Peninori School of Dance, and taught her first class there. She had healed from her injury, emotionally and physically. "It was like a healing of my whole life that I went through," she says. "A complete metamorphosis. The learning and maturing opened up many, many other areas of life that I never had when I was so sheltered just doing ballet." She related to the children with a depth of understanding she hadn't possessed before.

More responses to her letters came in and her reputation grew as she accepted other teaching assignments. Although still overweight for a dancer when she began teaching, the more she taught, the faster her body returned to its slender proportions.

Word of her skill spread to the New World School of the Arts, the biggest arts school in Miami. Daniel Lewis, Dean of Dance, invited her to substitute teach one class. The students adored her. After class, they asked Mr. Lewis if he could put Raffa on the faculty.

Lewis explained to Raffa that since the New World School of the Arts was an affiliate of Miami-Dade Community College, he could not hire her to a faculty position without a teaching degree and formal application. But he said, "Your credentials are far beyond what any degree could offer. Although there is no full-time opening on the faculty, I could use you as a swing-girl." Raffa responded, "Beggars can't be choosy. Whatever you can offer, I'll be glad to accept." In September 1994, she started teaching at New World part-time as an adjunct faculty member.

During Raffa's year of catharsis and healing, Miami City Ballet had established a School. One spring day in 1995 the phone rang. "May I please speak to Nancy Raffa?" asked the caller. "I assist Linda Villella, director of the Miami City Ballet School."

Raffa had avoided contact with the company, but Edward and Linda Villella had heard such glowing reports of her teaching, Linda was moved to call. She had hesitated at first, she told Nancy later, remembering Raffa's alarming emotional and physical distress when she left the company. Linda had wondered if Raffa would be stable enough to work with children. She decided to find out, and called.

She invited Raffa to teach a class. "They watched the class and hired me," says Raffa. "I was out of the depression. I was healed." Her enthusiasm for teaching and rapport with the children made it obvious that she was healthy.

"I started getting phone calls from almost all of the schools in Miami. At one point I taught part-time in nine different ballet schools. Gradually I stopped working at the gym to work in only the ballet schools. The following year, I narrowed it down to teaching in the two biggest schools, and finally narrowed it down to teaching only in the Miami City Ballet School."

Raffa eventually became one of the head teachers of the School's advanced division, then began to work in MCB's educational programs as Performance Outreach Coordinator of Ballet for Young People, a group of advanced students who learn company repertoire to perform in community lecture-demonstrations and concerts.

"I *love* working with the children," she says. "The unconditional love you get from them, the exchange of energy, ideas, and enthusiasm, and the knowledge that you get by working with them and that they receive from you—it's unexplainable, it's just an incredible reciprocity of energy. Working with children helped me to heal and is very, very satisfying to me."

The more she taught, the more she felt the urge to train herself again. Three years after resigning from Miami City Ballet, she worked herself back to her former weight and technique, and to a *higher* level of artistry.

"I felt I was at the peak of my dancing at this point, because I had a maturity I didn't have in my 20s. I went through a re-learning process by teaching. By applying the teaching to my own body, with the knowledge I had at 32, I was able to enhance my dancing so much more."

Brigid Baker, a New York choreographer who took a few of Raffa's MCB classes, significantly influenced her artistic development. Raffa developed a strong affinity with Baker when she learned that Baker taught rebirth breathing. She offered to give her time as a dancer for Baker's choreography in exchange for instruction in her breathing techniques.

"Her work in the American modern vocabulary had a profound effect on my perception of movement," says Raffa. "Brigid helped me to understand movement in a way I had never understood it before, lifting me to a higher, more expressive artistic level."

For two-and-a-half years—1996 to November 1998, while still teaching in the Miami City Ballet School—Raffa danced solo guest performances throughout the United States and France. Her fluency in English, Spanish, and French allows her to establish amiable communications with people wherever she goes.

She danced a few performances in Miami, which Linda and her students came to see. The critics raved. Edward Villella did not see her on stage, but when she took company class he said, "Nancy, you look great! What's goin' on?"

"I'm doing this for me," she said. "I was doing the performing for my own pleasure," she explains, "and my own love of dance."

Being constantly on the move guesting, alighting occasionally in Miami to teach before taking off again, gradually became a tiring, unfulfilling routine. She wasn't building toward a higher goal, just stepping from stage to stage. When Brigid Baker relocated to New York, which ended Raffa's close collaboration with her, "the guesting routine completely lost its appeal," she says. "Brigid has been one of the dearest people in my life, and my most powerful professional mentor since Ulysses Dove. When our meaningful working relationship stopped, the ballet gala stuff just didn't interest me anymore. It seemed so limiting and unchallenging."

Her ascent to stardom, decent to despair, and crawl to recovery had been a journey of self-discovery. She had taken the steps to continue growing as a dancer, now she wanted to take steps to continue growing as a person.

Raffa had never finished high school and at 34, it was something she wanted to do. With Baker's departure as the catalyst, she stopped performing and entered the tuition-free Working Solutions program at Miami-Dade Community College, a continuing education program for adults. She began to study for the GED (General Educational Development) high school equivalency test.

She did so well in all five subjects the exam tested—math, English, social studies, social sciences, and literature—her teacher encouraged her to take the practice test early. When she passed the practice test, the teacher said, "Go do the test. Have confidence in yourself. Try it."

Raffa took the official GED test in September 1998. The results came back in October with her GED certificate and a congratulatory letter. She had placed among the top 5 percent in the nation.

Her GED teacher suggested she go on to college, and her success on the test gave her the confidence to start taking college courses. Then she pondered, "What would I like to study, what would I like to major in? She called her Mom, who was working as a ballet pianist at New Jersey Ballet for former American Ballet Theatre principal Eleanor D'Antuono, then Artistic Advisor to New Jersey Ballet.

D'Antuono knew Raffa from ABT, and when Mrs. Raffa told her that her daughter was interested in going back to school, D'Antuono asked, "Does she know about Career Transition For Dancers? It's an incredible program. I'll get you the number—have Nancy give them a call."

Raffa arranged a phone interview with CTFD Director of Client Services Suzie Jary. "You're a perfect candidate," said Jary. Career Transition For Dancers (see Resources, page 250) granted Raffa college tuition to earn her Bachelor's degree, while she continued teaching at Miami City Ballet.

Like Linda Hamilton (see page 166), Raffa chose psychology as her field of study. "The children come to me daily with their questions and problems," Raffa says, "anorexia, depression, pressures of living up to expectations of excellence—I do kind of counseling work now, separate from being a ballet teacher. It's like déjà vu of so many things that I went through, I am able to pass on to the students huge experience in many different areas.

"But I felt, 'This is a serious thing, because what I say is going to influence these kids, and I would like to be more prepared, and more educated, to be able to help them properly. *That's* what made me get interested in psychology."

Miami-Dade Community College is a two-year school, and Raffa wanted her Bachelor's degree from a four-year program. She transferred to Saint Thomas University in September 2000 and graduated summa cum laude on May 18, 2002. She decided to postpone graduate school for a year to give herself a rest from the killer schedule she lived to manage a full course load and full teaching load concurrently.

Some days, for example, started at 3:00 A.M. She did her homework from 3:00 to 8:00 A.M., attended classes at Saint Thomas from 8:00 to 12:30, ate lunch, and taught at Miami City Ballet from 2:00 to 8:00 P.M.

After-class rehearsals often extended to 10:00 P.M. Once home, she talked with her husband for two or three hours and finally got to bed bet at midnight or 1:00 A.M. Three hours of sleep had to suffice most week nights. She caught up with eight hours on Friday and Saturday nights.

The yoga Julio Horvath and Geta Constantinescu had taught her 25 years ago and her study of Eastern philosophy helped her to cope with the 21-hour days. She had been initiated into Kriya yoga in 2001 by Swami Vidyadhishananda Giri and continues to study Kriya meditation with him.

"Meditation helps me in so many ways," she says. "It helps me to deal with stress, and it prolongs my span of working time because it increases my energy. Even in the two or three minutes I have between classes when the students are changing studios, I practice bringing my mind into a peaceful state that helps to regenerate the energy in my body."

Raffa's mission with her students is to build in them a strong foundation of self-confidence and love of the arts, beyond teaching them dance. That is also the mission of the Miami City Ballet School. Linda Villella's vision was to build a School that would develop the whole person, so students would leave personally and artistically enriched whether or not they pursued dance careers.

In her journey to fulfill her mission, just before Christmas 2001 Raffa collaborated with her mother and her brother Louis, who owns a recording studio, to produce a CD for ballet class. "Its title, *Music from the Heart*, derives from selections Louis wrote as inspirational pieces for events that happened during our family life," explains Raffa. "Like the adagio he wrote when I got married.

"My Mom plays piano on the CD, I organized the concept and the structure of the class, and my brother composed all the music. The twist to the CD is that the music contains unusual rhythms to help teach the students musicality. There are some beautiful pieces on there because they're inspirational, not just the typical music for ballet exercises."

Raffa returned to the stage for the first time since starting school in the fall of 1998, in the role of the Mother in Miami City Ballet's January 2002 company premiere of *Giselle*. "It felt like going home," she says, "and *woke up* in me my love of the stage and working in an artistic way."

The opening night of *Giselle* was an emotional moment for her. "While I sat alone in my dressing room before the show started, meditating to make contact with my higher self and spirit, I had a surge of emotion that flooded through my whole body. I began to sob and sob and sob as if a lock was unlatched and I was letting go of a something that had been locked into my cellular memory for the past ten years. I did not feel sad—on the contrary. I felt tremendously happy as if life, God, fate had given me the greatest gift on earth—the opportunity to appear

Nancy Raffa in rehearsal with Patricia Delgado, Jeanette Delgado, and Giselle Alvarez for *Swan Lake* Act II, Miami City Ballet School. (Photograph by Jorge E. Gallardo, 2002.)

with the company on that sacred stage, which I was never able to do with Miami City Ballet when I first joined it ten years ago and got hurt.

"I just sat there in awe of the magic that life can bring us. Who would ever think I would have the chance to get up on stage and dance with MCB after all these years? It was a gift, and when I went on stage I kept this in my consciousness. I tried to apply myself in the role of the Mother as if I was dancing Giselle, with that much respect and importance. I felt so happy to be able to give to the company, at least once, a bit of my artistic self."

Edward Villella came to her dressing room afterwards to offer special congratulations and thanks. Linda Villella gave her enthusiastic support like a second mother. Even the reviews applauded her performance, which she had donated to Villella to express her gratitude.

"I give everything with love," she says, "because I receive so much love back from Edward, Linda, and the students. Edward has been the most incredible, incredible support. He stood by me no matter what, all this time."

She pauses for a moment. "Dance is such a unique world, we help each other when we can. We're stepping stones for each other to make these transitions. An artist has the power to reach out and touch people on a soulful level, and that's what I want to aim for in anything I do. That's what I aimed for with my dancing, that's what I try to do with my students, and that's definitely what I want to do with psychology.

"I feel that there are so many people out there who are in pain and don't need to be, if they just had somebody to guide them, show them an easier path, and help them to understand themselves. Hopefully I can make the path for the younger kids easier, a bit less painful, and a lot more significant."

Linda Hamilton said of career transition, "The dancer is inside of you, and it takes time to get on the right path for a lot of people. What's important is that you find meaning."

Raffa found a new career path of profound meaning. "Dance is one of the most beautiful art forms," she says, "and dancers are very, very courageous people in electing that as their lifestyle. But unless you use dance to communicate something about yourself, to share your humanity and life with others, and as a tool for change and making life better, then it's superficial. If you are going to do it, then you need to do it with love, with integrity, and with a spirit of giving."

Part II

New Careers
Outside of Ballet

Some dancers leave ballet because of the way they are treated by their companies. Desire for a different future, an educational interest, or a new job pull others out. Still others are "pushed" out of ballet by injury, age, or feelings of frustration.

Whatever their reasons, all of the next four dancers turned away from the ballet life they had known and loved, and turned toward new friends, work, and mentors. At the average age of 34, they saw a world beyond ballet that they were eager, curious, or forced to explore.

All dancers develop personal qualities and adaptive skills that are highly marketable and valuable to any workplace as a result of their decades of rigorous ballet training and performing (see pages 243–246 for lists of these qualities and skills). The following four dancers used their competencies to advantage in their new fields.

Like Edward Villella, they gradually elevated the mental tenet of the Greek ideal above the physical. They updated their ballet expertise with further education or training, and conformed their lives to their career choices to create new identities for themselves.

Max Fuqua is a poignant example of using the competencies ballet gave him to redefine himself. After a career-ending injury, he felt he had no identity and that his life was "pointless." Gradually he felt special not having an identity. "It's kind of fun to think of yourself as anything. Whatever you want to be. You realize that being a dancer teaches you so many skills, so many practical ways of living, that you are able to do pretty much anything."

These dancers applied their ballet endowment to building careers that are often strikingly different from the ballet traditions that shaped their early years.

MICHAEL BYARS
From Barre to Bar

By the time he was five years old, Michael Byars had watched many a New York City Ballet performance from a ledge in the orchestra pit just behind the tympani, and thirty feet from his father, an oboist in the Ballet Orchestra. Craning his head from his perch, Michael could glimpse much of the magic unfolding onstage while feeling the power and beauty of the music reverberating around him. One of his favorite ballets was *A Midsummer Night's Dream*, and as the characters succumbed to Puck's magic flower, Michael similarly found himself enchanted.

"The ballet was always such a magical place, and I felt like I was a part of it from a very early age," says Byars. "Once when my mother had brought me to the theater for a brief intermission visit with my father, the conductor Hugo Fiorato suddenly came running into the musicians' lounge, crying 'Everyone into the pit! Everyone into the pit!' I learned later that the warning buzzer the stage manager uses to summon the musicians had failed to sound, so Fiorato had nearly walked into an empty orchestra pit to begin the next ballet. In the thirty seconds that followed Fiorato's frantic command, everyone scrambled into the pit—including me. I thought 'everyone' meant me too! My father was surprised, and there wasn't time to put me on the ledge. So I stood next to him and turned pages as he played *Symphony in C*."

Byars's father, James, loved to talk backstage with George Balanchine, New York City Ballet's founding choreographer, especially about the music and what he wanted to hear from the oboe section. During one of their talks, the conversation turned to the topic of James's two sons— Michael, then eleven, and his five-year-old brother Chris. Balanchine asked if Michael was interested in starting ballet. James said he would ask.

"I had been going to the ballet *a lot*—since my earliest memories," says Byars. "It looked like fun, but the children's roles in ballets like *The Nutcracker* and *A Midsummer Night's Dream* didn't interest me, perhaps because the children had been harder to see from my ledge in the orchestra pit. I wanted to be an *adult* dancer. It hadn't occurred to me until I was nearly eleven that I should start taking ballet classes, because I thought that when I got to be an adult, I would just be an adult dancer.

"Around the time of that fateful conversation between my father and Mr. B, I began to think to myself that I would really like to try dancing but didn't know how to bring up the subject. I was so startled when my father asked me whether I would like to start ballet classes that I initially said 'No.' Then I thought about it and a couple of days later said, 'Dad, I really meant "Yes," How do I start?'"

At Balanchine's urging, James called the School of American Ballet, took his son for an audition, and in January 1976, Michael was accepted. The School told him that he would start in the beginners' class the following September.

The next time James saw Balanchine backstage, Mr. B inquired about Michael's audition. "The School wants him," beamed James. "He will begin in September."

"That's terrible," cried Balanchine. "Your son wants to dance and my School says to wait nine months? He might lose interest. He might decide he wants something else. We must give him the chance *now*."

"Mr. B called the School, and I was in class the next week," explains Byars. The School initially placed him in the least advanced class, with eight-year-olds who had started the previous Fall. Three years older, four months behind, and six inches taller, "I felt like I was so obviously doing everything wrong, I was really, really attentive. If anybody got the slightest correction, I felt I'd better fix that too." His diligence and resulting progress earned him a quick promotion. His teachers moved him to the more advanced division with his eleven-year-old peers after just four classes.

Byars remained "tremendously focused" on his early dream of becoming a ballet dancer. In 1981, Balanchine selected seven promising sixteen- and seventeen-year-old students for a Special Men's Class, including Byars. Balanchine was too ill to teach the class himself, so he appointed two SAB faculty members in his stead: former Bolshoi Soloist Andrei Kramarevsky and former Royal Danish Soloist Stanley Williams. Balanchine occasionally visited; once, Byars remembers, he specifically exhorted the boys to learn everything that Williams had to teach, since mastery of the Bournonville technique would prepare them well for Mr. B's repertory.

"Of course, we tried extra hard," says Byars. "The level of concentration in that class was just out-standing. We did slow adagios at the barre on demi-pointe balancing throughout with both arms up in high fifth position. I always thought that adagios were really hard, yet we all did it—we were so focused. It was a very special time."

James and Byars's mother, Janita, were both educators as well as musicians—Janita was Principal Clarinetist for Leo-pold Stokowski's American Symphony before she turned to teaching and educational administration. Both parents supported their son's advanc-ing ballet career but wanted him to progress academically, too. In 1978 he entered the rig-orous Stuyvesant High School, one of three New York City public schools that screen can-didates through an entrance examination. He graduated from Stuyvesant in January 1982 with a Presidential Scholar's Medallion and the

Michael Byars as one of the nine men featured in Peter Martins's ballet, *Les Gentilhommes*, created for New York City Ballet in 1987 as an homage to Dan-ish teacher Stanley Williams (1925–97). (Photograph by Paul Kolnik, circa 1988.)

highest level award from the National Foundation for Advancement in the Arts, establishing himself as a top academic student as well as an advancing ballet student.

His parents suggested that he enroll in Columbia University's Gen-eral Studies program in the Fall of 1982 to maintain the flow of his edu-cation. He enrolled, but with five hours of classes on Monday, three on Wednesday, and a chemistry lab that went to 11:00 P.M., Byars left after completing just one term. "I didn't know where I was going with my dancing at that point in my life, and it was burdensome to have the addi-tional focus of school."

Within a year, Peter Martins invited him to join New York City Bal-let as an apprentice; the company extended a full *corps de ballet* contract to him the following April. He was promoted to Soloist in June 1989. "Looking back at my career, I feel very fortunate," says Byars humbly.

"I grew up to dance virtually every role that drew me to the theater as a kid—*A Midsummer Night's Dream, The Four Seasons, Tarantella, Symphony in Three Movements, Symphony in C, Fancy Free*—so it really was a dream come true for me." Puck became his signature role, his dancing transfixing others just as Puck had transfixed him twenty years earlier.

In late 1988, Byars received a letter from the American Guild of Musical Artists (AGMA), the dancers' union, that would lead him back to college and eventually on the path to his legal career. "The union letter said we were soon to vote on a dues increase. When I asked my colleagues about the letter, they answered, 'What letter?' or 'I just threw it out' or 'I thought it was just an audition notice.'

"I calculated exactly how much everybody would be paying if we enacted the new dues structure and thought, 'This is an awful lot of additional money for us to pay without anyone paying attention.' So I asked our ballet mistress to schedule a time for a company meeting to discuss the dues letter. Coincidentally, our collective bargaining agreement was about to expire, and at that meeting my colleagues asked me to chair the negotiating committee.

"I convinced seven other dancers to serve on the committee with me and asked each member to look closely at a different area of the contract, and at areas of our working lives that were not yet covered in the contract but might appropriately be subjects of new contract provisions. Another dancer and I looked into the issue of career transition: what happens to dancers when they retire. We realized early on that the information we were learning needed to be shared with our colleagues as soon as possible. The committee arranged a meeting specifically to address career transition and invited five former NYCB dancers to discuss their experiences with company members."

Forty NYCB members showed up for the meeting. One of the former dancers who came to share her experiences was Linda Hamilton, who brought the letter she had received that morning from Adelphi University informing her that she had passed her exams and earned her doctorate. She proudly announced in the meeting, "I got my Ph.D.!" (See page 172.)

"I promised myself after that meeting that I would go back to school once the contract negotiations concluded," says Byars. "In the Fall of 1990 I started back at Empire State College, because they had a labor studies program. I felt that if I were to go back to school after nearly eight years, it would be good to learn about something that I was involved in, and I also felt that I would better represent my colleagues if I had some instruction in labor negotiations. So there was a dual purpose: returning to college, through coursework immediately applicable to my union work."

Empire State College's joint program with Cornell University offered courses to union delegates and representatives in how to improve labor relations. Byars entered a class that consisted entirely of trade union members, such as electricians, steampipe fitters, and steelworkers.

"On the first day of class, one professor circulated a legal pad so that students could write their names, what union they were with, and what they did. When the pad reached the front, the professor read the information aloud. No one had any trouble figuring out who the ballet dancer was in the room, because I was about as big around as one of their arms. But it was a great experience. My classmates really appreciated hearing about labor relations from the performing artist's perspective, and I learned a lot from them. A few of them even came to see me dance."

The next summer, Byars joined a small group of dancers who were taking a summer course in literature at Fordham University, across the street from the New York State Theater. With the encouragement of several key NYCB supporters and Fordham administrators, the dancers developed a relationship with Fordham that allowed some accommodation of the dancers' schedules. Byars continued his labor relations coursework at Empire, but took liberal arts and economics credits at Fordham, eventually graduating from Fordham at age 31 after six years of study. He delivered the student commencement address at Avery Fisher Hall, the same stage on which he had graduated from high school fourteen years earlier, and directly across Lincoln Center from the State Theater stage on which he had danced the night before.

"After graduation, I took time to let my degree sink in. I let myself feel what it was like to have a college degree without making any immediate plans."

Byars had arrived at the brink of transition. He began looking forward to a graduate degree, so he took the GRE (Graduate Record Exam) and the LSAT (Law School Admission Test). He did well on both and ultimately decided to go to law school.

Around that time, a mutual friend in the David Parsons Dance Company introduced him to his future wife, Rachael Venner, after the three of them took ballet class together. "Rachael became a good friend with whom I could discuss my post-performing dreams without worrying that what I said would be repeated at the theater. When I got my acceptance letters from law schools, I shared them with her.

"At thirty-one, I became more aware of my future than I had been earlier on. I thought, 'If I stay with NYCB, I will continue to dance my favorite roles for a bit longer.' I really loved what I was doing, but after a certain point, I was dancing the same roles over and over. The marginal satisfaction of each additional performance was not enough to delay my future. I loved dancing Puck, but the difference between performance number 83 and performance number 82 was just not as great as between 18 and 17, or 33 and 32. In addition, I had always wanted to be thought of as a classical dancer and I had achieved that goal. When I started off my career, I danced Puck, *The Four Seasons*, and other character roles, but eventually I moved into more classical roles such as the Third Movement in *Symphony in C*, which was very special to me. So I felt that I had done everything I had wanted to do, and I was ready to move on to a new challenge."

Byars entered New York University School of Law in Fall 1997. At first he tried to attend ballet class whenever he could fit it into his law school schedule—which was rarely. "Taking ballet classes only occasionally was frustrating for me, because obviously, I rapidly lost my skill level without daily class. I realized that I had quit performing, in part, because I wanted to eliminate the physical stress that ballet places on the body, and trying to dance as I used to do, but irregularly, was a risky approach. I also felt the pressure of my tremendous transition into a completely new world that I would have to accept wholeheartedly to succeed.

"In some ways, I felt very much like I did when I was beginning my dance lessons: I needed to learn not only from my own experience, but also from the experiences of others. Many of my classmates had worked in the legal or related fields, or had post-graduate degrees." In an effort to learn more, Byars took a summer internship with a Court of Appeals judge on the Second Circuit and interned during the following academic year with a district court judge. "It was great to have their supervision on my writing and research, and to work with their clerks—recent law school graduates and young lawyers who were very bright and seemed to know how to do everything."

Byars took a summer job in 1999 with the international law firm Coudert Brothers. "While dancing, I had very much enjoyed the cross-cultural opportunities that came with touring, so Coudert's international practice especially appealed to me." That August, he met a friend and former dancing partner who had retired from New York City Ballet in her mid-twenties, gone to Harvard then to Wharton, and was now working in a top-level telecommunications position.

Byars recalls her reminding him that just as it takes a long time to become a dancer, it takes a number of years to reconceptualize what you are doing, and to feel as committed to something new. Byars says, "It's important for a dancer in transition to know other dancers who are a little farther along in the process, who can serve as role models and help you understand that you need to be patient about developing a new identity."

Byars graduated from NYU in May 2000, passed the bar exams for New York and Massachusetts in July, and was formally admitted to the bar in both states the following spring. Coudert Brothers welcomed him as a full-time associate that fall in their Intellectual Property and Media Law litigation group. He also worked on Coudert's bankruptcy, corporate internal investigation, and commercial litigation projects. In August 2001, he took a leave from private practice to gain additional litigation experience in the federal judiciary, first by working as a law clerk to Judge Reena Raggi, at the time a district judge in the Eastern District of New York. During the 2002-03 term he will continue in government service, by clerking for Judge Kim McLane Wardlaw of the Ninth Circuit Court of Appeals in Pasadena, California.

"The exciting thing about my life right now is that this is the time in a lawyer's career when there are

Michael Byars as a Law Clerk to the Honorable Kim M. Wardlaw, United States Circuit Judge for the Ninth District. Photograph taken outside the United States Court of Appeals building, Pasadena, CA. (Photograph by Rachael Venner, 2002.)

so many possibilities. I feel like the luckiest ex-dancer in the world. I had the dance career that I had always hoped for, and I am entering a great new profession. As one judge I worked for pointed out, dance is one of those professions where people have to stop at a certain time, but one's success as a dancer can be viewed as an indicator of future success. Non-dancers who are open-minded realize how the attributes that contributed to a successful dance career are going to translate into something new." (See Adaptive Skills and Marketable Personal Qualities, pages 243–246.)

With characteristic humility Byars says, "I feel really fortunate and hope that other dancers will find career transition equally fascinating and rewarding. Unfortunately I don't think everyone does at first, because some dancers don't start thinking about the process soon enough or can't find the right support." Byars's continued interest in dancers' career transitions is also reflected in his work with Career Transition For Dancers and with its affiliate, the International Organization for the Transition of Professional Dancers. As a union delegate, Byars helped coordinate informational meetings with CTFD. He served as a member of the editing committee for the IOTPD's 1995 book, *The Dancer's Destiny*, which summarizes the proceedings of the IOTPD's first international symposium. (See Resources, page 248.)

Equipped now with a law degree, he says, "I feel I am in a better position to help people. I always enjoyed the advocacy role of union representative and was gratified that my colleagues occasionally sought my advice in other areas too. I enjoyed helping people find solutions to their problems.

"Although I am not practicing law in a dance-related area right now, I did pro bono work for a dance company while at Coudert. And I still get the occasional call or e-mail from a former colleague. I am delighted and honored to think that people remember that I am willing to help them find the answers they need. That's very gratifying, and in keeping with one of my initial reasons for wanting to dance. My admiration for the dancers I saw on stage from the orchestra pit made me want to be one, and my admiration for what they do makes me glad to be able to help out now when I can."

Byars also remains involved in the dance world through his wife, a modern dancer. Their 2002-03 year on the West Coast is an adventure for both of them.

JEFF PLOURDE
Dancing into Accounting

Promotions at Deloitte & Touche from Staff Accountant to In-charge Accountant to Senior Accountant usually take three years. Former dancer Jeff Plourde leapt up the ladder in half that time, largely because of the personal qualities and adaptive skills he transferred from his ballet career to accounting.

"Accounting is a lot like dance," he says.

"In dance, you can work on a role for weeks and weeks, but no matter how prepared you are, if your costume doesn't fit, or isn't finished, or looks bad on your body and wardrobe refuses to adjust it, you're going to have a lousy performance. So the rule of thumb is, 'Never piss off wardrobe.'

"The support people—wardrobe, stage hands, prop master—play a much bigger role than most people realize. They are people with whom you always want to keep a good relationship, because the small things they do make a big difference to the quality of your performance.

"In public accounting, it's the same way," continues Plourde, "I'm an auditor, so when I prepare a financial statement, I give it to the report department to type, format, put in the right fonts, and put together. The report department is just like wardrobe. My report, and everybody else's report, of course, has top priority. So in order to get my report pushed through the system faster, or to have the report department help me with some of the technical writing, I don't piss off the report department."

He smiles. "I tell this story to my staff people. Some of the young licensed professionals with their CPAs and their Master's Degrees have a tendency to treat the administrative people as if they're at a lower level.

Jeffrey Plourde in a studio portrait that shows his clean, classic line. (Photograph courtesy of Jeffrey G. Plourde.)

Then when it comes down to getting their reports done, they miss their deadlines, because the report department won't support them. So I tell 'em that story: 'Never piss off wardrobe.'"

Plourde attributes a lot of his second-career success to the fact that he went through the full spectrum of his first career—from *corps de ballet* to principal. "There are so many nuances of knowledge that run throughout a dance career," he says, "and I try to bring all of those to the second career so I won't make the same mistakes. Having been through one career makes managing the second career a lot easier."

Plourde was born September 13, 1965, in Riverside, California. His mother was a music teacher, so she and her husband encouraged their son and daughter to study music. In high school, Plourde and his sister played in the band, but he longed to do something that his sister wasn't part of. At 14 he joined the theater department and began singing, dancing, and acting in the school musicals.

The music director was honest with him, "You don't have a lot of aptitude for singing, your acting's fair, but your dancing seems to be something you have a lot of talent in."

"Okay, what do I do?" responded Jeff.

"Talk to the girls in the department, find out where there's a good dance school, and get started," advised the director.

"I started off taking tap and jazz," says Plourde, "until the director of the dance school announced that in order to get a scholarship I'd have to take ballet."

Plourde reluctantly complied. "Once I got into ballet, I really enjoyed it. Eventually, I dropped out of tap and jazz. I had been taking those mainly to be in the school musicals. However, the *dance* school tap and jazz classes were very structured, with a syllabus. Some things I knew, but some things I was clueless about, which was frustrating, and I was already in the more advanced classes. With ballet, the teacher started at the very beginning and I progressed with the class."

Every spring, representatives from "the big ballet schools" came to audition students. Plourde auditioned in his second year of ballet and was accepted into Boston Ballet's Summer Dance Program. The next summer, he went to the National Ballet School in Toronto.

Pacific Northwest Ballet auditioned him when he was 17, and invited him to come to their School for a year. "Time to fly the coop," thought Plourde and moved from Riverside to Seattle, expecting to join the company. "We don't think you're quite ready for our company," said PNB administrators when he got there. Plourde nonetheless stayed—for two years. PNB includes students in their large productions, so he had opportunities to work with the company while training. He also danced in PNB's movie of *The Nutcracker.*

At the end of his second year in the School, Artistic Director Francia Russell had a conference with him. "You can stay in our School for another year," she said, "or you can get a job. We think you are at the level where you could get a job in a smaller company. You can always come back, but we think that you will learn a lot more as a professional than you will by staying in our School." Plourde thought that made sense.

"I auditioned around and my best choice was Fort Worth Ballet, a new company doing the Balanchine rep. So I headed down to Texas to begin my professional career at 19."

Plourde spent four fulfilling years in Forth Worth Ballet, from 1984 to 1988; he inspired Artistic Director Paul Mejia to create roles for him. "He created an *Afternoon of a Faun* that was real nice," recalls Plourde.

During his third year, Plourde began to think about college. He had finished high school and foresaw that at some point his dance career would end. He wanted to be prepared. He started taking classes at Tarrant County Community College during FWB's summer layoffs. "I didn't know what to major in, so I started picking up all the basic requirements. Then I met my wife. We got married in 1989; I was 23."

Plourde's wife Susan was building her own career in marketing for real estate investment trusts. A year after they married, an opportunity opened for her in Dallas. Plourde was ready for a change to another repertory, so in 1988 he joined Ballet Dallas and they moved out of Fort Worth.

Plourde stayed with Ballet Dallas for three years, but the company was small and he wanted more of a challenge. He and Susan also wanted to start a family, so Plourde pursued a career opportunity that would allow him to support them both. He landed a senior artist contract with

Ballet West shortly before his 27th birthday. The company's style offered him a new artistic frontier, and the contract was substantial enough to allow Susan to work part-time as a marketing consultant while preparing to have their first child. At age 28, Plourde became a father.

Their daughter Taylor was the one great joy of their year in Utah. Otherwise, "the company was not a good fit for me," he says. "The director worked the company in a fashion that I struggled to conform to. I was in the prime of my career, and I didn't want to be in an uncomfortable artistic environment." A dancer in the company provided a touch of inspiration, however. "He was finishing his degree in dance and also studying finance. He ended up retiring and working for a company doing financial analysis. I thought that was a smart move. He showed me that being a dancer didn't mean you couldn't be good with numbers, you couldn't figure out financial stuff. He was an inspiration."

Texas had been good to Plourde and his wife, so they decided to head back down South. Plourde negotiated a principal contract with Ballet Austin, and Susan became Director of Marketing for Schroeder Center Management.

Lambros Lambrou was Artistic Director of Ballet Austin when Plourde arrived in 1993. Lambrou liked Plourde, and responded to his talent and quick mind by choreographing a few ballets on him, a creative process that Plourde had always enjoyed.

"But my left hip started getting sore, and I wasn't sure why," he says. "You get older, you get a little creakier. I danced for a year, year-and-a-half, then decided to go back to school during summer layoffs. University of Texas at Austin is probably Texas's premier university, and the campus was just down the street from the Ballet. I enrolled in their Business School."

Plourde thought of majoring in management, "but the more people I talked to, the more people told me, 'Accounting is the vocabulary of business. Today you have to have a good financial understanding of how business works, and that's basically what they teach in accounting.'

"I thought accounting seemed awfully dry, and the stereotype of an accountant wasn't one that appealed to me—but I didn't know anything about it, really. It's funny that the stereotype would bother me after being a ballet dancer for 20 years!"

The professors convinced him that his stereotype of an accountant was false. "They told me that there are people in Congress who are accountants, and that there are more CEOs of more companies who have accounting backgrounds than any other. The occupation doesn't define you. If you're going to go through business school, you can go a variety of ways, but accounting might give me the best foundation in business. They were right, and that is the best decision I could have made."

Plourde's wife, a marketing professional, made another convincing point. "Jeff," she said, "when they start downsizing companies, it's always the accountants who are the last to be fired. Marketing goes first, then they take out half of management. But they usually leave the accountants in place, because the accountants are the ones who can tell you if the decisions you're making are costing you money or making you money. So there's a lot of longevity in it. It's a good career choice."

Plourde entered the University of Texas Business School in the accounting program. "The more I got into it," he says, "the more fascinating I found it, and the more I found that accounting is a lot like dance."

Plourde saw one parallel immediately. "The dancer," he says, "takes the images, feelings, and ideas of the choreographer and conveys them through the language of dance. In accounting, it's the same way. We take events that happen in business and put them into a language, a financial language. We try to put down on paper what a company is doing—how it's making money, how it's losing money, the sources of that money.

"When dancers go through school, initially they're just trying to learn steps, they're trying to learn the language of dance, the positions and the movements. As they get more advanced, they get better at it, and they try to take the language and express more and more. It's the same with accounting. When you're in school, you're learning all the rules and basics of accounting. But through practice, you can take the basics and the foundation, then see where you can utilize different interpretations to make a financial position change. So accounting just seemed very similar to what I was trying to achieve as a dancer."

In 1997, in the middle of Plourde's junior year, Susan was transferred to Orlando, Florida. She had marketed a mall in Austin for Schroeder Center Management, which they successfully sold, then asked her to market a mall for them in Orlando, their biggest property. It was a great opportunity for her and they needed the paycheck, so they decided to move to Florida.

Plourde planned to stop dancing at the end of the Austin season, finish his junior year at the University of Texas, then join his wife in Orlando. Without a dance job, he would have plenty of time to complete his senior year at the University of Central Florida and prepare for the grueling CPA exam. He laughs, "Since she made four times more than I did, that tended to be a motivating factor."

Mid-season he consulted an orthopedist about his left hip. The diagnosis: arthritis. He was told that despite anti-inflammatory medication, he should expect problems until he retired from dancing.

Even with the medication his hip hurt. "When the prescription drugs aren't keeping the pain or the inflammation down," says Plourde, "you've really run out of options. You can get steroid shots, but then you've got a bigger problem. I wasn't ready for that. I was 32 and had danced for just about 13 years. I thought, 'It's okay, I've had a good career,' and was pretty much ready to retire."

Plourde and his wife visited Orlando several times before they moved, and he discovered that there was a small ballet company there—Southern Ballet Theatre (now Orlando Ballet).

"It turned out the director was a friend of mine from Dallas," says Plourde, "and he told me he could use a principal dancer. We worked out a deal, and I danced for one more season—1997-98."

Susan's career blossomed in Orlando. She joined Colonial Properties Trust and became their Vice-President of Retail Marketing. As the year proceeded for Plourde, his dancing days seemed numbered. By the close of Southern Ballet Theatre's season in May, he had five good reasons to end his ballet career.

First: pain. "I was in a *lot* of pain," he says.

Second: repertoire. "The company that year decided to go with a classical repertoire. As you get older, it becomes harder and harder to stay with classical ballet if you're a principal dancer. That's body-pounding stuff! I think audiences like to see younger, more virtuoso dancers do those roles, too. I think that almost all dancers would prefer to go from a classical repertoire when they're younger to a more contemporary format when they're older. They can utilize their artistry and maturity on stage, but the work isn't as physically treacherous."

Third: schedule. "I was going to school at the same time I was dancing, and my school hours didn't always work with the company schedule. The director was okay with that, but it made for a difficult working relationship."

Fourth: standards. Plourde strives to achieve the highest standards of excellence in all he does—a principle exemplified by the fact that he graduated Magna Cum Laude from the University of Central Florida. "You set a standard," he says, "and the last year or two of my ballet career, it was getting harder and harder to meet a standard that was fulfilling, let alone one that would give me a little self-respect.

"I think you hit that standard physically around 27, 28, then in the later years you struggle to keep up with that standard. You start to see that standard slip, and rather than growing as an artist, trying to get better and better, you see that your instrument is deteriorating. You realize that your best years have gone by, and that you're never going to be able to fulfill your goals *physically* as an artist. Your muscles hurt, your joints hurt, and although the passion for the art form is still there and you still love to do it, the physical part just becomes more and more difficult.

"That's why the repertoire is so important. If it's physically demanding, I know right away that it isn't going to be fun—that I'm going to be out there killing myself, and I'm not going to meet my standards." He preferred to quit than dance sub-standard.

Fifth: life. "I wanted more out of life. I wanted a family, a house, material things. I'd had a good, full career. I'd danced all the classical roles, a lot of neo-classical roles, a bunch of Balanchine roles. I'd danced with a lot of great ballerinas, did ballet competitions in Russia and Japan, traveled all over the world—and made a decent living at it.

"Now I'm making a transition into another field, and I may or may not come back to ballet ever again, I don't know."

Plourde started working part-time at a local accounting firm in January 1999. After his Magna Cum Laude graduation in June 1999, he began the fifth-year requirement of 150 class hours mandated by the state of Florida to sit for the CPA exam. Deloitte & Touche hired him as a full-time Staff Accountant in September 1999; he scheduled his CPA exam for that November.

The CPA exam—that rite of passage into the exclusive club of licensed Certified Public Accountants—is the most difficult board certification test of any kind, tougher than the bar exam for lawyers or the state boards for doctors. The four-part, fifteen-and-a-half-hour marathon takes two days to complete, and fewer than 30 percent of those examined pass all four parts on the first try.

By November Plourde was ready. He walked into the examination room completely confident that he would pass the entire exam the first time. He had applied his ballet discipline and perfectionism to his exam preparation and expected a great performance. "Our profession is one where not meeting a deadline, being sloppy or lazy, has enormous consequences," he says. "If you are not well prepared—you don't know your role, forget what you're doing, or blow it when you walk out on that stage in front of 3,000 people in nothing but tights and make-up—there's nowhere to hide.

"When you start at a young age in that kind of environment with that kind of pressure, mistakes, lack of concentration, or just small errors are all magnified. You know that it's your responsibility to be the best that you can be on that stage, or you'll look bad, the whole company will look sloppy, and the director's going to be at your dressing room door, you can count on it.

"So you approach everything with that same kind of intensity—'I've just got to know this, I've got to *know* this'—that intensity carries on into your school work and pretty much everything you do."

Plourde passed the CPA exam that November, 1999. "It's not impossible to pass," he says modestly, "you just have to be well prepared." Deloitte & Touche rewarded him with a promotion to In-charge Accountant a few months later. Benford's law replaced *battement frappé*, attestation reports replaced *attitude épaulée*. He adhered to GAAS (generally accepted auditing standards) as vigorously as he had avoided sag, controlled policies and procedures as precisely as he had controlled his body.

Fortune Magazine has named Deloitte & Touche to its list of 100 Best Companies to Work For in America every year since the list's inception in 1998. The company's quality performance is harmonious with Plourde's work ethic. The similarities he sees between accounting and ballet allow him to apply the wisdom he gained from his first career to his second.

To the three similarities he described earlier—valuing support people, building from the basic language, and preparing well—he adds three more: the concepts of similar skill sets, optimum performance in your role, and what he refers to as the "no-glory" roles.

"All dancers in a company do the same thing," he explains, "the only differences are male, female, and rank. Everyone dances ballet, so all male dancers or all female dancers have an opportunity to be cast in any given role. Your title or rank may give you a better shot at it, or qualify you or disqualify you for certain roles, but for the most part if the director feels that one dancer is the perfect match for a certain role, the director will give that dancer that role. Each time a ballet is cast, dancers compete with their peers.

"Public accounting is pretty much the same way. Say you've got an office of 40 professionals. They're all accountants, they're all CPAs. You might differentiate between tax and audit, but among the 30 auditors, you're all up for clients and engagements because you all have similar skill sets. That's a lot like dance."

Plourde managed the competition in dance, and continues to manage the competition in accounting, by striving to be the best he can be in his current role. "When you come into a ballet company, all you want to do is to be a soloist. So you work hard to become a soloist. When you become a soloist, all you want to be is a principal. So you work hard to become a principal. But you're not really working hard at being a good soloist, you're working hard to try to be a principal. The same with the *corps de ballet*. You never really evaluate your position in the *corps* and its importance in the grand scheme of things. All you are thinking about is the next best role, when am I going to get to dance with so-and-so, when am I going to get promoted to soloist or principal.

"When you get to be principal, you think, 'Gee, I'm only as good as the *corps* behind me.' When people come to watch the ballet, they see the whole thing and unfortunately the weakest links stand out. If the principals are great, but the *corps* is not solid, that weakness will stick in their minds.

"I think that's a concept you can take to the client engagements. Each person at each level—Staff Accountant, In-charge Accountant, Senior Manager, and Partner—has a very valuable role in working hard on their respective skills to make or break your performance. Your performance in *THAT ROLE* is the most important thing. If you focus on executing what you've got to do, the promotions will come.

"The odd thing about my promotions within the firm is that they were never something I pushed for, never something I asked for, they just *happened*. Each role that I took, I thought, 'Well, my job is to do my best to make my performance in this position the best.'"

The sixth similarity Plourde sees between ballet and accounting and worked to his advantage is the concept of no-glory roles. "There are always roles in a bal-

Deloitte & Touche Senior CPA Jeffrey Plourde in a picture that captures his brio. (Photograph courtesy of Jeffrey G. Plourde, 2002.)

let that nobody wants to dance. The *no-glory* roles. The ones the critics never write about, or that are not technically challenging, or, for the men, bravura. There are a lot of roles that don't get any recognition, yet are key to the story or cornerstones of the ballet, like character roles, or parents in the first-act *Nutcracker* Party Scene. If the parents in Party Scene are engaging, they will carry that whole first act.

"In accounting, there are always clients we don't want to work with or engagements we don't want to work on. A lot of times those clients or engagements are cornerstones to the office, yet because they have become such disasters, they carry no opportunity for recognition, and people try not to take them on.

"I've found that if you take the opportunity, and you turn that cornerstone into significant performance, then you *can* get recognition."

Plourde's rapid rise in public accounting continues. Especially remarkable about his achievements in both his previous and his present careers is the fact that his progress is largely self-guided, achieved without mentors. "There have been dancers along the way who have gone a certain path that I thought looked pretty good, like the dancer at Ballet West who worked in finance. My wife is also a tremendous role model. But on the whole, my careers have been pretty much self-guided." Ballet success can certainly beget life-long success.

In the spring of 2002, Plourde offered to mentor a young Cuban dancer who was about to retire from Orlando Ballet, Plourde's former Southern Ballet Theatre. "He asked me about getting into accounting," says Plourde. "He loves numbers and loves doing his own taxes, so he asked me about going to school and getting into accounting, finance, and bookkeeping. I told him about Career Transition For Dancers (see Resources, page 250), the local community college, and got him started in both. He transferred his diplomas from Cuba and will try to enroll in the fall."

Plourde found a new aesthetic in accounting, a career at first glance quite different from dance, yet in fact remarkably related to it. "Accounting contrasts completely to the art world," he says, "with its choreographers, classical ballets, romance. That world involves more abstract thinking and creative concepts. Accounting is far more concrete, absolute, number-oriented, and factual. The contrast has been refereshing.

"And I enjoy the people. After the ballet, we all went to the parties, fundraisers, and events. The people there were usually executives, or business people who had had significant success in their respective fields. You could either talk about what you knew, or talk about what they knew. Usually they didn't know anything about what you did, so you tried to steer the conversation towards what they did. I have always been interested in the money side of business, so I found talking to those people about business fascinating.

"Now that I'm *in* it, as a CPA, I see a lot of different businesses, and I'm down into details quite a bit. It's been very rewarding to learn about all these different companies and businesses, from a numbers perspective and an operations perspective, but mostly from the people perspective. I enjoy the opportunity to engage with a lot of people all the time, and I enjoy learning from them."

Plourde's transition from ballet, and all the transitions in this book, show that, in Plourde's words, "You can do it. You can make the transition into something else.

"You just have to take it one year at a time. You have to say, 'Okay, I am now going to make the transition, what do I need to do? I need to go back to school. Well, the first step is I've got to register.' So you call up the school, you find out what you need to do. You take one step at a time. Instead of thinking out six years, just think, 'What do I have to do today, tomorrow, this year.' Chip away just a little, tiny bit at a time, and next thing you know, you've done it."

ERIN STIEFEL INCH
High EI

How relevant that Erin Inch and *Emotional Intelligence* begin with the same letters. Psychologist Daniel Goleman, author of the bestseller *Emotional Intelligence: Why It Can Matter More Than IQ*, defines EI as the totality of characteristics beyond intelligence that a person brings to life: "abilities such as being able to motivate oneself and persist in the face of frustrations; to control impulse and delay gratification; to regulate one's moods and keep distress from swamping the ability to think; to empathize and to hope...."

"Emotional aptitude is a *meta-ability* determining how well we can use whatever other skills we have, including raw intellect.... Much evidence exists that people who are emotionally adept—who know and manage their own feelings well, and who read and deal effectively with other people's feelings—are at an advantage in any domain of life ... emotional competence is the master aptitude, facilitating all other kinds of intelligence."

The dancers in this book made successful career transitions because they possess emotionally intelligent traits, among them, writes Goleman, "being able to motivate themselves, feeling resourceful enough to find ways to accomplish their objectives, reassuring themselves when in a tight spot that things will get better, being flexible enough to find different ways to get to their goals or to switch goals if one becomes impossible, and having the sense to break down a formidable task into smaller, manageable pieces." The coincidence of initials in Goleman's concept and Inch's name bids use of these traits as benchmarks for her life.

Born November 3, 1971, in New Haven, Connecticut, Erin Mima

Stiefel's first 29 years were as mobile as Robin Hoffman's (see page 203), and for the same reasons: her father's career and her own. "Alan, a graduate of Yale Divinity School, had decided law enforcement was a more practical way to improve the world and had begun working his way up the ranks in the Federal Bureau of Prisons, where promotions usually require frequent moves across state lines," wrote Harris Green in his December 1995 *Dance Magazine* article, *Ethan Stiefel: Prodigal Son of City Ballet*. When Erin and her younger brother Ethan decided they wanted to be professional dancers, "[Our] father considered whether ballet schools were available before accepting a transfer," says Ethan in Green's article.

The Stiefel's moved to Sinking Valley, Pennsylvania, when Erin was nine months old; Ethan was born in nearby Tyrone, PA, February 13, 1973. The family moved to Houston, Texas, before Erin's second birthday, and to Porter, Texas (where Alan was a state trooper) when she was two-and-a-half. She started kindergarten in Milwaukee, Wisconsin.

The Stiefels settled in Portage, Wisconsin, when Erin was six, where Mima Stiefel enrolled her two hyperactive children in gymnastics to channel their diffuse energy. The kids were good. So good, that their instructors pushed them to train three-to-four times a week for competitions. "My parents thought the rigorous training was too much for young children," says Erin Inch. "They were concerned that we would burn out too fast and asked us to choose a different activity."

Ethan chose pee-wee football. After seeing the Wisconsin Dance Ensemble perform *The Nutcracker*, Erin wanted to start ballet. "When you're a little girl and see the tutus, point shoes, and makeup, it's a *beautiful* world," she says. "All of that really inspired me. My parents thought, 'Ballet would work. Give her some grace, soften her a little!'"

In the summer of 1981, Stiefel started with one class a week at Jo Jean Retrum's Monona Academy of Dance, 50 miles south of Portage in Madison, Wisconsin. Retrum had formed the Wisconsin Dance Ensemble to tour schools with lecture-demonstrations and performances of popular children's ballets such as *Peter and the Wolf*, *Peter Rabbit's Ballet*, and *Coppélia*. A Wisconsin Dance Ensemble advertisement Mrs. Stiefel had seen in the local paper brought Erin to Retrum's *Nutcracker* and studio.

"I was hooked from the first class," she says. "I've always been very physically active, and I liked the sport aspect of it. I liked the music, the focus, the competition—everything.

"When my brother saw guys jumping around and having a good time in a summer class I was taking, he wanted to start, too." Former Pittsburgh Steeler Lynn Swann had taken ballet lessons in the 1970s to give him grace, agility, and leg power. Ethan figured ballet might help *his* football, too, and joined his sister in Retrum's Academy. Laughs Inch, "My Mom said, 'Great! He's breaking furniture so I hope that ballet will soften him, too!' He got hooked as well, and after that we pretty much went through classes together."

Erin Stiefel danced her first Wisconsin Dance Ensemble *Nutcracker* at age 11. Most memorable for her about those 1982 *Nutcrackers* were guest stars Gilma Bustillo as the Sugar Plum Fairy and Charles Maple as her Cavalier. "They were soloists with American Ballet Theatre and became my idols. Whenever they toured to the area with American Ballet Theatre I would go to every performance to see them.

Erin Stiefel as a Zurich Ballet dancer in the third *pas de deux* of Hans van Manen's ballet *Polish Pieces*. Her partner is Giorgio Madia. (Photograph by Suzanne Schwiertz, 1995.)

"When they went to Switzerland to join Basel Ballet in 1983, I became very intrigued with that company and with the idea of Americans dancing in Europe" (Bustillo was born in New York City, Maple in Pasadena, California).

By age 12 Stiefel's self-motivation and dedication to ballet convinced her parents that she was serious about dancing. When she successfully auditioned for the Milwaukee Ballet School and won a full scholarship, they gladly drove the two hours each way to allow her to study there. "My parents were extraordinarily supportive," says Inch. "I have never seen parents who would give up anything for what their children really wanted to do. But they were not stage parents, they never *pushed* us to do something. *We* had to want to do it, and *we* had to make the sacrifices.

"After school, my Mom would be waiting with dinner in the car, drive me and my brother from Portage to Milwaukee for our ballet classes, then drive us home. We did our homework in the car on the way, on the way back, and when we got home."

Stiefel studied at Milwaukee Ballet from fall 1983 to fall 1985 with Ted Kivitt, Paul Sutherland, Brunhilda Ruiz, and Basil Thompson. "I also studied from '83 to '85 at the William Reilly Dance Academy in

Milwaukee," she says. "The Reilly Academy taught a different style of ballet, and I wanted to be versatile."

When Alan was ripe for his next transfer, he knew his children had their eyes on New York. The closest opportunity for him between Portage and Manhattan was the Lewisburg Penitentiary in Pennsylvania. "We consulted with Paul Sutherland and Brunhilda Ruiz," says Inch. "They thought the Selinsgrove [PA] area would be fine, because they knew that Barbara Weisberger, founder of Pennsylvania Ballet, had been teaching in Scranton.

"Unfortunately, Barbara was not teaching at the time, but she recommended us to Marcia Dale Weary, director of the Central Pennsylvania Youth Ballet, which had studios in Carlisle and Harrisburg. We studied in Carlisle from October 1985 until the end of June 1987." CPYB has good credentials: it has produced professional dancers who have joined the world's top ballet companies, and is the only regional company in the country licensed to perform George Balanchine's *The Nutcracker*.

"Carlisle was 70 miles from Selinsgrove, so we did the same thing we did in Milwaukee: went to school every day, my Mom picked us up after school with dinner in the car, drove us to our ballet classes in Carlisle, then drove us home." The car was their dining room and study hall.

Weisberger created the Carlisle Project in 1984 to offer gifted ballet choreographers "funding, time, mentors, artistic collaborators, studio space, and showcasing opportunities essential to the creative process." she encouraged innovation and provided dancers for choreographic inspiration. Upon the high recommendations of Paul Sutherland and Brunhilda Ruiz, Weisberger chose Stiefel and her brother to be two of the Carlisle Project dancers. "I felt like the clay that the choreographers could mould to their ballets," says Erin Stiefel. "Because we were advanced, they knew they could give us any steps and we could perform them."

Carlisle provided a stepping stone to New York, but Stiefel's ultimate goal was the world. Resourceful enough to find ways to accomplish her objectives, in 1986 and 1987 she attended the School of American Ballet's summer course with her brother, and started an accelerated academic program in high school that included language courses in French, German, and Spanish.

"SAB was very, very interested in us," she says, "and after the 1987 summer course invited us into the full-year program." Wrote Green in his article, "In 1987, Alan hit the big time—warden of the Metropolitan Correctional Center in Manhattan—and Erin and Ethan could take advantage of the scholarships they had just won to the School of American Ballet." The Stiefel's moved to Somerset, New Jersey. At 4:30 A.M. Monday through Friday, the whole family piled into the car and drove the 30 miles to New York City. Alan and Mima went to work at the Metropolitan

Correctional Center—he as Associate Warden, she in the financial department. Erin and Ethan went back to sleep in Alan's office until 7:00 A.M., when it was time to take the subway uptown to school.

Stiefel and her brother went to the Professional Children's School where her schedule was similar to Patricia McBride's at the Lodge School (see page 36): "I would go to school for an hour or so in the morning, then go to ballet class at SAB, then go back to school, then go back for another ballet class, then go home. I did most of my courses by correspondence.

"I had doubled-up on my academics in my first two-and-a-half years of high school and worked hard to get all of my coursework done before we moved to New Jersey. When I got to PCS, I didn't have much to worry about. New York law requires four years of English, so in my senior year I just had an English course and a Health course to take to get my diploma.

"I always knew that school was important. My parents stressed academics because ballet is like any sport: you don't know when it will end. You could have an injury, so you need something to fall back on."

A full schedule of ballet and scholarship didn't allow much time for a teen-age social life. Says Inch, "Because I started dancing at such a young age, I didn't really know what I was missing. Not having a social life didn't phase me. I had a wonderful life in ballet doing what I loved, so I just never thought of that." Jacques D'Amboise once said, "Use the art of dance to express the beauty of being a human being," and that's what Stiefel was doing. Casual socializing couldn't compete with that beauty.

Stiefel's teachers at SAB included Suzanne Farrell, Suki Schorer, Merrill Ashley, the venerable Alexandra Danilova, and Stanley Williams. Said Ethan of Stanley Williams in the February 3, 2003, documentary *Born to be Wild: The Leading Men of American Ballet Theatre* (produced by Thirteen/WNET New York,), "The great thing about [Stanley's] class is that you have to do a great number of things on your own. That makes a very intelligent dancer."

Erin Stiefel had stayed in touch with Gilma Bustillo and Charles Maple and followed reviews of Basel Ballet. When the Basel company came to perform in New York's City Center January 31–February 5, 1989, she went to as many performances as she could.

"I met Gilma and Charles, and they told me that Basel Ballet was having an audition for the company. They encouraged me, 'You should try, see what happens.' I auditioned to get experience but wasn't expecting much. It was my first audition. By luck, I was chosen.

"I had always had a fascination with Europe; when I took three languages in high school I kind of already knew where I was going. I decided that this was a wonderful opportunity, and that I was going to go for it. I figured, 'I'm American, I can always come back to my country,' but I wanted to experience new lands and to see the rest of the world.

"I was given a contract, and three weeks after the audition I moved to Europe. They said they needed me in three weeks."

Stiefel and her mother landed in Basel, Switzerland, located on the Upper Rhine in the Dreiländereck—the triangle formed by France to the west, Germany to the north, and Switzerland's northwest point. "My Mom came over for the first week. As she was leaving and I was waving good-bye, it hit me that that my close family would now be far away. It was strange. Suddenly at 17 I was in a world where I didn't know anybody and didn't speak the language very well—Swiss German is *very* different from the high German I had learned in school!—so it was overwhelming.

Stiefel developed a supportive group of friends within the company which helped her to adjust. "The dancers were all very, very nice," she says. "I was the youngest one, and they kind of put me under their wing, especially Gilma and Charles. They helped me out and watched over me to make sure I was okay."

Artistically, the road was rougher. "Shortly after I joined Basel Ballet, artistic director Heinz Spoerli informed me that I would be on in two days. I had two run-through rehearsals to learn the entire *Swan Lake* ballet. These were not teaching sessions, and there was no video. These were purely run-throughs for the company. It was my wake up call to the world of professional ballet. In school, I was so used to taking half-a-year to rehearse for *The Nutcracker* and the other half for the spring show. But no matter how scary learning *Swan Lake* was, it was one of the most exhilarating feelings. I was now a pro.

"Heinz was so impressed with my ability to learn a ballet virtually by osmosis that he kept throwing more at me. We had a hard touring schedule during the first few months after I joined the company, and by the middle of April my body gave me another wake up call. One night after a performance of *Swan Lake* I barely made it home before collapsing. A few hours later when I came to, I called a good friend who was the only company member with a car. He rushed me to the hospital where I found out that I had a 107-degree fever.

"The doctors thought I possibly had leukemia so kept me in the hospital. 'Sleep well,' they said. At 17, with only two months in a foreign country, no family there, and not speaking the language, it was frightening. It turned out that I didn't have leukemia, but I will never know why they kept me in the hospital for a week then on restrictions for the next two weeks. I learned that my body was not a machine I could turn on and off at will or simply leave on all the time. I had to figure out how to take care of it if I was going to last in this profession."

When Spoerli became Basel Ballet's artistic director in 1973, he had single-mindedly set to raising the company's technical standards while building his reputation as a choreographer. He created over 80 new works during the next 18 years, developed his own versions of traditional classics such as *Giselle, A Midsummer Night's Dream,* Prokofiev's *Romeo and Juliet,* Henze's *Ondine,* and *Coppélia,* and introduced works of Balanchine, Maurice Béjart, Paul Taylor, John Cranko, and other choreographers. His original full-length narrative ballets won critical acclaim for their drama and characterizations; his abstract works ranged from the comic *Chäs* (1979) based on Swiss folklore, to the heavy tour de force *Die Nacht aus Blei* (The Night of Lead, 1985).

One can see the huge demands that such a vast, varied repertoire placed on the dancers in dramatic versatility, technical range, and learning speed. Stiefel persevered, reassuring herself that things would get better as she adjusted. They did. "After about six months I had adapted to the professional pace, had my own apartment, and understood how it all worked over there. I never learned Swiss German very well but managed to communicate and adjusted fine."

Stiefel had joined Basel Ballet to "experience new lands and see the world," and see the world she did. "The company toured extensively throughout Europe, but the most exotic place we went was to Taipei, Taiwan for nine days, November 10–20, 1990." Basel Ballet displayed its prowess in a program comprised of Balanchine's *Concerto Barocco,* Paul Taylor's *Esplanade,* William Forsythe's *Konzert für Violine und Orhester pas de deux,* and Heinz Spoerli's *Settings.* Stiefel danced *Concerto Barocco* and *Settings.*

One of her most rewarding Basel Ballet experiences was working with Bernd Roger Bienert in December 1990 on his ballet *2 trazoM* (Mozart spelled backwards). "I enjoyed the way Bienert worked," she says. "He was unpredictable. His youthful enthusiasm allowed him to try absolutely anything, because he wanted to be different and unique." I got to know him very well."

Jochen Schmidt wrote in his 2002 Internet article, *Heinz Spoerli and the Zurich Ballet,* that by 1990 "Spoerli began to feel somewhat confined by his hometown of Basel. Having resisted previous offers to entice him away, he now gave in to the Deutsche Oper am Rhein in Düsseldorf." Spoerli's farewell program for Basel Ballet included none of his own works but those of William Forsythe (*Steptext*), Bernd Bienert (*2 trazoM*), and Dietmar Seyffert. A *Festschrift* commemorating Spoerli's long Basel reign was published and a copy given to each dancer. Inch treasures hers among her career keepsakes.

Spoerli invited his Basel dancers to go with him to Düsseldorf, but Erin Stiefel declined. "I didn't really want to go on to Germany with him," she says. "I had worked with him for two-and-a-half years and wanted to try something new. I wanted to expand a little bit, try another company.

"Quite honestly, Spoerli had been a hard-driving director to work for. He put us through unmerciful stress to achieve the perfection he wanted, stress that drove many dancers eventually to hate ballet. He chastised dancers to become thinner and thinner, and in front of the whole company would insult those whom he considered "overweight." His response to an injury was, 'Take a pill and dance. Strengthen your mental toughness.' When one dancer's father died, he refused to allow her to go to his funeral. She went anyway, although when she returned, he permitted her to continue with the company as soloist only because he knew that soon he would be leaving Basel for Düsseldorf. He controlled by fear, and notoriously preferred younger dancers because he could control them with iron authority. Experienced dancers seldom worked with him for long, and I, too, didn't want more of this."

Stiefel left Basel Ballet in July 1991 for Bonn, Germany, where she successfully auditioned for the Operballett der Stadt Bonn. She joined the Operballett in September 1991 under Hungarian-born artistic director Youri Vamos. Vamos' choreographic strength was dramatic ballet, based on literary models (*A Midsummer Night's Dream, Romeo and Juliet*) and novel psychoanalytical retellings of ballet classics (*Cinderella, The Nutcracker, Swan Lake*). "His ballets have a lot of EQ," she says, "a lot of Emotional Quality." Vamos' work is rich with narrative expression and explorations of human relationships.

Stiefel didn't stay in Bonn long enough to experience much of Vamos' choreography. "I was only there for five months. It was a difficult time for Germany and I didn't feel comfortable in the country, especially being an American. The Berlin Wall had come down [on November 9, 1989], and Germany was going through reunification and moving its capital from Bonn to Berlin. A lot of changes were happening so I thought, 'Let's see, where else can I go?'"

"I knew that Bernd Bienert had become artistic director of Zurich Ballet and heard that he was holding an audition. I had enjoyed his work very much, liked him as a person, and thought it would be nice to work with this man again. So I went to Zurich, auditioned, was given a job and a contract. I left Bonn at the end of January 1992 and started dancing for Zurich Ballet in February. Just about when I had started to pick up the German language, I moved back to Switzerland!"

Schmidt wrote in his Internet article that "the young Bernd Roger Bienert from Vienna ... stood out for his collaborations with several of Europe's most renowned architects and for setting up some beautiful reconstructions of early modern dance works."

In the summer of 1992, Ethan Stiefel joined Zurich Ballet as a guest artist for the 1992-93 season. Wrote Harris Green, "Bernd Roger Bienert promptly built a new, far-out production of *Nutcracker* around him [as the Cavalier] and the company issued a commemorative T-shirt emblazoned with his photo." *A Strange Nutcracker in Zurich* was the title Bert Wechsler aptly gave to his Winter 1993 *Attitude* review of Bienert's October 24, 1992, performance.

A photograph which Erin Stiefel Inch has hanging on her wall to this day captures one of her most memorable moments of that 1992-93 Zurich Ballet season she spent with her brother. "We were cast as the leads in the ballet *La Vivandière*." Arthur Saint-Léon's *La Vivandière*, which premiered in London May 23, 1844, is set in a little village in Hungary. Kathi, the camp-follower, loves Hans, the son of a tavern-keeper, but they have to overcome the jealousy of the Burgomaster and the Baron, who are both pursuing Kathi, before they can get married. "It is the only time Ethan and I ever danced as partners professionally," says Inch, "and the first time I had danced as a principal."

Bienert designed a program around the Stiefels that included the *pas de six* from *La Vivandière*, a reconstruction of Nijinsky's *Afternoon of a Faun*, Bienert's *Lej Dals Chöds*, and Jorma Uotinen's *Rendering*. "I was in all four of the ballets that evening," says Inch. "The photo that I have was taken at the final dress rehearsal for press releases.

"What meant so much to me, in addition to the unforgettable experience of dancing with Ethan, is that I look up to him so much. Although he is 15 months younger than me, his level of dancing has always been inspiring. When I look at him and know what a kind, gentle, humble person he is, it only adds to the awe. My parents were thrilled to know we were dancing together, and for a surprise we sent them a video of the opening night. I think it was beyond their wildest dreams we would ever be in the same company, let alone dance together.

"Also thrilling was that this was my first leading role in a ballet. I had done solos, but this was a 20-to-25 minute piece in which I had two solos and a *pas de deux*, and got my big break to prove I could handle the pressure. After this performance my career took off. Dancing with Ethan helped. I knew I could completely trust my partner and didn't have to build that rapport that many new partners do."

Ethan returned to New York City Ballet at the end of the '92-'93 season, but another American arrived in the fall of 1993 whom Erin befriended: Max Fuqua (see pages 144–145). In her April 1995 *Dance Magazine* review of Zurich Ballet's October 30, 1994, program, which included Bienert's *Autumn Sketches*, Mats Ek's *Old Children*, and Hans van Manen's *Concertante*, Irene Wydler-Roth commended Zurich's eight young soloists, among them Max Fuqua and Erin Stiefel, who "won special attention" from the audience and critics.

Wrote Wydler-Roth of the program's third ballet, "Van Manen undoubtedly presented the jewel of the evening with *Concertante*. His art of visualizing Frank Martin's *Petite Symphonie Concertante* aroused undivided admiration and enthusiasm. The varied movement patterns, the changes of direction and speed—what a breathtaking choreographic event!"

Says Inch, "I danced quite a few of van Manen's ballets—*Five Tangos, In and Out, Visions Fugitive, Concertante, Polish Pieces*—and enjoyed each one equally. I admired him and his choreography so much. I love the simplicity of his steps, the range of emotions I had to portray, his use of music. His ballets are clean and minimalist, emphasizing the dancers' movements and expressions, rather than relying on props or extravagant sets and costumes to distract. He has a clear, precise vision of what he wants, yet he is very passionate. You have fun because you know he is having fun."

Said van Manen in Renee Renouf's March 1, 2001 interview with him published on the website http://www.ballet.co.uk/magazines/yr_01/mar01/, "I love to work with dancers. I love dancers. They inspire me most of all. Every time I make a ballet for a certain dancer, [he or she] often [makes] a name because of the ballet. That is the most wonderful thing that can happen. When someone thinks of a certain ballet they think of a certain dancer. I like that." In Zurich, Erin Stiefel earned that renown for her performances of *Polish Pieces*.

"When I was cast in the third *pas de deux* of *Polish Pieces*," she says, "I got to have a rehearsal with Hans van Manen. He worked me to the bone in the rehearsal, but he also told me how much he enjoyed watching my dancing. I was honored. It was my happiest moment dancing."

November 24, 1994, was just another day in Zurich, but Americans everywhere were celebrating one of their favorite holidays. "For the 10 years that I was living in Europe, I only celebrated Thanksgiving once," says Inch. "I always worked that day and would never remember it was Thanksgiving until my parents called to wish me a happy one. European markets did not sell turkeys especially for that day, and there were no decorations lining store windows to remind me.

"In 1994, however, there was an unusually large number of Americans in Zurich Ballet. Many of them were homesick, so I hosted a Thanksgiving. We made tons of food and laughed until our stomachs hurt. Being with friends was so heartwarming for all of us."

Life was comfortable and happy for Stiefel in Zurich during the first half of the 1990s. Her career was thriving, enriched by creative choreographers, she had a circle of good friends, and had pleasantly adapted to the European lifestyle. "The pace of life in Europe is generally slower than in America," she says. "Dinner can take three hours easily. Sundays, if you do not work in the theater, are devoted to taking walks, sitting in cafés where you inevitably meet friends, enjoying good food, and truly rejuvenating yourself before the work week begins."

At the end of 1995 while rehearsing Bienert's *The Moldau* for its January 7 premier in the Zurich Opera House, Stiefel felt a twinge in her right knee. She thought little of it, sure that her body heat would relieve the discomfort as the rehearsal progressed. It didn't.

She consulted friends who said, "No big deal. Just keep working, you'll get over it." Stiefel kept working, but her knee hurt more. "Dancers have a great ability to overcome pain," she says. "When you get on stage, the adrenaline starts flowing and blocks out the pain. But when you get *off* stage, all of a sudden you feel it."

In the April 1996 *Dance Magazine,* Irene Wydler-Roth reviewed Zurich Ballet's January 7, 1996, performance, opening her review with, "Zurich Ballet made the beginning of the new year memorable with an evening that included the reconstruction of Jean Börlin's *Skating Rink,* the Swiss premier of Ed Wubbe's *White Streams,* and the premiere of artistic director Bernd R. Bienert's *The Moldau....*" Of Wubbe's *White Streams* she writes, "The dance is a free, unconstrained translation of [Arvo Pärt's] score consisting of perpetual chains of movement and reactions to it. Graceful bodies constantly form new, unexpected duets, trios, and quartets.... Among the dancers, Mariëtte Redel, Erin Stiefel, and Luiz Bongiovani stood out....

"The event of the evening was undoubtedly the premier of the reconstructed *Skating Rink.*" Wydler-Roth proceeds to describe *Skating Rink*'s history, choreography, costumes, scenery, and dancers. "...What a feast for the eyes and ears!" she concludes. "The entire company ... earned lasting applause."

"My biggest thrill as a dancer," says Inch, "was when I looked out at an audience as I was taking my bow and saw someone smile. I knew then that they had thoroughly enjoyed the performance, and that for the brief amount of time they were in the theater they forgot about their own problems and were whisked away to another, magical world that I had helped to create. That is what I wanted as a dancer and what brought the greatest satisfaction: knowing that I could help people to forget their own pain and suffering for a couple of hours and totally enjoy themselves."

She couldn't forget her knee pain, so finally consulted a doctor who prescribed travel to a warm place during her two-and-a-half-week January break. "He advised me to go someplace where I could relax and not be tempted to take class. I picked Africa. He gave me a cortisone shot and I boarded the plane for Mombasa with some friends from the company."

Mombasa, the largest port on Africa's east coast, is a bustling city of mixed cultures with superb beaches lining its northern and southern shores. From there, the Zurich dancers traveled the Masai Mara for a safari in the Kenyan portion of the Serengeti plains, where they saw exotic wildlife and spectacular scenery.

When they returned to Zurich, they learned that Heinz Spoerli would be replacing Bernd Bienert at the end of the 1995-96 season as Zurich Ballet's artistic director. Stiefel dreaded the prospect of working with "the abysmal boss" with whom she had started her career. Good news was that Ethan had decided to join Zurich Ballet again for the 1996-97 season.

Spoerli opened his first Zurich season with the intense, neoclassical *Goldberg Variations* he had created for Düsseldorf in 1993, featuring Ethan Stiefel as one of the leads. Recalls Erin Inch, "*Goldberg Variations* premiered September 1, 1996. There was such a short turn around time—only a couple of weeks to adjust to a new director, new ballet, and almost an entirely new company, for there were only 10 of us left from Bienert's company—so it was all business!!"

Wrote Michael Merz in his Spoerli interview article in the PricewaterhouseCoopers Switzerland *CEO Online* Edition 3/2002, "Heinz Spoerli was given the job of making the ballet of the Zurich Opera House into a world-class company. And he succeeded," transforming it into an ensemble of world renown in only a few years." Said Spoerli in Merz's article "For me, dance is like a marriage, and I am always considering how long I can keep the relationship up. Each new piece is also a birth—a beautiful experience, but full of difficult moments. After all, before I can even think about pleasing an audience with a piece, I have to gain and maintain the enthusiasm of my dancers. I can't just repackage an old piece. This constant self-renewal requires a great deal of effort. I'm ... a disciplined craftsman."

Spoerli achieved Zurich Ballet's enormous leap in standing from so-so to stellar by concentrating on, according to Jochen Schmidt, four interlinking factors: careful choice of dancers, first-class training, intelligent choice of repertoire, and his own choreographies. Spoerli lives by the motto: "Excellence is the only answer."

His disciplined approach to building the company took its toll. In October 1996, with the company way behind schedule, Spoerli was pushing Max Fuqua and his partner hard to get Hans van Manen's *Concertante* onto the stage, even though they had just learned the ballet the day before (see page 146). The injury Max suffered as a result of the pressure ended his career. Stiefel's knee pain kept getting worse with Spoerli's intense agenda, although she tried to toughen herself against the escalating agony. A pleasant sojourn in December 1996 gave her a brief respite.

"My parents came over to Europe for a two-week holiday to celebrate Christmas. Their wedding anniversary is December 22, and coincidentally I had the weekend free. We boarded a night train for Paris on Friday the 20th. From the moment we arrived in Paris it was role reversal. I spoke enough French to get by, but they spoke none. I knew where everything was and how to get there; my parents had only to follow my lead, enjoy and soak up the surroundings. We all had one of the best times of our lives, and Paris will always hold a special place in our hearts."

The new year brought increased demands. Spoerli's choreography had become more and more intricate and bodily textured, requiring pliancy, speed, athleticism, off-balance direction changes, and exacting precision from his dancers. The ballets of guest choreographers Spoerli employed, specifically those of William Forsythe and Hans van Manen, required similar fireworks and brio. Critics marveled at how the dancers could deliver such brilliant performances of this challenging work with the minimal rehearsal time Spoerli allotted them.

Had Spoerli forgotten the meniscus operation he has suffered in 1963 precipitated by the choreographic demands of Waslaw Orlikowski, then Basel Ballet's artistic director? In her excellent June 2003 article for *Dance Magazine*'s Health and Fitness for Life series, Suzanne Martin describes the kneecap, or patellofemoral, problems that plague dancers of forms that accentuate the use of turnout. For example, "The kneecap rides in a specific groove of the thighbone, and if the muscles are unbalanced, pain can begin from the kneecap grinding on the groove the wrong way. In a worst-case scenario this tightness can pull the entire kneecap off of the groove."

Martin covers cartilage disc (meniscus) tears, overuse problems that lead to patellar tendonitis, anterior and posterior cruciate ligament (ACL and PCL) injuries, and much more. She gives postural and physical therapy tips to help dancers maintain good form and avoid injury, and offers advice for mental control of body mechanics.

Stiefel had pushed her mental control about as far as she could. "By the spring of 1997," she says, "I couldn't block out the pain anymore, even on stage. It was unavoidable whenever I danced." She still had to perform Forsythe's incredibly complex *In the middle … somewhat elevated* before the season ended. "It was my premier in that ballet. On stage, all of a sudden something just didn't feel right. I knew it was the knee. I bit my tongue and finished the ballet, as dancers do, but in my head it was not comfortable.

"On June 11, 1997, I had knee surgery in Zurich. It was scary, because I didn't speak the language well enough to understand all the medical terms, so I didn't know exactly what was happening to me. I kept thinking, "Are they understanding the problem? Is everything going to

Erin Stiefel Inch with her son, Kieran Stiefel Inch, born December 4, 2002. (Photograph courtesy of Erin Stiefel Inch and Scott Inch.)

turn out all right? Am I going to be the same? Am I going to be able to dance the same?' All that uncertainty added to the anxiety I was already feeling about the operation.

"I was lucky, because I got to see a lot of sports medicine doctors who were used to working with athletes, and Switzerland has a good reputation for their medical care. Most Swiss doctors come to the States for medical training and I had a few doctors who had, so that made it a little easier to comprehend what was going on. But I just had to go in with confidence, reassuring myself, 'They've studied all their lives to do this. They're professionals, just like I'm a professional dancer. People accept that I am going to give them top quality, so I have to accept the same from these doctors.' They were in fact very, very attentive and made sure that they did an excellent job."

The surgeons explained that she had developed a growth on her patella from built-up scar tissue, and that removal of the deformity required taking off part of the kneecap. They also repaired damaged tendons and ligaments. "I still have the part of the kneecap that they cut off," says Inch. "It's in my medicine cabinet!

"It should've been a very routine operation, but I tried to come back too quickly. I felt a lot of pressure from my boss, Heinz Spoerli, to return to dancing. I should've been off for about five months, but I tried to dance again two weeks after I got rid of the crutches. The knee just couldn't hold it. We had a month off that summer, so I came back to America and tried to train in New York to get my knee in shape for the 1997-98 season.

"I went back to Zurich at the end of the summer and for about three months tried to take classes and perform. It just didn't work. I was trying to do too much and the knee wasn't ready. I just couldn't do it. I tried to rehabilitate for the rest of the season so I could get back, but with the extent of the injury and the rigors of ballet, the knee never got to the point where I felt confident. I always felt that it might go again, and that fear kept me from being able to recover properly." Wrote Martin in her article, "What we think translates into our bodies."

"Much as I tried, I just knew that I would never feel like myself again.

The knee was too weak now. I could have gone for more surgery, or tried to make a life doing some other kind of dancing, but I couldn't even walk! Walking was very painful, and I couldn't run. There were a lot of things I couldn't do, so I just thought it wasn't worth it any more.

"The doctors were hopeful that we could restore my knee for normal life, so I did physical therapy in Zurich until July 1998 then came back to America. I'd had a wonderful career, especially under Bernd Bienert. I had done wonderful ballets, danced many, many soloist roles, and worked with great choreographers, so I had fulfilled what I had wanted to do with my career. I was satisfied and thought, 'If this is a sign, it's time to make a change. I've got to do something else with my life.'"

Spoerli's knee operation had diverted his career path from dancing to directing and choreographing; Stiefel's operation diverted hers from dancing to "normal life." Being flexible enough to switch goals if one goal becomes impossible, she embarked on the challenge of how to make normality special.

Stiefel moved from Zurich, Switzerland to Selinsgrove, Pennsylvania. "My brother lives in Manhattan, and the only other people I really knew at the time were my parents, who lived in Selinsgrove."

Her parents and brother have been her lifelong support group and helped to ease her transition. "We have always been very, very close," she says. "No matter what, we always support one another and are able to talk with one another openly. Nothing has ever ended that. My parents and my brother are my best friends. Having the support of these three people who are closest to me eased the difficult change."

Nonetheless, America gave her a culture shock. "After living in Europe for 10 years, America seemed like a foreign country to me. I had been so focused on dance during my adolescent years that I didn't socialize or experience much of normal life. I was totally immersed in the dance world in Europe. Dance was all I knew, and when that and my identity as a dancer were gone, it was hard to return to normal surroundings."

"Especially living in a small town, people were not familiar with what I had done in my life, so I couldn't say, 'I was a dancer and I did this—.' They didn't comprehend what I gave up and the road that I had to take to get there. It was a big shock. It was *hard*."

In Jochen Schmidt's article, Spoerli said that he attempted to express with his *Goldberg Variations* "the life that passes you by" in dance, the interrelationships of people who meet and part, exchanging perspectives and insights. Wrote Schmidt, "the length of the path open for them to travel [provides] an extraordinary wealth of possibilities." Stiefel's life was now open to innumerable possibilities.

She broke down the formidable task of building a new life into smaller, manageable pieces. As Jeff Plourde advises (see page 120), "You have to say, 'Okay, I am now going to make the transition, what do I need to do? ... You take one step at a time.... [Ask yourself] 'What do I have to do today, tomorrow, this year?' Chip away just a little, tiny bit at a time, and next thing you know, you've done it."

Stiefel asked herself those questions. "I knew I needed a means of [financial] support," she says, "needed to go back to school, and needed to find an apartment. My parents are my best friends, but I think if we lived in the same house at this point we would destroy our friendship. We're all such individuals; they have their ways, I have mine."

Her father networked through friends and learned that the Bon Ton department store was looking for someone to sell their new line of Ralph Lauren women's wear. Stiefel got the job, found an apartment in Selinsgrove, and enrolled in the Bloomsburg University evening school as a freshman—where she quickly became a straight–A student, as she was throughout high school. She chose subjects that interested her from the spectrum of courses, intellectually dancing a varied repertoire of disciplines hoping to find the most fulfilling one for self-expression. A university is an intellectual prism refracting enlightenment.

"I haven't declared a major, because once you know what it's like to get up every day and say, 'I am so lucky, I *want* to go to work,' you don't want to settle for anything less. The wonderful feeling I had when I was dancing I just knew was *me*. It just clicked. I knew I was succeeding, at least for that part of my life, and it was like an addiction drug. I gave up my life and made sacrifices to become a professional, and I *loved* what I did. Finding another profession that I have the same passion about is going to take time.

"What is neat about coming from a dance background, though, where you have traveled throughout the world and met many different people, is that when you finally sit down and start studying different subjects, you can really grasp their depth. I think dance gives you a great, great foundation for going out into the world and learning about different possibilities for work careers. I've realized that there is a whole other world of wonderful things outside of ballet. Dancing is just one of them."

In the summer of 1999 while Stiefel was working at Bon Ton, one of the Bloomsburg University mathematics professors stopped by, Scott E. Inch, Ph.D. "I had seen him on campus and knew who he was. His parents lived close to the mall where I worked, so he would shop at the mall when he came down from Bloomsburg to visit them.

"He often stopped by to talk and we got to know each other. After a while he would ask if I wanted to have coffee or dinner and I'd say, 'Okay, sure.'" Friendship blossomed into romance. On December 9, 2000, Scott and Erin married and moved to a house in Lewisburg.

Erin gave birth to a baby boy on December 4, 2002, Kieran Stiefel

Inch. "Scott and I have Irish backgrounds," she says, "and Kieran is an Irish name. So he has a name that's individual, a name from the mother's side of the family, and one from the father's side." After a difficult pregnancy and birth, Erin Inch is reveling in her new role as a mother. She put aside her University studies for a while, knowing that she can always return, with tuition reductions, because her husband teaches there. "I will go back to school when Kieran is a bit older," she says. "Right now I want to experience the joys of his first step, first words, first everything."

Her knee is fine for normal life, although she still feels it and must be careful not to overstress it. "It will never be the same as before the injury, but I've learned to live with it and make do." That emotional intelligence is the pattern of her life: she is self-motivated, finds resourceful ways to accomplish her objectives, reassures herself when in tight spots that things will get better, finds ways to achieve her goals or switches goals if one goal becomes impossible, and breaks down big tasks into small, manageable pieces.

When asked what she would like her legacy to be she replies, "I hope people will say, 'She gave her all to whatever she did. No matter what it was, she really poured her heart into it and gave it her all.' I gave something with dance, and now it's time for me to move on to something else, to contribute to the world in a different way, and hopefully to make it a better place. I believe that I have so much to give the world."

Inch is delaying her own career gratification for the deeper gratifications marriage and motherhood. "Professionally, I have not found anything to fill the professional void dancing left," she says. "I am sure I will, but I understand that it takes time. Personally, my life is so much richer. Being close to family, having time for family and friends, meeting my husband and experiencing that relationship are things I would not trade for the world. The birth of my son has only intensified this sentiment. I am a very lucky woman. I have had the exciting, jet set lifestyle, but now I also get to have the excitement of slowing down and enjoying such simple but awesome pleasures. Sometimes I am not sure if I have actually slowed down!

No confining proscenium, no demanding boss, limit her exploration of all life has to offer. "It's time to move on."

MAX FUQUA
Soared Again by Diving

Max rolls over the edge of the boat backwards and slowly disappears into the sea. He rights himself with a graceful torque of flippers and enters a paradise teeming with exotic life and landforms. His wavy blond hair undulates in the underwater currents like a thicket of sunlit eelgrass as he moves about with the weightless ease of a fish, independent of the surface world. The gravity that hurt him as a dancer cedes to buoyancy that heals him as a diver. Amid this life, he finds good in everything.

No confining proscenium limits his exploration of nature's impressive variety: anemones and angelfish, crabs and coral, sponges and starfish. But nature is akin to dance, for like the fundamentals of ballet, she uses only a few basic forms in many different contexts to create her overwhelming diversity. Spirals, 120-degree joints, pentagons, hexagons, meanders, branching patterns—nature builds upon these basics, so that even among creations that seem superficially the same, each is different in subtle ways.

Dressed in scuba gear—s(elf) c(ontained) u(nderwater) b(reathing) a(paratus)—Fuqua swims in harmony with the sea's diversity and his fellow divers. He says, "Diving in the ocean environment is for me similar to being among other dancers on stage. "We are all doing our individual things but are also working together."

Rock singer and scuba lover Jerry Garcia said diving was the only thing he got as high on as he could on drugs, and the high was all the more beautiful because it was a totally natural high. For Fuqua it is the same. Looking seventy feet ahead through sun-filtered waters he thinks, "What could be better than this?"

Max Fuqua as Zurich Ballet soloist leading the corps de ballet in Bernd Bienert's choreographic work *Bolero*. (Photograph by Suzanne Schwiertz, 1996.)

With the air in his tank getting low, Fuqua prepares to exit the clear Key Largo waters and enter a murky world teeming with tourists crowding shops for dry, high-priced versions of the marine exotica he has just experienced in their natural state.

He drives back to Alex's apartment in Miami Beach after three days of diving Florida's upper Keys. Alex Brady is soloist with Miami City Ballet, a promising choreographer, and Max's best friend. Max is down from Dallas for a visit on this January 1999 weekend.

Brady and Fuqua became buddies when they met as thirteen-year-olds at the School of American Ballet in 1982. Says Brady, "The first time I saw Max was the first day of my first summer course at SAB. At one point during class, Mrs. Glebhoff [Nathalie Glebhoff, then associate director of the School] and another woman came in to take attendance and there was this big hubbub surrounding this little boy, a skinny little kid with this huge head of hair like a blond Afro. I heard, 'Max, this ...' and 'Max, that ...' Max had come in to take the summer course and nobody knew he was going to be there, so there was this big commotion. But everybody liked him and wanted to help." After class, Brady met Fuqua in the locker room and it was instant friendship. "Ballet here is going to be fun," thought Max, "and I already have a cool friend." Max and Alex have been best friends ever since.

Max Fuqua was born May 5, 1969, in Highland Park, an established, moneyed, traditional suburb of Dallas, Texas. He began gymnastics when he was four. "We had a coach who started us competing really young," he says, "competing with other little kids. He recommended that I do some ballet to get more coordination and strength in my legs. So that was how I got into it. We got Tootsie Rolls every day, and being the only boy in the Dallas Metropolitan Ballet School, I got a lot of attention—that's one of the main things that kept me there.

"Ballet was challenging, but it didn't yet have a competitive aspect to it. It was much more individual expression and less pressure to *win*. I appreciated that more. It was more the exploration than the competition. That appealed to me a lot."

Fuqua did gymnastics and ballet concurrently until he was twelve, then dropped gymnastics. "I had done pretty much everything in school— baseball, football, gymnastics. I had always been competitive and did pretty well with that stuff, but I had also been performing with the Dallas Metropolitan Ballet. They had a company that is pretty well-known, at least five or six girls who have been in New York City Ballet came from that school. One of the reasons they consistently produce good dancers is that they have performances all the time. I really enjoyed that. I loved being on stage with them. That's what won me over: the performances."

He adds with a grin, "My favorite role was as an Indian in *Peter Pan* because each performance was more mischievous than the last."

The founding teachers of the Dallas Metropolitan Ballet school had danced in the New York Metropolitan Opera Ballet, but they based their Dallas curriculum on Balanchine's. "These teachers were not in New York City Ballet," Fuqua explains, "but what made them different and so good is that before they taught a single class, they studied how Balanchine and others at SAB taught. Many ex-dancers just start teaching class. These people learned from Balanchine how to make dancers." This careful teaching shaped Max from his very first classes on.

In 1980, Heather Watts came to Dallas to audition young dancers for the School of American Ballet. Pint-sized Max decided he *had* to go there. To him this was the best school in the country.

When he became one of the Chosen Ones at age eleven, he experienced the first of six major career transitions that would occur in the first thirty years of his life. He stepped from the threshold of puberty into New York and Men's Intermediate class at the School of American Ballet.

Richard Rapp was his teacher that first year, a low-keyed even-tempered man who works on essentials with a straightforward lack of flourish. Fuqua recalls him now as "one of the best teachers at SAB."

Classes became more demanding, and more competitive, as Fuqua progressed. Siren songs of adolescence enticed him outside of class. He describes the challenge of his six years at SAB.

"My years in SAB were indeed challenging. I went from a small town to Manhattan, and I lost my focus on dance for some time. There were distractions everywhere. Some very typical for a teenager such as drinking beer, smoking cigarettes, and flirting with girls. But a lot of the distractions were good.

"I spent countless hours in the museums, became an avid fan of classic films, hung out in the jazz clubs downtown, and got to talk to Herbie Hancock and Wynton Marsalis about what it's like to be a performer. I went to the ballet practically every night of the week. I learned photography and sold my pictures on the street. I was exploring life."

Fuqua is likeable guy who doesn't hesitate to introduce himself to the likes of Herbie Hancock or Wynton Marsalis or bend the rules a little to learn. Alex Brady reflects on his personality, "He was always getting into trouble then, but everybody knew who he was and was rooting for him, Peter Martins, everybody. People knew he wasn't an evil kid. They championed him even though they knew he might get into trouble every once in a while. He'll be in New York now and people will call up, 'Hi Max! How're you doing?' "

Fuqua reflects on Martins, "I really *liked* Peter Martins. Liked him immediately. I liked his style. He was somebody that I always respected. I've liked almost every Dane I've ever met, they're all really friendly, really fun, but I had especially good rapport with Peter Martins.

"When we were filming *The Magic Flute*—Peter was resetting it, rechoreographing it to put on film—there was one instance when I was standing on the stage and he came over and stood next to me, and we started talking. It was strange to me to be just a thirteen-year-old kid with the whole company out there, and he came over to talk to *me* about the steps, the costumes, and to make a joke. He was very friendly with me and we always got along."

Former New York City Ballet principal Sean Lavery reflects on thirteen-year-old Fuqua. "He was terrific. In *Nutcracker*, he really could do anything."

In 1984, Fuqua was given a scholarship to Edward Villella's summer camp on Cape Cod. His right hip had begun to hurt earlier that spring, but he danced through the pain hoping it would go away. Doctors and therapists varied in their opinions of what was wrong and suggested remedies, but nothing helped.

Fuqua carried his pain to Cape Cod, but he was there less than a week when his hip gave out completely. The final diagnosis was a cyst, and surgery to remove it was the only solution. The surgery set back his dancing considerably.

After hobbling about on crutches for several weeks, he became mobile enough to get a job in a restaurant cleaning tables. He says, "This experience helped me to see how special the life of a dancer is and motivated me to work harder." He returned to class that fall and worked himself back into good shape.

Fuqua was granted a full scholarship for the 1985 summer session at the San Francisco Ballet School. He says, "San Francisco taught me discipline." His teachers noticed. Teacher Anatol Vilzac and school director Richard Cammack, in particular, encouraged him. Teacher Henry Berg predicted that he would become a principal dancer.

Fuqua's academic education was fragmented compared to his disciplined ballet training. Fortunately his Highland Park schooling gave him a strong academic foundation, proven by the fact that he passed his GED (general educational development test) by recalling what he had learned up to the seventh grade in Dallas. "The public schools in Highland Park are rated among the best in the U.S.," he says. "The level of teaching is extremely high. In math and science subjects I was at best a B or C grade student, but I relished English, writing, social studies, and languages—and did well in them." His aptitude for subjects involving communication and human relations would play an important role in his later career transitions.

The three schools Fuqua attended in New York while studying at the School of American Ballet taught him life lessons far more significant than the material he gained in the classroom. Like Mark Twain, he never let his schooling interfere with his education.

Mt. Pleasant Christian Academy, his first New York school, was run by a Baptist church whose congregation was exclusively African American. He says, "The academic material was secondary to the friendships I made, but it was one hell of a culture shock at first. When we went to a gym to play, it was on 125th Street. When we went to a library, it was a library in Harlem. The other students' lives were so different from mine. It was difficult, but very interesting, to be introduced to their world.

"One beautiful thing that happened there was that I lost all traces of the bigotry that is so pervasive in the southern states. We had frequent parent days when families would come to see what we were working on. They brought food and got to know each other. It was an atmosphere of love and respect."

After a year at Mt. Pleasant, Fuqua switched to a catholic school for the next year-and-a-half. "Again, the academics were secondary to the relationships I made. One priest and I frequently ate lunch together and talked politics. He was very liberal while my views at the time were conservative. He convinced me many times, though, to accept his point of view. These conversations were a valuable lesson in learning to listen to other peoples' opinions and to think about them."

Fuqua started correspondence courses in 1985 after his cyst operation but stopped them the following spring when he was accepted into the Professional Children's School. However, he had also started guest-dancing that year with companies in the New York area and was enjoying making money as a dancer. He says, "I knew that I would become a professional, so against my parents' wishes, I dropped out of PCS. At the time, I remember thinking I would save them the tuition money."

Seasonal guest-dancing was not a job, however, and New York's enticements still often blurred the seventeen-year-old's career focus.

Fortunately, one of his best friends his last two years at SAB, along with Alex Brady, was John Selya, an award-winning dancer who became a member of American Ballet Theater's corps after graduation. Says Brady, "John was really a hard worker. He had a clear focus about what he wanted to do and was going for it. That made *us* want to work harder and better, so John sort of pulled us both up to his level. We all realized that if this was what we were going to do, we had to get our shit together, to start to focus. You only have one chance at ballet, and John helped us to see that. I credit the big change in Max's whole approach to dancing to our friendship with this guy."

Fuqua worked, focused, and was promoted to the Advanced Men's class. Now he would be among SAB's most gifted students for the next two years.

After his sixth year at SAB, he was advised to stay yet another year on the chance that there might be openings in the Company. Peter Martins had taken over directorship of New York City Ballet after Balanchine's death and wanted to build his own base of dancers. Martins liked Fuqua, but couldn't guarantee him a job.

Fuqua wasn't sure he wanted to wait around. He decided go to San Francisco for the summer to think things through, but had missed all the auditions for the 1988 summer session. He talked to Stanley Williams, New York City Ballet's most revered teacher, about what to do. Stanley talked to San Francisco Ballet's Director Helgi Tomasson and got Max in. His second major career transition was imminent.

"The first day I was in class," says Fuqua "the secretary from the company came down and said I should leave class after the barre and go upstairs and take company class, which started an hour later. I thought, '*Wow!*, that I should go up and take it!' So I started class again with the company and took the whole thing. Afterwards, Helgi offered me a job.

"It was a big surprise. I have a feeling—I never really knew this—

but I have a feeling that Stanley explained the situation [of New York City Ballet's transformation under Peter Martins] to Helgi because they're such good friends. I didn't contact the company at all, they just came down and grabbed me out of class, so I think that Stanley had spoken to them quietly about me."

Getting into City Ballet had been Fuqua's goal for so long, going to San Francisco was difficult at first. "But I've always felt it was a good move, instead of staying in New York and taking a chance."

As usual, Fuqua made friends and won hearts quickly. "I'm still in contact with a lot of the company," he says. "I go back as often as I can. I'm a pretty friendly guy, I guess. I like to socialize. Friendships are a great thing."

After five years in San Francisco, Fuqua started to feel restless. California felt far away and he started thinking, "What else is there to do? Where else in the world is there to go." San Francisco's mixed repertoire of modern and contemporary work as well as Balanchine ballets and the classics opened Fuqua's mind to new dance possibilities.

He started taking modern classes on his own and expanded into taking African dance, improvisational dance, and even tap. He saw that there was much more he could do with his dancing than ballet.

Over the six years that Max knew Richard Rapp at SAB, they had become friends. A couple of years after Fuqua joined San Francisco Ballet, he and Rapp got to talking and Rapp told him that he had the *whole world* to dance in, not just New York or San Francisco. "You can go anywhere you want to. It's all about enjoying your career anyway. Enjoying your ability to dance."

Rapp's words resounded in Fuqua's head as he imagined where besides New York or San Francisco he could dance.

He came back to New York for the summer of '93 to take class. His third major career transition lurked on 51st street. "I was in David Howard's class, 51st Street studio," he reminisces. "It's always a great class because you see dancers from every different company, as well as non-professionals…. I was there, and this guy comes up to me and says, 'I like your dancing. Where are you working?' … He was the director of the Zurich Ballet and was looking for dancers for that company."

Fuqua talked with the Zurich director—then Bernd Bienert—over a long lunch. Although Max thrives on novelty, he doesn't rush into things blindly: he knew all about the School of American Ballet before he went there; he had first-hand experience with San Francisco Ballet and talked to Stanley Williams before moving to California. Now on the brink of another career change, he studied the videotapes Bienert gave him and had long conversations with ABT principal Ethan Stiefel who had just returned from a year in Zurich.

"Everything just told me to go," he says. "The company had the reper-toire I was looking for, with emphasis on contemporary choreographers like Hans van Manen and Mats Ek. They also offered a *huge* increase in money, and it is a great country to live in. Bienert initially offered me a corps contract, but I told him I would only go as a soloist. It took a little bit of negotiating, but eventually I got the solo contract."

Fuqua's first six weeks in Zurich were stressful: new people, new lan-guage, new repertoire. But when he met a girl, began to learn the lan-guage, and really had a life there, everything was fine.

His experience of cultural adaptation at Mt. Pleasant Christian Academy as a twelve-year-old served him well here. "I use that experi-ence every day in Europe," he says. "It allows me to understand and be comfortable with the many and various cultures here."

His method for learning German was typically Max. "I went to school for about a week and couldn't stand it. I've never had the patience for school. I can do the work, but I can't stand being in a classroom. It just drives me crazy. So I learned German myself from tapes and books—and I really insisted on talking to people in German. Speaking with peo-ple is the best way to feel comfortable in your neighborhood, or with the people in your building. I just like to talk to people."

Fuqua thrived dancing with Zurich Ballet. He passionately recalls his favorite ballet experience there, as the man in Swedish choreographer Mats Ek's *Gras*. "The whole learning and rehearsing process with Mats was a dream. He is so intelligent, so deep-feeling and human. He was extremely demanding but worked with such respect for my partner and me that we would have danced for him all day and night. The ballet is a series of *pas de deux* and solos, showing the story of a man being born from the Gras*, exploring his new world, falling in love, then becoming unsure and uncomfortable with himself and his surroundings. He loses control and in the end, returns to the Gras where the woman cannot fol-low, and dies.

"Every step in this ballet is filled with nuance. The smallest gesture has meaning and gives insight to the man's state of mind throughout his 'life.' It is physically demanding and emotionally draining. The chore-ography is so powerful that the dancer should not act the role; that would be too much. Yet I have never danced anything where my thoughts and emotions were so intimately connected to the steps I was doing. It was as if the steps were feelings pouring out of my soul onto the stage."

In October 1996, Fuqua and his partner were rehearsing Hans van Manen's ballet *Concertante* in the empty Zurich Opera House. The specter of his fourth career transition lurked in the wings. With the company way

*Gras *is the German noun for grass. In the USA this ballet is called* Grass.

behind schedule, Heinz Spoerli, who assumed the artistic directorship from Bienert at the end of the 1995-96 season, was pushing them hard to get the ballet on stage, even though they had just learned it the day before.

Max and his partner hurried through the complex movements, trying to perfect them. They decided to repeat the most difficult move one last time. Max bent forward and his partner bent backward to lie down on Max's back. They were supposed to remain in constant contact, her body lying over his shoulders as he dropped to face flat on the floor, carrying them both down simultaneously.

They had done the move right once, but this time, halfway to the floor, his partner stayed suspended over him for a second—then came crashing down on his hips. Max screamed in pain as he struggled to get up. At last he stood, and felt severe pain in his left hip.

"Usually I heal really fast from injuries. But I knew this one wasn't such a light one. After a month, I started to think, 'It's not getting better,' but I was doing the leads in most of the ballets and they weren't able to replace me at the time. So I had to finish the season."

He modified steps and modified classwork to get by. But by the end of the '96-'97 season he couldn't walk down the street anymore, the pain was so great. He had to stop dancing.

Fuqua refused to admit defeat and for the next year did physical therapy and consulted first with doctors in Zurich, and then in New York, Paris, and San Francisco to find out what was wrong. He spent all of his money on "every test in the world"—bone scans, MRIs, CAT scans—to discover the problem, yet every result was inconclusive. He desperately wanted to dance, but every time he tried to go back to class, the same pain would come back in exactly the same place with the same intensity. Doctors recommended arthroscopy, but Fuqua refused, especially when they told him he might not be able to dance again. He knew that surgery would be extremely risky, because arthroscopy of the hip joint was a new procedure. He wanted to keep it as a very last resort.

"You never realize how important your work is to you until you can't do it anymore. I don't mean just ballet dancing, I mean waking up with a purpose and having work to do. And besides that, it's what I love to do: *dance*. It was *really* difficult—*very* very hard.

"I went through a big, long depression," he admits. "When your life is just kind of pointless for a while, it depresses you. But I wasn't so devastated that I couldn't function anymore. It helped a lot to know I was doing everything I could do, seeing the best doctors and therapists. Though I would not recommend spending all your savings on trying to find a solution, knowing that the leading specialists were exploring every possibility certainly made it easier for me to accept the situation. I've always had kind of a balanced mentality towards ballet which allowed me to put my mind and energy into new things."

One of those things was scuba diving, his fourth big transition physically and mentally. He had actually made his first dive in the Indian Ocean in 1994 while vacationing in Mauritius, near Madagascar. The following year he took a beginner scuba certification course in the Ionian Sea while on Corfu, northernmost of the Ionian islands. He took an advanced certification course in 1996 in the Ligurian Sea during a trip to Portofino, Italy.

Fuqua began diving in Zurich in 1997 after increasing pain from his injury had forced him off the stage. "I was just trying to keep it together by getting into other things," he says. He was miraculously pain-free underwater, which intensified scuba's appeal.

"During the injury time, I really poured myself into more challenging dives. I dove to fifty-five meters in the pitch black lakes, or in rivers with currents so strong we had to use ropes. I dove under the ice of frozen lakes in the Alps. On one of my favorite dives in Lago Maggiore, a large lake that stretches across Italy and Switzerland, I found the bottom half of a Roman amphora almost 2000 years old!"

Fuqua suddenly saw the whole world in a grain of sand: he could travel the planet by diving as well as he could by dancing.

After a year-and-a-half of searching for "every theory under the sun" to explain his hip pain, he submitted to an arthroscopy which revealed the answer. Torn cartilage had lodged in the hip joint, an injury difficult to identify externally. Repair was impossible. Cutting away the centimeter of splintered fiber was the only option for pain-free mobility.

For six weeks following surgery, Fuqua worked out in the gym getting back into shape, then returned to class. He tried for three months to come back. "I got pretty much in shape, but I still couldn't work past class. I could only go for about an hour-and-a-half, and then I would start to feel like I shouldn't do any more, that it would be dangerous to do more. The last thing I wanted to do was to re-tear my hip or irritate it again and have constant pain like I had had.

"So I just decided to go ahead and stop. To make it a permanent stop." It was summer, 1998. His fifth career transition became real. The "fantasy job" he had loved since childhood ended in a split second at age 28. He lost his identity but found pleasure with his pain-free body. Gradually he felt special *not* having an identity. "It's kind of fun to think of yourself as anything. Whatever you want to be. You realize that being a dancer teaches you so many skills, so many practical ways of living, that you *are* able to do pretty much anything. The choices are overwhelming in a way. So the problem is not anymore that you've lost your identity, but rather what do you want to do out of all the possibilities? That's a great position to be in."

Switzerland is unique in that it requires every company to pay full

Max Fuqua, owner of Plaza Health Foods, Inc., with employees and two frozen yogurt fans from Dallas Metropolitan Ballet. Standing from left to right are Michael Scott, Meri Tesfay, Max Fuqua, Allen Lalumia, and Sandy Drehsen. Seated are Sara Austin (left) and Eleanor Washburne. (Photograph by Don Shipman, 2003.)

salary to injured or laid-off employees until they are retrained and fully functional in other productive work. Fuqua will be fully compensated for college courses or whatever specialized training he needs.

His long-range plan is materializing. In September 1998 he and a Swiss friend started a business in Zurich of importing organic health foods from the United States to Switzerland. "I just wandered into a health food store in Zurich," he explains, "and saw the stock they had was really out of date compared to what's going on in California.

"I had been in the States that September, and I just started calling manufacturers, telling them what we were doing. Everyone was into it and they all sent me samples. I got samples from about sixty different manufacturers and had them shipped over to Zurich." When Fuqua returned to Zurich, he and his partner rented an office and their company was born. They named their fledgling enterprise Cross Import.

"A friend of ours in Zurich, an incredibly wealthy guy, let us use his warehouse," he says. "So far, every time we turn around, there's an open door. Everything we've needed to make this thing work, we've gotten."

One of Fuqua's work requirements is mobility. He envisions traveling world-wide to market his business, and to dive wherever he goes. He's excited about making his long-range plan of international marketing happen. "It's something you can make a lot money in," he says, "which is appealing. I've done the starving artist thing. It would be nice to make a little money. And you have to be mobile, you have to go around to sell and to buy within Europe and the world. That really appeals to me. And also, the business is based on relationships. You meet people, you make deals, you talk about things, you negotiate." Facility with people has been Max's secret to success in everything. It's his ace-in-the-hole during his sixth transition from dancer to successful businessman.

Businessman? "I'll never think of myself as a '*businessman*,'" he says with disgust. "I hate the sound of that. Just being able to make things happen is very, very satisfying. Being able to accomplish things."

The valuable lesson Fuqua learned in 1984 during his lunchtime conversations with the catholic school priest—of listening to others and really understanding their points of view—had been reinforced by working with many different choreographers throughout his career. He developed this lesson into a powerful skill over the years and puts it to use daily now in his negotiating, selling, and working with teams on projects. The world is his oyster as he looks to the future.

Pain-free biped in a bivalve world, Fuqua explores the deep. Jacques-Yves Cousteau invented scuba gear—aqualung and wetsuit—in the 1940s, allowing humans to explore freely under water. Divers make continual discoveries in the undersea world, and the possibilities for exploring our underwater planet are limitless. Fuqua sees his possibilities above and below sea level as limitless, too.

Max Fuqua made six career transitions within twenty years: from Dallas Metropolitan Ballet to the School of American Ballet at age eleven, from SAB student to San Francisco Ballet professional at age nineteen, from San Francisco to Zurich Opera Ballet at twenty-four, from dancer to diver at twenty-seven, from diver to start-up "businessman" at twenty-eight, and from start-up to established entrepreneur at age thirty.

And he is in the process of another transition. In early 2000, Fuqua began to take school seriously and to apply his ballet discipline to his academic education. He is working at an accelerated pace toward degrees in language and business with a keen eye on his goal of a second career in international marketing.

"Thankfully my injury occurred in Zurich, and I now have this great opportunity to retrain," he says. "I will study German and French at the Dolmetscherschule Zurich (translator's school) and obtain diplomas from the Goethe-Institut and Alliance Française. I will then study in German at a Swiss business school to obtain a Handelsdiplom, the basic Swiss business diploma, equivalent to an associate's degree. Then I will study at the Graduate School of Business Administration to obtain a bachelor's degree. My courses include finance management, accounting, management of information systems, industrial/business project management, marketing, economics, leadership, and personal psychology."

Fuqua is unique and fortunate in his "balanced mentality towards ballet"—and toward life. If one thing doesn't work, he does another. And his engaging personality allows him to open doors to what he wants to do.

Although five thousand eight hundred miles separate Max Fuqua in Zurich, Switzerland, and Amanda Ose in Stanford, California, and their lives and reasons for career change are dramatically different, they are alike in this respect: their interpersonal skills make them magnets for good fortune.

Part III

Non-Ballet Careers Related to Dance

Margot Fonteyn wrote in her book *The Magic of Dance* (Alfred A. Knopf, Inc. 1979, page 4), "People influencing dance have been of two kinds: those who advanced the art by contributing to its evolution one way or another and those who spread the knowledge." I say there is a third kind: those who give back to dance, who support and preserve the art, by helping its people, archiving its products, or managing its organizations.

The next six dancers are of this third kind. They have a deep sense of giving back to the art form they love by choosing non-dance careers that allow them to harmonize their work with ballet.

Their lives, like a chaconne, are a series of variations on an unvarying ground base. The melodies and rhythms derived from their different careers unfold over the deep chordal theme of ballet.

A modern practice which is exactly similar to the chaconne in technique is the "blues," where a series of chords supplies the theme upon which the players create melodic patterns. The dancers here who were pushed out of ballet by injury knew the "blues," but gradually attuned themselves to non-ballet careers consonant with their underlying ballet passion.

Others foresaw that their stage careers would not last forever so voluntarily pulled themselves out with focused education or on-the-job training. They figured out how to have their art and eat too by choosing work that assures career security, but allows them to continue to serve their fellow dancers.

151

All of these dancers, at the average age of 43, know how to support themselves while supporting the heritage that made them what they are.

AMANDA OSE
Her Dream Came True

Like Max Fuqua, immersion in water was Amanda Ose's baptism into career change.

Under blue skies on the fifth of May, 2000, the spirited dance of Ose and her four high-kicking friends rouses the gathered crowd to cheers. The dancers strike their final pose in front of the campus fountain, when suddenly a guy rushes forward, swoops up Ose, and dumps her into the fountain. The other four dancers are quickly thrown in, too, and half the crowd jumps in after them.

Ose's short white dress billows in the spray, its red spaghetti straps relax, and water seeps through her sneakers and socks. Her russet hair laps her shoulders and laughing face. How different this scene from that of a year ago! There was Amanda at the barre, disciplined and poised in leotard and pointe shoes, working toward a ballet career in Pacific Northwest Ballet's Professional Division. *Ten* years ago as Clara in PNB's *Nutcracker*, she never would have dreamed she'd end up sopping wet in a college fountain.

Amanda Ose, born December 3, 1980, in Seattle, Washington, first saw PNB's *Nutcracker* when she was five, with her mother. Says Ose, "I just decided right there that I was going to start ballet." Mrs. Ose had studied ballet, piano, acting, and singing as a child, continuing ballet in college, so she understood her daughter's passion to dance. She enrolled Amanda in Creative Movement, Pacific Northwest Ballet School's class for five-year-old beginners.

Wrote Lincoln Kirstein in *The Classic Ballet: Basic Technique and Terminology* (Alfred A. Knopf, Inc. 1952, page 8), "A childhood vision of

153

Amanda Ose in a *Paquita* variation in Pacific Northwest Ballet's June 19, 1999, school performance. This was Ose's last performance with PNB. (Photograph by Rex Tranter, 1999.)

the dancer's glory must somehow be cradled and preserved, for the daily duty is onerous and the result slow to appear." PNB faculty cradled Amanda's vision and nurtured it into a passion for dance. She loved the physical movement, the challenge of working hard, meeting the demands of her teachers, and performing. Her teachers quickly recognized the child's natural gifts. Even at five years old, her concentration, determination, and memory were exceptional.

Says Ose modestly, "Probably the strong point of my, uh—'talent'— was being able to watch the teacher give a combination and then to replicate it, being quick. I was not necessarily the most physically gifted kid in the class, but I never had any trouble picking up the combinations or the corrections."

Mrs. Ose contemplates family genetics as an explanation for her daughter's facility. "My sister was known as being a quick study in ballet class—she shares Amanda's talent in math, too—while I was musical. My 82-year-old father has a strong mathematics background, exceptional physical co-ordination, and is a great dancer!"

In Amanda's first *Nutcracker*, she distinguished herself as the Little Girl in Act I's party scene. She blossomed into the role of Clara two years later. When she out-grew children's roles, she danced Snowflakes and Flowers. Amanda danced in every PNB *Nutcracker* from 1986 to 1999 and, says Pacific Northwest Ballet School teacher Vikki Pulkkinen, who has known Amanda for over thirteen years, "She was *always* totally professional, even as a child. She gave 100 percent to every teacher she had. That was her attitude."

Ose simply loves to dance. "I *love* it," she says. "I just really like all aspects of it. Every chance I got to perform was good, exciting. As I got older, the challenge to perfect certain movements was exciting and I developed a greater appreciation for dancing, so the passion grew."

When fourteen-year-old Ose entered high school, friends, academics, and extracurricular activities became as important to her as ballet. She began to lead a dual life, and kept her two lives separate. When at PNB, she gave herself 100 percent to PNB. When at school, she gave 100 percent to school. She never talked about ballet to her high school friends because she thought they would think it was "weird," and she rarely stretched at home. Says Mrs. Ose, "I used to think, 'If she really wants to be a ballerina, seems to me she'd be stretching *constantly* at home,' She rarely did. She had a completely different life at home. You'd never know there was ballet going on."

Her participation in Drill Team when she was a sophomore revealed a hint of her ballet talent at school. The thirty-two women on Drill Team— the high school dance team—perform in formation at football games, basketball games, and school assemblies. They met every morning at 6:00 to learn and perfect their routines.

Ose's tenth-grade schedule during *Nutcracker* season got her up at 5:00 A.M. for Drill Team practice, and some mornings she had French Club or student government meetings after Drill Team. She was in school from 7:30 A.M. to 1:20 P.M., then dashed off to PNB for ballet class and rehearsal. She got home around 7:30 P.M., later if she had a *Nutcracker* performance. She ate a fast dinner, finished homework she couldn't tuck in during the day, and had her head on the pillow by 11:00 at the latest. She *always* got straight A's. Says her mother, "She was a 'quick study' and just very disciplined about her life."

Throughout high school, Ose danced up to eight hours a day as a student and performer at PNBS, yet in addition to maintaining a 4.0 grade point average, dancing on Drill Team, and being in the French Club, she was class secretary her sophomore year and secretary of the National Honor Society her senior year. At graduation she was presented with a National Merit Letter of Commendation, a Puget Sound Association of Phi Beta Kappa Award, Washington State Principals' Scholars

Award, and recognized as one of Bellevue High's six Tandy Technology Scholars.

Says Ose, reflecting on her high school years, "It was a challenge to balance school with ballet, because I wanted to maintain a normal high school experience and be with my friends, too. I'd come home from PNB and be really tired and not want to go out, but I thought, 'Hey, I want to see everybody and I want to have good memories of high school,' So I went out with them and went to all the football games and all the dances. I think I was lucky because I had really supportive friends, but also I was willing to make the effort to stay connected to them." Her friends responded in kind—she was popular.

Although Ose was enjoying school, enjoying ballet, and getting top grades, the hours that dancing took away from daily high school life made her begin to question ballet as a career. Unlike previous years when dancing was *everything* to her, says her mother, "Tenth grade was the year Amanda was completely on the fence about ballet."

Another compromising factor was at work in the background. Says Ose, "My family's always been adamant about my being well-rounded and able to do normal sporting activities and stuff. We have a ski house in Idaho and go there a lot. That probably wasn't so good for my dancing, but I did it anyway. My family's really into tennis, too. I have to give them credit for making me learn how to ski and play tennis. Now I'm happy that they did.

"My dad especially was always exposing me to different activities. He had an appreciation for ballet, but he really wanted me to go to college, I'm sure. He never really *said* that, but I just knew that he thought there was a lot more out there for me.

"So all the while I was growing up, both my parents were instrumental in helping me branch out, and I'm so glad, because I know many girls who stop ballet and then don't know where to go with their lives. They think that that's the end, but luckily my family taught me otherwise."

She says this in retrospect, but in 1997 at the end of her sophomore year, she was still going full tilt into ballet, trying to see how far she could go with it, trying to see if she could get to the point where maybe she could dance professionally.

Powerful influences pulled her into ballet, despite her parents' emphasis on being well-rounded and her own expanding interests.

In 1995 and 1996 when she was fourteen and fifteen, she attended the School of American Ballet Summer Program. SAB opened her eyes to the sophisticated New York ballet scene and Ose set her goals higher.

During the 1994-95 school year at the tender age of thirteen, an important influence arrived in Seattle. PNB hired Truman Finney to teach Level 6. Finney had danced with New York City Ballet when he was very young and had been greatly influenced by the legendary teacher Stanley Williams. Williams' potent messages of the precision, clarity, and accuracy of each step, of the relationship of one step to the other within the musical phrase, of execution with energy but without strain, of presentation and carriage that were pleasing to the eye—and Williams' very presence—shaped Finney's dancing and teaching. Williams made him feel the challenge and importance of being a dancer, and Finney later instilled these same feelings in his own students.

Ose entered Level 6 on the brink of womanhood to encounter Finney as her first male teacher. Her quick mind, hard work, and musicality captured his attention, and they developed instant rapport.

"Truman Finney was incredible with students," she says, "and an incredible influence on me. He understood musicality, unlike anyone I have ever known, and when he saw a musical dancer, he 'connected' with her. He also approached ballet in a way that was very different from what I had experienced with anybody else. He looked for very specific qualities in dancers and for intricacies of movement rather than technical feats. For example, he was never impressed with someone who did a quadruple pirouette, because he would rather see a perfectly executed double that fit within the music.

"I understood his approach right away and connected with it. He responded to me for recognizing what he was trying to teach and we had a good relationship. I've had so many amazing teachers at PNB so I wouldn't want to single one out, but he was definitely an important mentor."

An extraordinary support system of parents, friends, academic faculty, and ballet teachers has complemented nature throughout Ose's life to make her the success she is. Her father is an exemplary bond trader, tennis player, runner, and skier. Her mother is just as active, has polished interpersonal skills, and is a full-time mom to her three children—Amanda has a brother two years older and one four years younger. Her friends are there for her. School faculty adore her, and her math teacher in particular took an interest in her dancing, for she linked her analytical reasoning ability to her success in ballet.

Ose's distant mentor and quintessential role model at PNB is coartistic director Francia Russell, a brilliant, remarkable woman. She and her husband Kent Stowell founded Pacific Northwest Ballet in 1977 and have grown the company into one of the top five in the United States. "I never had a lot of contact with Francia," says Ose, "but I always looked up to her. She had danced for a couple of years in New York City Ballet before going on to college.

"She was always extremely composed and professional no matter how busy she was. I especially loved watching her work. She could enter a rehearsal room to set a ballet on Level 7 kids and after an hour and a half turn those teenagers into professional-looking dancers. It was incredible watching her stage a ballet, because she knew the entire thing inside and out. Also, she never forgot anyone's name. She knows everyone in the school, all the way down to the smallest children. I watched her throughout my childhood at PNB and saw how much she did—she works twelve-to-fifteen hours a day or *more*—and I thought, 'Wow, she is one smart woman.'

"What she has accomplished, and what she and Kent have done with the company, are incredible to me. I definitely look up to her."

Truman Finney taught at PNB through Ose's tenth grade year, 1996-97. She missed him when he left, but one of her gifts is adaptability. She determined to work all the harder for her new teachers, still envisioning a possible ballet career.

As she progressed through her junior year of high school, she says, "I started to realize that there was a lot out there I wanted to explore, and that if I kept dancing, even just for a couple of years, I might miss out on the valuable experience of being a college freshman. I had to decide what was going to give me a better experience and what was going to be more exciting for me"—a ballet career or college.

In the summer of 1998, Ose enrolled in Boston Ballet's Summer Dance Program. Class standards were high, competition tough, and she gave it her all. Her technique advanced as a result, and she came back filled with conviction to become a professional dancer. Francia Russell invited her into PNB's Professional Division (PD) as Amanda prepared to enter her senior year of high school. She was seventeen, one of the youngest of the PDs.

Only a select few Level 7s enter the Professional Division—Level 7 is the highest PNBS level before PD. Ninety percent of the approximately twenty-five PD students are from American cities other than Seattle or from other countries. Entrance is by invitation only; Francia Russell has the final say on who gets in. PDs perform with the company in *Nutcracker*, in big ballets where a large corps is needed, and often rehearse with the company or understudy.

Maintaining her dual life became an even greater challenge for Ose in her senior year. Now she had to leave Bellevue High at 10:30 A.M. to fulfill her professional-level class and rehearsal responsibilities at PNB. At school, she was taking advanced placement calculus, English, history, and French and still trying to "maintain a normal high school experience." College application deadlines loomed near.

"My mind started to wander thinking about colleges," she says, "but at that point I didn't really know yet...."

Six-to-eight hours a day Ose was with girls who had already graduated from high school or were working on their GEDs (general educational development test). The few who were in high school were certainly not taking four advanced placement courses. Amanda was the *only* one who was seriously thinking about college.

Stress built as she tried to keep up with her commitments at Bellevue and at PNB concurrently. Stress grew when she added the weight of completing all of her own college applications.

"It was rough," she says. "Halfway through my senior year, there were a couple of days when I was approaching an application deadline and I'd be racing from school to ballet and thinking, 'Why am I doing this?' But those were just a couple of isolated days. I never went through a period where I just said, 'I want to stop doing this.' I think if I had felt that way, I would've quit. I had enough interesting me in high school and other activities so I could have said, 'Hey, this isn't for me anymore,' but it kind of always *was* for me, so that's what made this decision extra hard at the end. I never ever said to my parents anything like 'I don't like ballet anymore'" But when she seemed inclined toward a ballet career, they would ask, "Well, are you sure this is what you want to be doing?'"

Ose applied to nine colleges—Vassar, Boston College, Dartmouth, Brown, Amherst, Stanford, Occidental, Santa Clara, Claremont McKenna—but she had still not resolved her dilemma of ballet vs. college.

Unsure of where she would be accepted, and unsure of what she wanted to do with ballet, she voiced her dilemma to Francia Russell and Kent Stowell during her mid-year conference with them in January 1999.

"Francia was so incredibly supportive and said, 'Whatever you do, we'll be behind you in it.' I think she recognized the devotion that I had to school and the success I was having in academics, so she really helped by encouraging me to pursue college. She reminded me that not many dancers have the opportunity to go to a really good college, and if it ended up that I had that opportunity, then I should take it.

"I think at that point I knew in my heart that I was going to go to college, but having her say that helped me to affirm my decision. Just knowing that they were there supporting me with whatever direction I chose was really nice. Being in the PNB school for so long, I got to know a lot of the teachers and dancers really well. Knowing all of *them* would support me really helped, too."

Reflecting on her thirteen years at PNBS she adds modestly, "There are only a couple of people who have gone on that long. I'm sure they were tired of me by then."

As winter flowed into spring, the Professional Division students were busy learning excerpts from the repertoire—*Firebird, Paquita, Silver Lining,*—to dance in their annual School Performance. At home, letters began to appear in the mail from the colleges to which Ose had applied. Boston

College accepted her, as did Vassar, Occidental, Santa Clara, and Clare-mont McKenna. Brown and Amherst wait-listed her. She still hadn't heard from Dartmouth and Stanford. She held out hope for her first choice.

"I knew I had the potential to get into a pretty good school, but one important criterion for me was proximity to home. Of all the schools I applied to, Stanford was the only one where the quality of education is totally top notch and the school is not completely across the country in the east. I wasn't quite sure what I wanted to pursue as a major and Stan-ford has a broad core curriculum, so I felt that there I would have a chance to figure out what interested me. Also, I've known quite a few people who've gone down there and absolutely loved it, had an amazing expe-rience."

Stanford was her dream—but her chances of getting into Stanford were slim. "I was sure I wouldn't get in because at my high school, it was very rare for anyone to get accepted. Maybe every two years we'd have one person get in, and my really good friend had already gotten accepted early decision in January. I thought, 'Okay, so that's it for our school. They only accept one person and that was the end. I'll live with that.' I started getting other acceptances, and it was exciting, but I kept hoping, '*I want to see that one envelope from Stanford.*'"

Ose received a letter of acceptance from Dartmouth in March. She thought with a sigh, "Well, I guess I'll go there."

Friday, April 2, 1999, Amanda left school and hurried to her PD class and rehearsal. The PDs were learning *Firebird* with the company, and the level of intensity and professionalism in the studio was high. When the principals came forward to rehearse their *pas de deux*, the sparks of their emotion and virtuosity electrified the room. Everyone in the studio stood transfixed by their performance.

Vikki Pulkkinen was concentrating on student evaluations in the school office. A sudden bolt of energy running up the stairs startled her. She looked up to see Mrs. Ose at her door. Recounts Pulkkinen, "I hadn't seen Amanda's mom in a while because for the last couple years Amanda had been coming to her conferences by herself, she didn't need her *mom* there anymore. Her mother came running into the office and I said, 'Hi, what are you doing here?' She said, 'Vikki, Vikki, Amanda got accepted in Stanford!!' I went, 'Oh, you're *kidding*! Does she know?' She said, 'No, but she's been waiting to hear. Where is she?' I said, 'She's in company rehearsal. Wait a minute. I'll pull her out for this.' She said, 'Oh no, you can't pull her out of company rehearsal.' I said, 'Wait, I'll see if she's stand-ing in the back understudying or whatever.' 'Are you sure?' 'Yeah.'

"So I knocked on the window and got somebody to get Amanda and Amanda kind of looked at me and I waved her over. She came out the door and I said, 'Amanda, your mom's here and she wants to talk to you.'

Amanda's face went white and I said, 'No, no, everything's fine. There's nothing wrong.'

"Amanda went up to her mom, and her other classmates who weren't rehearsing were watching out the window. Her mother said, 'I just wanted to tell you that you got your letter today.' Amanda just *freaked out*—'Oh! Oh!...' She was just *so* excited!

"Then everybody in the building came out—the kids, the office staff—they were hugging and kissing her, people had tears in their eyes, she was jumping up and down; then the company members found out, and Francia found out—it was just so incredible. It was like *our* kid, our child. It was so nice to see *everyone* so excited. There were parents of little children sitting in the hall waiting to go into Creative Movement, and they said, 'What happened? What happened?' We said, 'Amanda Ose, one of our PDs just got accepted in Stanford!' They said, 'Oh, that's *wonderful!*,' and they didn't even know her.

"She is truly a PNB success story," concludes Pulkkinen. "When you have somebody like that, boy, she was so easy to teach. So easy to teach. She raised the whole level of the class, and she was consistent for every teacher that walked into that room.

"For example, if she were having a down day, say, perhaps maybe her pirouettes weren't right on, she would rise above it and then work on her *port de bras* or on something else—she always found *something* to work on. An "off" day never got her down, which is why people speak so highly of her. She really was one of those rare students. I don't know what might have been going on inside her, but boy she got into that ballet studio and she left everything else outside the door.

"I cannot say one negative about Amanda Ose," continues Pulkkinen. She was always very focused, a meticulous worker, articulate, a positive leader in class, and worked to 100 percent of what she could do. If I needed anyone to show a combination or remember what was done three weeks before that, Amanda knew it.

"In her progress reports, we were always trying to find a different way to say excellent. We got to the point of saying, 'Hey, wait a minute, excellent is *excellent*. We really do not need to go further than that.'" Pulkkinen pulls out a report from 1996 and reads, "'Effort. Excellent. Amanda is a remarkable student. She is a pleasure to work with.' I think Amanda is going to be someone *very* successful in whatever path she takes."

Says Ose humbly of her Stanford surprise, "We didn't mean it to be such a big production, but it was. We had another hour of rehearsal, and I went back in and was smiling the whole time. My parents took me out to dinner afterwards to celebrate. It didn't sink in for a couple days.

"All of the events leading up to the acceptance were telling me that I wasn't going to get in," she reflects. "My friend had already gotten in and I heard people saying, 'You know how high selective they are,' and 'But you never know....' There were actually four people from my graduating class who got in that year, which was some kind of huge record at my high school."

No more uncertainty. No more doubt. Her dream came true. She decided then and there: 'I'm going to go to school.' "I don't think the transition could have been easier. I remember telling my mom, 'Well, I'm not so sure if I'm going to quit ballet unless I get into Stanford,' and that was before I'd even applied. It almost seems ridiculous how easy the transition was."

Her parents were relieved. Her mother had always been bothered by the "looks" part of ballet. Says Mrs. Ose, "If a director likes your look, then you keep going. Some students are so long-limbed, so thin, so hyperextended; they have that really exaggerated, sculpted look. That wasn't Amanda's look."

Her father recalls attending a ballet performance with his wife some time later in which one of the girls fell. Simultaneously they turned to each other and he spoke for both of them, "Aren't you glad she didn't go into this? The *pressure* to be perfect."

Ose's last ballet appearance was June 19, 1999, in PNB's School Performance. "It was a lot of fun," she says, "we got to wear the big tutus and the tiaras, and we danced variations from the repertoire I really liked." She was awarded a solo variation from *Paquita* for her graduation. "I was so grateful to be able to do that, it made it a nice final performance, a good way to go out."

Long, loud applause modulates into stadium yells as Ose sits in the stands watching the Stanford-UCLA game her first week on campus. She was actually watching the Dollies—the official dance team of Stanford's marching band—more than the game. They appeared to be having a great time, and after working in Starbucks in Seattle all summer, the urge to dance inspired her to think, "Maybe *I* could be a Dollie! I love dancing and performing and am a huge fan of Stanford sports. Being a Dollie would give me the opportunity to do both all the time."

The five young women who comprise the Dollies perform wherever Bandsmen play, dancing their way to Harvard, Graceland, Little Rock, even Australia.

Most Dollies have grown up as ballet, tap, or jazz dancers; some have been cheerleaders, a few, figure skaters. All choreograph. They collaborate, making new dances for each performance and practicing up to three hours a day. Their time commitment is thirty hours a week for a year.

The Dollie tradition dates back to 1922, and over the years, the Dollies have been panned and praised, inspired dirty jokes and kudos. Some feel the institution "reeks of exploitation." However, most people see these multi-talented performers as remarkable, capable women. Wrote senior political science major Stephanie Pieczenik, in 1998 a Dollie herself, "We are headed to M.D. and Ph.D. programs, starting companies in the Silicon Valley, and we are graduating with honors. If anything, I think we are models for this enlightened age." Amanda Ose personifies these words.

She decided to try out. Fresh from Pacific Northwest Ballet School's Professional Division, Ose's dancing shone at the Dollie audition, but when band members interview prospective Dollies, they place as much importance on an interesting and dynamic personality as they do on skilled dancing. They quickly saw that Amanda Ose has both and more.

Her dancing held their attention, her intelligence bowled them over, her irresistible brown eyes and russet-red hair turned their heads, and her personality sealed the deal. She was chosen from dozens of talented hopefuls to be

Amanda Ose as a Stanford University Dollie dancing at an autumn 2000 Stanford football game. (Photograph ©2000 Robby Byers, used with his permission.)

one of the five Stanford Dollies. The annual Dollie Splash is the first public appearance for each new Dollie quintet.

Dancing now at football games, Ose's "second-balcony smile" rises to the top row from the pure joy of doing the two things she loves most as a Stanford sophomore: dancing and representing her school. With her red hair gleaming under the stadium lights, she is a beacon for Dollie merit. She is also a born performer, suited to life on stage or in a stadium. Her charisma drives audiences wild.

Pacific Northwest Ballet Technical and Lighting Director Rico Chiarelli recalls Ose dancing in *The Nutcracker* and says, "I loved Amanda onstage. I loved lighting her hair!" Chiarelli and Ose became pals over the thirteen years she danced at Pacific Northwest Ballet School, and he saw her potential bloom. "She used to come by my office all the time to see what I was doing. Asked me very good questions. She is obviously very bright."

When Ose first entered Stanford, she had thought of riding the train to San Francisco three times a week to take class at San Francisco Ballet.

Her interest in being a Dollie made her want to stick close to campus, however, so she explored opportunities for ballet in the Stanford dance department. Stanford's dance director Kristine Elliott, a former soloist with American Ballet Theatre and dancer with the New Amsterdam Ballet and Stuttgart Ballet, was delighted to welcome Ose into class.

The philosophy of the Stanford Dance Division is that dance plays a vital role in self-definition and an individual's understanding of the person in relation to the world. The goal is to "develop a trained body, cultivated mind, and passionate engagement through movement experience." There is no pointe work—Ose has not had on pointe shoes since her farewell performance. Said her mother a full year after that performance, "She is happy that her feet are looking almost normal!"

Ose takes three classes a week. A few of her fellow students are as advanced as she; one was recently with San Francisco Ballet. The remainder of the students were competent dancers in their home towns but did not aspire to anything beyond that.

Coincidentally, her sophomore year, John Winfield, a former PNB dancer who joined New York City Ballet, applied to Stanford in his twenties as a transfer student. He and Ose struck up a friendship. Their rapport and similar competence inspired choreographer Charles Moulton, founder of New York's Performance Space 122, to set his *pas de deux*, entitled *Home Away From Home*, on them for the May 2000 Student Concert.

Ose is having a great time at Stanford dancing, learning, being a Dollie, and making friends. "It is a wonderful place—it's hard to say what my favorite part about it is. I would have to say that the people I have met are what make this place special. I have made so many new friends, and everyone is unique and interesting."

She ponders what life would have been like as a professional dancer. "I think to be a dancer, you have to have so much drive and so much desire to be the best at what you're doing, and you have to focus exclusively on ballet.

"I had that desire and I had that drive in ballet, but also in a couple other areas, like academics and social events. You need to ask yourself why you're there eight hours a day, why you're working on perfecting each little step over and over. You have to be 100 percent passionate about ballet or it's hard to do it. Once you lose that, or your interest starts leaning a little bit, it's almost futile to keep pursuing it. You'll just get more and more despondent. At least that's what I found with myself. I was questioning it, 'Why am I doing this? Spending my time doing this?' Thinking about, 'Should I not be going to school?,' If you're interest is wandering, if something else is calling you, go explore. Life is too short to keep it in one area."

She will always be grateful for what ballet has given her, though. "I think a lot of the reason I was successful academically is because ballet teaches you some amazing lessons in discipline. I have to credit it for helping me do well in other areas, too—there are just so many positive things that came out of it."

Kermit the Frog's advice to Harvard's 1982 graduating seniors was, "As you set sail on the great vacation of life, think of Harvard as your travel agent." Rephrase this, "As you travel on your journey through life, think of ballet as your guide." Ballet instills positive personal qualities in dancers (see pages 243–246) that serve them in everything they do.

Ose chose education over ballet at eighteen, but her love of dance may bring her back to Pacific Northwest Ballet after graduation as a member of the administrative staff. She grew up at PNB, and it is her second home. "That would be really cool to go back and do something with the ballet company," she says. "What better way to put your ballet training to use? It's hard to find people who have gotten a good education, have the dance background, and have a desire to work at the administrative level. To come back sometime would be an excellent goal to have."

Ose was active in PNB's *Discover Dance* outreach program, especially as a dancer in the Discover Dance Student Company, dancing in outreach performances in community centers around Seattle. She is interested in public relations now at Stanford, has terrific interpersonal skills, and would certainly win favor for Pacific Northwest Ballet in an outreach position.

"You never know," she says. "I could come back and work with the company some day. I have such an appreciation for the arts and can see myself always being active in the arts community. Once you get that appreciation, you want to help out the arts because they're struggling. I could see myself helping out with something like *Discover Dance*—it's an amazing program."

Many dancers feel they want to give back to the art they love. At nineteen, Ose is young to be contemplating a similar future, yet her blend of intelligence, personality, and compassion for ballet would be welcome in any company.

Linda Hamilton's blend of intelligence and compassion with psychological expertise make her way of giving back quite different.

LINDA HAMILTON, PH.D.
Solutions in Psychology

When New York City Ballet was performing in the Soviet Union in 1972, corps de ballet dancer Linda Homek found a little kitten that had infected eyes. She took pity on the helpless stray and brought it back to her hotel room. Surveillance was very tight then and the dancers' comings and goings were monitored constantly, but when the company boarded the plane for Moscow, Homek could not bear to leave the kitten behind. She snuck it on the plane and when they got to Moscow, located a veterinarian.

Compassion overcame fear, and she ventured alone over unfamiliar roads to get a prescription from the vet. She discovered upon her return that the prescription was written in Old Russian. She asked Mr. Balanchine to translate it, obtained the medicine, and nursed the kitten back to health. When the company left Russia, Homek found the kitten a home with one of the matrons who watched the dancers on each floor of the hotel.

The kitten is but one of countless injured pigeons, birds, lost dogs and cats that Linda Homek—Linda Hamilton by her 1984 marriage—has rescued over the years. She admits, "It's hard to ignore them when they're suffering."

Hamilton feels the same deep compassion for people. "When I was eight, I noticed the shoe salesman was stressed out and having a hard day with a lot of people to wait on. I didn't want to tell him my shoes were too tight, much to my mother's unhappiness when I got home."

When she was nineteen, a dancer in the company whom she did not know well started having a drinking problem, breaking up with her boyfriend, and "really falling apart." Hamilton invited the dancer to stay with her for several days until she could get her life back together. "We talked a lot and I tried to be as supportive as possible. Soon after, she started doing better."

Hamilton's early successes helping animals and people, and her success today as a clinical psychologist, spring from her ability to feel what another creature is feeling or put herself in another person's shoes. Although inclinations toward her current calling emerged in childhood, her first love was dancing. She put herself into dancing shoes long before she put herself into others' shoes as a therapist.

When she was two, she saw the Royal Ballet perform *Sleeping Beauty* on television and told her mother that's what she wanted to do when she grew up. The decision was natural, for Linda was exposed to the arts from birth. Her father was a portrait painter, her mother a violinist, and they took their daughter to opera and ballet regularly from the age of four. Her mother brought her to the School of American Ballet when she was eight, and dancing became the focus of her life from then on.

Linda Homek was born in New York City in 1952. The family moved to Woodside in Queens for several years when she was in grade school and junior high, but she was a promising student at the School of American Ballet and her mother had a premonition that she would get into the company. Mrs. Homek wanted to be near her daughter at SAB, so the family moved back to New York when Linda was fourteen. Mrs. Homek's premonition was right. Linda was accepted into New York City Ballet at sixteen and dropped out of high school to devote herself full-time to dancing.

Ballet became her reason for living. She worked hard to win the approval of her teachers and Mr. Balanchine, and the thrill of performing made her work harder. Her body soon began to rebel, however, against the demands she placed on it. She suffered her first sprained ankle and had to stop dancing, but she did not let the injury keep her out for long. A second sprained ankle some time later, then a third, threw her into despair—why do these keep happening? What mind-body miscommunication is going on here? She tried to figure out the mind-body connection.

In her late teens and early twenties, Hamilton sought deeper understanding of herself and her place in the world, too, by reading self-help books such as *I'm OK, You're OK* and *Passages*. She became fascinated with trying to solve personal and interpersonal problems as well as with the mind-body connection.

After *six* sprained ankles, Hamilton finally realized that she was not giving her ankles enough time to repair themselves. Too eager to return to dancing to let the ankles heal, the sprains kept recurring. It took a severe

Linda Hamilton as a corps de ballet dancer costumed for the ballet *Suite #3*. (Photograph by Arthur Elgort, 1979.)

stress fracture in her back when she was twenty-four to get her off her feet—she was forced to stop dancing for three months to recover.

"I was doing *The Cage*," she explains, "one of my favorite ballets. Jerry Robbins was a good choreographer, and I love Stravinsky's music. I was doing the Mother role when my partner, the Novice, let go and didn't hold herself when I was carrying her. That's when I did it."

Hamilton began thinking about getting a second career at this point, but recovered, returned, and kept dancing.

Two years later, several things happened that made her think seriously about the future. "I was twenty-six, which made me think about thirty. I was in the middle of going through a divorce—my early marriage to a musician had failed—and that also made me think about the future. I'd be on my own, and how was I going to take care of myself after I stopped dancing? And I had a *bad* injury with my ankle and couldn't dance for several months—a bone chip.

"So here I was not able to perform, not having my personal life in order, and imagining that I'd have to leave dancing in the not-too-distant future, and I didn't even have a high school education."

But if she left ballet, how would she earn a living? Fortunately, her husband had asked her to see a psychologist before they divorced. "The intensity of the sessions, with their focus on self-expression and personal growth, reminded me of the stage," she says. "Therapy offered solutions to many of my problems, though not to my marriage. These experiences motivated and inspired me to study psychology with a focus on the performing arts."

Hamilton finally resolved to become a clinical psychologist.

"I went to what I knew," she explains. "I knew about training—I had trained at the School of American Ballet for eight years—and that was sort of my model for how you became somebody, you went to some kind of school. And I had chosen something I loved. So my question was: What do I like to do besides dancing? I always seemed to gravitate towards helping animals or people in distress, and because of my injuries I was always trying to figure out the mind-body connection, how they related. Clinical psychology just seemed like a natural thing to do.

"So that was the extent of my exploration. I didn't do any of the things I would recommend now, like talk to other psychologists, research the job market, find out how much you make—things like that. I just chose psychology."

Once Hamilton made that decision, it seemed like everything "just fell into place." Fordham University was right across the street from Lincoln Center and by 1980 had arranged flexible course schedules for several City Ballet dancers. Also, Hamilton's brother had gone to Fordham for a couple of years before switching schools, so she knew of the university. She decided to go there, too.

After studying for a several months to make up the high school courses she had missed, she passed the exam to get her high school equivalency degree. She then applied to Fordham and took a full coarse load—three classes—on Monday, her day off.

The rest of the week she took class with the Company in the morning and did her homework in quiet moments at the theater. "You make, you find time. There's a lot of time during the day, and if you're disciplined, it's amazing what you can get done. And I got straight-A's, so it's all doable." She also had a lot of support from her parents and mentors.

"Neither of my parents had college degrees. Still, there was always emphasis on education and getting A's when I was growing up.

"And the mentors I had were wonderful. They were women, which I hadn't really thought about one way or the other, but I suppose it's good to have strong role models as women. I had them in dancing and I had them in psychology. They were the ones who encouraged me—Dr. Michelle Warren particularly, who is an endocrinologist and a specialist on eating disorders in dancers."

Impressed with Hamilton's work ethic and willingness to take on extra projects, Dr. Warren invited her to assist with a large study that she and a social psychologist were doing on dancers' eating disorders and menstrual problems. "I started by opening doors for Dr. Warren and helping her to collect data at Professional Children's School and SAB. When the data collection was finished, she let me stay on as her assistant helping to code and analyze the research. She taught me everything from questionnaire development to coding to statistical analysis.

"At one point Dr. Warren said, 'You know, you have to do *your* study.' I was comfortable where I was, but I said, 'All right.' So I did an independent study for more credits at Fordham, and we basically replicated what she had done on adolescent dancers with professional dancers. Every time I went on tour, I would go study the dancers. So we had data from Western Europe, Germany, and England, and New York City Ballet, ABT, and Dance Theater of Harlem—so on a lot of professional dancers. The premise was that regardless of the culture, you would see the same kinds of occupational stresses, the same pressure to be thin, the same incidence, roughly, of eating and menstrual problems."

Hamilton earned her bachelor's degree in psychology in 1984, dancing full time throughout her four years of college. In fact, dancing was how she paid for her education, college *and* graduate school. "I was working and getting a very good salary in New York City Ballet, so I never took out a loan," she says modestly. "I paid for everything."

The prominent orthopedic surgeon in dance medicine, Dr. William Hamilton, was City Ballet's orthopedic consultant at that time. He and Linda Homek had become good friends, but he was drawn to her with new admiration during her college years when he saw how dedicated she was to her studies. *She* developed heartfelt admiration for him in return, for her work in psychology and performing arts medicine gave her deeper understanding of his work. "Bill felt about his work the way I have felt about dancing. And he could see that if you found something that you cared about, it can inspire the same dedication and meaning. He is a great inspiration." Their mutual admiration soon turned to love, and the two married in December 1984.

The study Hamilton did with Dr. Warren motivated her to continue doing research, "because it was just such a positive experience," she says. "I was able to bring my knowledge of dancing to something new, and I learned as much about psychology and research as I knew about dancing, which was exciting." The study also led to six published papers, one in the *New England Journal of Medicine*. Just six years earlier Hamilton faced an uncertain future with a minimal high school education, and now she was on her way to triple competence.

She chose Adelphi University for graduate school because it offered a doctorate in both clinical and research in psychology. The dual doctorate "was an extra year of school, but I thought it would be worth it. And you were required to do two publishable papers and present at conferences, so it forced me into being very active in those ways, as well as in seeing patients."

Fordham University is across the street from Lincoln Center, but Adelphi is in Garden City Long Island, so Hamilton's schedule became even "crazier" than in college. "I had to commute for forty-five minutes each way, sometimes twice in one day, depending on my staff schedule. And towards the end of graduate school, I would add things on, because I wanted to be prepared for my new career. Something you don't get in clinical psychology is a lot on the physiological side, like menstrual problems. I thought that was important, so I did a neuropsych externship at Beth Israel Hospital in addition to dancing and going to graduate school.

"The craziest time was when we were dancing in Orange County, California. I had my neuropsych externship on my day off, and I would fly in from California, do it, and get on the next plane and go back so I could dance. I did that for two weeks, which was crazy, but I'd sleep on the plane. It was actually very exciting. It was a challenge to see how much I could get done and do it well."

Hamilton's divided life would soon have a single focus. The next step in her training was an internship at Roosevelt Hospital in New York City, which was a nine-to-five job. When she began her career transition in 1980, she had planned to retire from dancing in eight years when she got her Ph.D. She was still a year away from her degree, but she couldn't dance with the full-time internship schedule.

"So it was a choice I made. Psychologically, I was ready, and I was moving towards something versus being pushed out. I had a new identity, which helped, and I had published papers at that point, given talks, become invested in being a psychologist. Those factors made leaving dancing a positive experience for the most part.

"But it was still a huge transition. The first year was very peculiar, because I went from being a professional to being an assistant psychologist making much less money—I was still a student, an intern. And I had to find out about things I never bothered about as a dancer, like, is this health insurance good? Life was different, and it was uncomfortable. I was about as prepared as you could be, but it still took a while to adjust. Certainly it got easier as I got my degree, got my practice going, and started writing books, but I was building from scratch.

"The hardest part of the transition was not knowing what was going to happen. I had to make peace with the fact that the future was ambiguous. With the Company, everything was structured and you knew where you'd be from week to week. People told you what your schedule was and it was all up-front. Now I felt like I was out in the real world with no structure other than what I imposed on it. But that was *very* exciting. Actually I like that, but at the same time it was scary, because I didn't know where I would end up."

Hamilton made her decision in June 1988, a week before the end of New York City Ballet's Spring season. She was dancing *Chaconne*. "I did my last performance and threw out my toe shoes that night." She left a culture where people rose to distinction by choice of the master as much as by talent, and entered a culture where she could rise to distinction through self-directed choices of her own. She walked out of the theater in the shoes of a clinical psychologist.

The beauty of her transition was that she did not have to drop ballet, she incorporated it. "I was a former dancer, and I was a psychologist, *too*. As time went by, I specialized in the performing arts. I just sort of pulled my whole life to get there. It worked very well."

Hamilton's internship at Roosevelt was in the eating disorders clinic, and her first post-graduate job as a psychologist was on the eating disorders inpatient unit at the Fair Oaks Hospital in Summit, New Jersey. Although she focused on eating disorders in college, graduate school, as an intern, and as a clinician, she had no such problem of her own. "I was not even a dieter. I was naturally thin and ate whatever I wanted, but also was not particularly interested in food. My mother was not a great cook, so eating was something you did just to get by."

Her interest in eating disorders came from her mentor's interest, endocrinologist Dr. Michelle Warren. Also, Hamilton's best friend when she was growing up had an eating disorder, and she was aware that the dancers around her were suffering. Her innate compassion said, "Dancers have these problems, why aren't we doing something about them?" The only problem Hamilton had as a dancer were injuries.

Hamilton received her doctorate from Adelphi in January 1989. Her colleague Michael Byars at New York City Ballet (see page 106) had volunteered to chair a dancers' committee that January to negotiate with AGMA for a better contract that would compensate for the dancers' financial, educational, and psychological needs during career transition. Byars called a general meeting of the dancers to discuss their AGMA negotiation which Hamilton attended.

"She had just that morning received her doctorate from Adelphi," recalls Byars. "I think it gave her great satisfaction to be able to say, 'You guys can do it, and by the way, this morning, I got this great piece of paper—I got my Ph.D.!' It was an inspirational moment for all of us." The dancers eventually won what they wanted from AGMA.

After earning her doctorate, Hamilton became a regular consultant to the School of American Ballet and the Alvin Ailey American Dance

Center. She also wanted to start her own private practice treating dancers and other performing artists. She had begun training to be a therapist in her third year of graduate school by seeing patients in the campus clinic who were not dancers. During her supervised internship at Roosevelt, she saw patients from the general population who were not dancers, and also did a six-month rotation at the Smithers Alcohol Treatment Center with non-dancers. It was not until 1992 that she felt ready to work with dancers as private clients.

"But," she says, "at the beginning of any practice, nobody's exactly knocking down your doors to see you. I was trying to figure out what to do, and I remember thinking, "One thing I know I'm good at is giving advice, and I know more about dancing than I know about anything." So early in 1992 she sent a letter to *Dance Magazine* proposing to write an "Advice for Dancers" column. She had never written for a magazine, but gave examples of the kinds of questions readers would ask and how she would answer them, and enclosed her curriculum vitae which showed the many academic articles she had written. "They took me up on it, and I was published two months later." Her first column appeared in the April 1992 issue and "Advice for Dancers" has been a monthly feature in the magazine since. The goal of the column is not only to help readers with their mental, physical, and life adjustment problems, but also to educate the dance community about the stresses involved in the profession.

Clients came to Hamilton from a variety of art forms, including comedians, actors, dancers, and musicians. By the mid-90's, her practice was thriving. She decided to compile the knowledge she had gained from her practice to date, and from her research, consultations, and conference presentations, into an academic book on performing arts medicine aimed at the treatment and prevention of performers' occupational stresses. *The Person Behind the Mask: A Guide to Performing Arts Psychology* (1997, Ablex Publishing Corporation) was the first book of its kind to take a psychoeducational approach to the problems performers confront.

Social psychologist Dr. Harold Takooshian at Fordham University heard about *The Person Behind the Mask* and invited Hamilton to teach a course based on her book. She had begun teaching right after getting her doctorate with undergraduate psychology classes, but stopped a year later when her life became too busy. It was hard to refuse Dr. Takooshian's invitation to teach now: he had been a mentor to her in college—encouraging her work, endorsing her entry into the psychology honor society—and a course on performing arts psychology had never been offered anywhere before. Hamilton began to envision a curriculum and saw that the course would meet the needs of many students.

"It's cross-disciplinary," she explains, "so we get students who are in the drama department or the dance department, and it appeals to psychology students who need to take a cross-disciplinary course. They think, 'When I graduate and get my degree, maybe I'll work with performers, too.' But performers who take the course learn about occupational stress and ways to prevent it." She launched Performing Arts Psychology in September 1998, and it has become a popular course.

Hamilton started her career transition as a student at Fordham almost two decades earlier, now here she was back again as a professor. She smiles, "It looks like I've come full circle."

While working on *The Person Behind the Mask*, Hamilton became involved in a four-year study at the School of American Ballet that examined the reasons why dancers leave the school. The results showed that an alarming fifty-five percent of the students drop out due to a variety of anatomical and psychological problems.

She presented this study at a 1997 conference of the American Psychological Association. After her presentation, an editor from Simon and Schuster walked up to her and said, "How would you like to write a book?" to be published by Schuster's subsidiary Jossey-Bass Inc. Hamilton agreed, although she had barely finished the manuscript for *The Person Behind the Mask*, for as with her course, she saw how helpful a book offering counsel, guidance, and resource information would be. *Advice for Dancers: Emotional Counsel and Practical Strategies* (1998, Jossey-Bass Inc.) draws somewhat on the School of American Ballet study, but it is based primarily on her *Dance Magazine* "Advice for Dancers" column.

Hamilton did the inevitable book signings for *Advice for Dancers*. Her mother attended one at Barnes & Noble in the spring of 1999 with camera in hand and proudly took pictures while her daughter signed. "My mother was my greatest mentor, in the sense that she really supported me, encouraged my transition, and saw what I needed each step of the way. She is still encouraging me." Mrs. Homek motivated herself in the process, returning to school in her sixties to earn a bachelor's degree at Hunter College.

The dedication that opens *Advice for Dancers* reveals Hamilton's deepest inspiration: "This book is dedicated with heartfelt love and affection to my husband William G. Hamilton, M.D. His love, constant support, and own exemplary work as an orthopedic surgeon in dance medicine have been a shining light in my transition from dance to my career in clinical psychology."

Linda Hamilton is a shining light in her own right. She paved her career transition with hard work, professional articles, advice columns, and private counsel, and widened her path with the publication of her two books. The prolific output of her career allows more and more people to travel to peace in their lives through her guidance.

Hamilton forged her transition from gut feelings, education, and practical experience, "but there is no one way to do it," she says. "What's important is that you find meaning. The dancer is inside of you, and it takes time to get on the right path for a lot of people. Probably the utmost difficulty is fear. So I would always recommend that dancers have enough time to prepare financially and psychologically before they leave. And there are a lot of ways to keep dance in your life even if you give it up. But you could do all of the things that people would say are right, like go to school or get a great job, but if you don't care about what you're doing, it doesn't really matter.

"There are many more resources for students now than there were when I started," she continues, "and there are more dancers with second careers they can talk to. The more information you can find out, the better."

Meaning fosters motivation which attracts mentors

Linda Hamilton, Ph.D., now a clinical psychologist and associate professor at Fordham University, with a private practice in New York City specializing in the emotional stresses of performance. (Photograph by Howard Schatz, 1997.)

who can facilitate transition. "One thing I realized early on is people are very open to helping other people starting out, if you're willing to give them your time. Everything I did with Dr. Warren, I did for free. She was paying people, but I refused to accept any money. I just wanted the experience. And I think when you put that kind of work and effort behind it, people want to help you. People like nurturing people who want to work. There are always people like that out there who will give you opportunities. But," she cautions, "if you don't work and measure up, there are not [opportunities]." As Edward Villella says, "That's what life is all about: opportunity and missed opportunity."

Hamilton's career transition resembles her ballet career. Once she had decided to become a dancer, she worked intently, step by step, year by year, opportunity by opportunity, to shape herself into the person she wanted to be. Once she decided to become a clinical psychologist, she shaped herself by the same behaviors, only this time avoided injury. Stardom eluded her at New York City Ballet, but her renown as a clinical psychologist has grown steadily.

In honor of her leadership role in performing arts psychology, Hamilton's work is featured in a 1997 documentary by the Netherlands' European Media Support entitled *A Vision to Heal.* Her biography is also in the *Marquis Who's Who of American Women.*

Hamilton has found the ultimate mind-body connection in psychology by using her mind—through education, research, articles, columns, books, and therapy—to connect with the minds and bodies of the performing artists she serves and to help them to make healthy mind-body connections of their own.

What about her own body? How does she maintain the instrument that once was her sole means of existence? Wiser now, she takes good care of herself. "I always made sure I got eight hours of sleep during college and graduate school," she says, "and I have stayed in shape by doing Pilates three times a week and using a stationery bike almost every day. I'm in good shape for a lay person—I do a minimum to get the results I want. A half-an-hour on the bike and an hour three times a week with weights feels good to me now."

Dance Magazine Executive Editor Richard Philp printed in the January 2000 issue quotes from nineteen of his good New York friends stating what they wished for dance in the twenty-first century. Linda Hamilton said, "Greater communication between the dance community and dance medicine. We've learned so much about occupational stress in dance medicine, but that information doesn't always get translated into the dancer's life.

"When it comes to dancers' wellness," she continues later in the issue, "the theme for the new millennium is 'treat the whole person' ... the benefits to the profession are likely to be artistic as well as personal."

JOYSANNE SIDIMUS
Canadian Collaborations

When the doctor told Joysanne Sidimus that recovery from her left knee anterior cruciate ligament operation would take nine months, she contemplated having another baby or writing a book. "It's too soon to have another baby," she thought, "so I guess I'll write a book."

Sidimus reflected on her life that day in 1981 as she faced the long recuperation. Who was she? Wife, mother, former dancer, ballet teacher, Balanchine *répétiteur*. She also reflected on the lives of her friends who were former dancers. "It occurred to me that a lot of my former dancing colleagues were doing *very* interesting things totally unrelated to dance. I found that just astonishing, because at that point in my life I couldn't imagine doing anything unrelated to dance."

"Some of these people were very good friends and I thought, 'There are enough of them to make a book—on dancers' career transitions.'" Sidimus started interviewing for her book in 1983 unaware of how the book research would change her life. In 1985 as a result of the research, the Dancer Transition Resource Centre came into existence. *Exchanges: Life After Dance* appeared in bookstores four years later, published by the Press of Terpsichore Limited in 1987.

Joysanne Sidimus was born June 21, 1938, in New York City, into a Russian-Polish household where dance was part of the culture. "When music was turned on," she says, "I *had* to get up and move to it.

"We lived in a large apartment, and as a young child, after playing with my friends when I came from school, I had a very specific routine. I did homework first, practiced the piano for a half-hour, then was free to do what I wanted. I would go into the living room, put on records and

A studio portrait of Joysanne Sidimus as Arabian in *The Nutcracker*. Jack Mitchell relates the story behind this photo: "This picture of Joysanne was taken during a four day shoot of the entire Pennsylvania Ballet in March, 1969, for a Souvenir Program Book. She was one of many attractive soloists I photographed in PB's Philadelphia studio. She was very adept at doing off-balance positions for me, a technique I use to imply movement in what would be a static pose. I ask dancers to attack the still pose with extra energy to go past the point of balance; this lightens the weight on the supporting foot, forcing the arch. It shows feet to great advantage!" (Photograph © Jack Mitchell, reprinted with his permission.)

just dance, before my dad came home. I lived the whole day just for that time. I loved it."

When Sidimus was seven, her parents took her to the Metropolitan Opera House to see Alicia Markova and Anton Dolin dance *Giselle*. Enchanted, she announced to her parents, "I want to be that lady on that stage." She reflects back, "I just thought it was the most beautiful thing I had seen in my whole life. I still do—not just *Giselle* of course, but the enchantment of ballet."

She asked to go to ballet class. Her parents said, "Fine, if it doesn't interfere with your school work." They took her to the School of American Ballet, but at seven years old she was rejected. Too young.

"I went to study with Vera Nemchinova for a year at Ballet Arts in Carnegie Hall. I auditioned at SAB the next year and got in. Eddie Villella and I were in the same children's class." Sidimus trained at the School of American Ballet until 1958, when she was invited into the company. From 1955–57 she tried to continue her academic education at Barnard College, but the school schedule and work load proved too difficult to combine with ballet classes.

After five years in the New York City Ballet *corps*, "Even though I loved working with Balanchine, I felt that I was doing just about everything I could do, and that I was not going to go much further. I didn't have the perfect Balanchine body, and I wanted to dance in different styles and try dramatic roles. But I also wanted to keep my connections with Balanchine and his repertoire, which I adored."

She approached Balanchine about dancing in another company. "He was wonderful. He said, 'It's probably a good idea. Go. Try.'"

In the spring of 1962, Violette Verdy helped her to meet John Gilpin, then Artistic Director of the London Festival Ballet, which Sidimus' childhood idols Alicia Markova and Anton Dolin had founded as Markova-Dolin Ballet in 1949 (see page 66). She was hired as a soloist for the 1962-63 season. "I went to London but stayed with the company for only six months. It just was not my cup of tea."

Several London Festival dancers were ex-dancers of the National Ballet of Canada and told Sidimus of founder and Artistic Director Celia Franca's dramatic bent. Sidimus was fascinated. By fortunate chance, National Ballet choreographer Grant Strate and National Ballet School Principal Betty Oliphant were in London at the time. "I let it be known that I was interested," she says, "and they spoke to Celia about my joining the company. To my great surprise Celia took me, sight unseen, as a principal."

Sidimus arrived at the National Ballet of Canada in 1963. "I really enjoyed it," she says, "and had five *fabulous* years there, 1963 to '68." Her only setback was a torn cartilage in her left knee. "But I had it repaired, went on dancing, and it seemed fine.

"After five years, Celia wanted me to do primarily character roles, but I still wanted to dance; I was only 30 and felt that was too young to stop. So we had a parting of the ways and I came back to New York."

The day after Sidimus arrived in New York, she went to the ballet at City Center to see the newly-created Pennsylvania Ballet perform, among other repertoire, John Butler's *Carmina Burana*. She thought, "Wow. That's a work I would *love* to dance."

She went backstage to see Pennsylvania Ballet's founder and Artistic Director Barbara Weisberger. Boldly she asked, "Can I join your company, please?" Weisberger responded, "Where have you been all these years?"

"She knew me from New York City Ballet," explains Sidimus, "and it just so happened that in six months one of her principal dancers would be leaving to have a baby. At the end of the '68 season I joined Pennsylvania Ballet—and got to dance *Carmina Burana*."

Pennsylvania Ballet was a small, pioneering company then, so Sidimus was called upon to teach company class and rehearse the company as well as dance. She staged her first Balanchine ballet there, *Serenade*, in which she also danced one of the principal roles.

Her debut as *répétiteur* for Balanchine works reveals the intimate network of the ballet world. In 1969, Erik Bruhn, who was then Artistic Director of the Royal Swedish Ballet, wrote to Balanchine to ask if Sidimus could come to Sweden to stage *Serenade* for his company. Sidimus had danced with Bruhn when he was a guest artist with the National Ballet in the mid–'60s, and he liked the way she moved. "When Barbara Horgan [General Director of The Balanchine Trust] told me of the request, I was enormously flattered and *very* surprised, as I'm sure Mr. B was!"

Sidimus did not go to Sweden, but Barbara Weisberger heard of Bruhn's request and asked Balanchine if Sidimus could stage *Serenade* for Pennsylvania Ballet. Balanchine agreed to take the risk. "Erik (and of course, Mr. B) started that part of my career," says Sidimus. "Sometimes it's just timing—and luck."

She speaks fondly of her two years with Pennsylvania Ballet, 1968–1971. "Barbara Weisberger was doing amazing things there. The company was wonderful, the repertoire exciting, and my fellow artists were fabulous. But the *touring* was really, really tough. I'm a homebody. I like home and hearth. Coming at the end of a career, when I was older rather than younger, I didn't fare very well with all that touring. I never liked living out of a suitcase—I'm not good at it and don't enjoy it.

"After a while, the circumstances of dancing became more difficult than the joy of dancing, and when that goes, it's time to stop." Sidimus left Pennsylvania Ballet and stopped performing in 1971.

"I went through a very, very rough time when I stopped," she says. "I just couldn't come to terms with it. I didn't know who I was, what I was, what to do, or where to go. My identity in every way, shape, and form was shaken to the roots. It was a moral, spiritual, financial, identity, and career crisis. You name it, I went through it. I was pretty shaky, for a long time." She went home to New York and stayed with her mother. "Being at home was helpful."

Sidimus returned to dance in 1972 when her good friend Sharon Wagner helped her to get a summer job teaching at the Briansky Saratoga Ballet Center at Skidmore College. There she met John Selleck, one of the pianists for her classes. "I think I fell in love with his music first," she says. "He was just an absolutely marvelous musician."

Selleck was a composer working on his doctorate in composition at Columbia University and playing for summer ballet classes in Saratoga to earn money. Love of his music led to love of the man—he and Sidimus married in 1975.

They lived in New York, where she got a job as ballet mistress of American Ballet Theatre's second company, then called Ballet Repertory Company, whose Artistic Director was Richard Englund. When Selleck earned his doctorate, the couple moved to Winston-Salem, North Carolina where Sidimus taught ballet at the North Carolina School of the Arts and Selleck became a systems analyst for the city of Winston-Salem.

"I *loved* the School of the Arts," she says, "it was an incredible place and the students were extraordinary. I worked for the Dean, Bobby [Robert] Lindgren"—New York City Ballet dancer from 1957 to 1959 when Sidimus first joined the company—"and taught alongside Mimi Paul, Duncan Noble, Gyula Pandi, Gina Vidal, Dick Kuch, Dick Gain, and other colleagues from the dance world. I had Anya there." Their daughter Anya, born January 3, 1979, is now 24 and studying for a degree in life sciences at the University of Toronto.

"I stayed on the faculty for seven years," says Sidimus, "but missed the stimulus of a larger place. I had always been happy in Canada, and the marriage was getting a little shaky." She had an opportunity to return to Canada when York University, which had a very good dance department, offered her a faculty position as ballet teacher.

"We shuttled back and forth for a year while I was teaching at York. It seemed there was a lot going on in Canada, and I was *much* happier. I felt there was much more opportunity for Anya to develop educationally, too, because in Canada parents can send their children to school in French or English. I thought that was an amazing opportunity and sent her to a French school. She is now functionally bilingual, which is a great gift."

Selleck eventually joined Sidimus and Anya in Toronto, but the marriage didn't last. They divorced in 1993 after 18 years of marriage. "Ironically, we spend quite a bit of time together now," she says. "My work is enormously fulfilling, of course, but it's the balance that makes life worth living, for me anyway. Some people are consumed by what they do and that's enough for them, but I find I'm happiest when my life is in balance."

Since her retirement in 1971, Sidimus had been constantly on her feet teaching or staging for ten years. She felt her left knee weaken over the years, and her pregnancy exacerbated the old injury even more. Her knee finally became painful and unsteady. An ACL (anterior cruciate ligament) operation was necessary. She underwent the procedure in 1981 and the nine-month recovery, then in 1983 began research for *Exchanges: Life After Dance*, the book she had planned during her recuperation.

"I began interviewing the people who ended up in the book, but when I turned off the tape recorder and started the game of 'Whatever Happened To—' I discovered suicides, addictions, breakdowns, and dancers, who quite simply, had vanished. Many people had a *really* hard time with transition; the more people I talked to, the more I uncovered this fact.

"It seemed to me that there was an imperative there, that something had to be done about this. That you couldn't just uncover all this and write a book; you had to *do* something about it.

"It was a fertile time for action in Canada, because the Canada Council, which is our national arts funding body, had commissioned two reports on dancer transition issues previously, in 1976 and 1982. The latest report had said that career transition was the only thing in dance that had never been addressed and needed to be." Ideas for establishing a dancers' transition center in Canada took shape in Sidimus' mind.

In 1983 Erik Bruhn arrived in Canada to be the National Ballet's Artistic Director. "He was very strongly supportive of my ideas," says Sidimus. "He said that helping dancers in transition was something that had to start happening worldwide, because he, too, had seen tragedies in his native Denmark."

Dance education pioneer Betty Oliphant brought Sidimus' dream to the attention of the Canada Council. With the support of several government organizations and departments, Sidimus initiated action to launch the Dancer Transition Research Project in December 1984. She conducted a national survey that polled 258 dancers in 23 companies, and about 100 independent dancers, on their perceptions of career change, lifestyle, desire for and thoughts on a transition center.

The survey results revealed a clear need. The Dancer Transition Centre, which changed its name to the Dancer Transition Resource Centre in 1994, opened officially on September 1, 1985, with founder Sidimus as Executive Director.

Although management of the DTRC became her full-time job, Erik Bruhn invited her to stage Balanchine works for the National Ballet. "I guess he respected me as an artist," she says. "He certainly liked my dancing, then asked me to stage, and he was very, very supportive of my work with the Transition Centre. We had a connection that, for me, was profoundly meaningful."

Bruhn's invitation started a relationship for Sidimus with The Balanchine Trust which continues to this day. She is the Balanchine *répétiteur* for the National Ballet of Canada, staging Balanchine works herself or assisting other Trust *répétiteurs*. For example, in 1998 she staged *Episodes* and was ballet mistress when Suzanne Farrell staged *Mozartiana*. In 2002 the Trust flew her to Rio de Janeiro to stage *Serenade* for the ballet company of the Teatro Municipal, Rio's opera house. "I *love* staging Balanchine works," she says. "From the age of eight, Balanchine and his work were my primary inspirations."

Exchanges and the DTRC were just the beginning of Sidimus' post-performing career achievements. By the end of 2002 she was involved in several more. She conceived and helped to establish an Artists' Health Centre which opened in November 2002 at the Toronto Western Hospital, and the Artists' Health Centre Foundation which supports the Centre. On the international front, she helped to involve the DTRC in the aDvANCE Project, a study of professional dancers' career transitions commissioned by the IOTPD (International Organization for the Transition of Professional Dancers). She is now co-authoring a book on the role of the artist in Canadian society with choreographer and dance writer Carol Anderson. Her initiatives continue to pour infinite benefits into the dance world.

The need for a health center for artists became evident by 1993. "By then," says Sidimus, "80 percent of the dancers who came into the Dancer Transition Resource Centre were telling me that they were spending up to 60 percent of their income, which was often below $16,500 a year, on health care."

In 1995 a group of artists, medical professionals, and corporate people met to investigate the possibility of starting an artists' health center in Toronto. They obtained a donation from the management consulting firm McKinsey & Company for a survey of Toronto artists representing a broad range of arts disciplines. The goal was to find out what services artists would want, should such a center be established. The survey revealed that artists choose mostly alternative treatments not covered by Ontario's health insurance plan. The envisioned artists' health center began to take shape.

First, Sidimus organized a meeting of representatives from Toronto's "Big Five" arts organizations—Toronto Symphony Orchestra, National Ballet of Canada, Canadian Opera Company, Stratford, and Young Peoples' Theatre. She asked the representatives, 'If we had something like an artists' health center in Toronto that would provide and partially subsidize a combination of traditional and alternative treatments, would that interest you?' Unanimously they responded, 'Absolutely. We definitely need this.'"

Later that year Sidimus and Wendy Reiser, a family practice doctor who had been a soloist with the National Ballet of Canada, went to London to talk with people at the British Performing Arts Medicine Trust (BPAMT), which was doing what they hoped to do in Canada. "They also published a very good journal, had a hot line, and held clinics for artists which combined medical and alternative therapies."

Back in Canada, she and a core group formed two boards: a Board of Directors and a Steering Committee of Artists that included 22 artists from across the disciplines. The founding President of the Board of Directors, Graham Savage then of Rogers Communications, raised $90,000 from his corporate colleagues; Sidimus negotiated additional seed money from foundations and private sources. They eventually convinced Toronto Western Hospital to house the complex, to be named the Artists' Health Centre.

Shortly thereafter, a donation of $1,000,000 for research was found

Joysanne Sidimus, Founder and Executive Director of Canada's Dancer Transition Resource Centre. (Photograph by David Street.)

through the Toronto Western Hospital Foundation and the center had a name. The Al and Malka Green Artists' Health Centre officially opened on November 6, 2002 and includes a dance studio, music studio, clinical rooms, a mental health room, and a full repertoire of medical, and alternative/complementary services. It is the first of its kind to have been designed by artists in collaboration with medical and alternative health care providers and other professionals.

The Artists' Health Centre Foundation which created the Artists' Health Centre supports it with funding, advice, names of alternative practitioners, and in a variety of other ways. Sidimus serves as vice-president of the Artists' Health Centre Foundation Board, supporting current Board Chair Elise Orenstein.

"Joysanne is definitely a visionary," says Chryssa Koulis, Administrator of the Artists' Health Centre Foundation. "When she sees a need, she fights for it and fills it."

Says Sidimus, "I really enjoy cooperative work, and I've had some very, very wonderful collaborations. I like bringing people together to work on projects, and bringing things to fruition in teams. I *love* the creative ideas that get bounced across the table, and we always seem to come up with something good. I truly believe that artists' creativity has been largely untapped in the world of practical solutions such as the creation of organizations, and things not usually associated with artists."

In February 2002, the DTRC invited representatives from the other three existing transition centers—New York's Career Transition For Dancers, London's Dancers Career Development, and Amsterdam's Netherlands Dancers Transition Programme—to discuss the new aDvANCE Project research initiative commissioned by the IOTPD. Professor Joan Jeffri of Columbia University's Research Center for Arts and

Culture heads the project, which researches dancers' transitions world-wide.

To complement this research project, the DTRC is working with the New York, London, and Amsterdam transition centers to help create Dancers International, an organization that assists dancers who have had primarily international careers. "More and more dancers are emerging who perform for a long time—15 to 20 years—but they go from country to country," says Sidimus. "They don't dance long enough in any one country to avail themselves of the transition program in that country, so we are trying to create Dancers International to deal with their needs. We'll give them counseling to start.

"It is very difficult to get international money, however," she adds, "because a service that may be charitably incorporated in one country may be administered in another."

In March 2002, a gift from the Canadian government crowned the DTRC's remarkable achievements to date. "Funding for the Dancer Transition Resource Centre was doubled," says Sidimus. "It was our first increase in 16 years; our last one was in 1986, the year after we opened. Now we can expand: our grants have gone up, our staff has increased, and our office space has grown. We opened part-time offices in Vancouver and Montreal, and we published two books."

Sidimus took a five-month sabbatical in September 2002 to co-author with Carol Anderson a book entitled *Reflections in a Dancing Eye.* "It is a book of interviews with some of the top minds in Canada," she explains, "about the role and value of the artist in contemporary Canadian society—a *huge* topic."

Sidimus re-energizes herself physically most mornings with a workout at the YMCA that includes Pilates mat work and swimming. She recalls one of her favorite proverbs—"In dreams begins responsibility"—and that means responsibility to her body as well as to her work.

But ask her, "What is your top priority?" and she answers, "To be a mom, and to be a good mom. To me, that's my most important job in life." Anya is a lucky girl.

Sidimus' Dancer Transition Resource Centre spawned all of her subsequent achievements, and its widening embrace assists increasing numbers of dancers into, within, and from their professional lives. Orthopedic surgeon Dr. Daryl Olgilvie-Harris calls Sidimus the "mind" of the organization. Former DTRC Board of Directors Chair Lynda Hamilton calls her its "life force." Current Board Chair Garry Neil calls her its "guiding spirit."

Says Sidimus, "I just do my work and hope we can help some people."

JIM SOHM
Mentored Mentor

"Possessed to choose a single word to describe the current San Francisco Ballet," wrote journalist Christine Temin in *The Boston Sunday Globe* April 2, 2000, "I'd pick 'integrity.' That's due to the leadership of Helgi Tomasson, who came to San Francisco to head the company fifteen years ago."

When Tomasson became Artistic Director in 1985, Jim Sohm, a similar model of integrity, was in the prime of his career as a San Francisco Ballet principal dancer.

Sohm's integrity germinated in childhood with the mentoring of his parents. His ballet career germinated in class with the mentoring of his first ballet teacher. Timely mentoring throughout his life elevated his ballet career to stellar heights and developed him into the successful San Francisco Ballet School Administrative Manager he is today. "I had a lot of people pulling for me all along the way," he says. "If you are mentored properly, you can do anything. I really believe that. You just need someone behind you who believes in you."

Jim Sohm was born April 9, 1955, in Fremont, California, the fourth of five children: he has two older brothers, an older sister, and a younger sister. "Both of my parents imbued in us very strong ethics," he says, "and taught us to look at all sides before making decisions.

"My father worked for the same company from the time he left college to the day he retired. His job was what used to be called industrial relations—he negotiated and oversaw union labor contracts for most of his career. At seven years old we were negotiating with each other. He'd say, 'What time are you going to be home, Jim?' 'Well, I'll be home at

four o'clock.' He'd say, 'You realize that you have set that goal for yourself, so if you aren't home at four o'clock you have failed yourself, not
me.'

"That's how I grew up. It's a tricky thing to live through, but it worked
on me." An uncompromising adherence to ethical principles was woven
into the fabric of his character.

English psychologist and author Havelock Ellis said, "The sphere of
ethics for the Greeks was not distinguished from the sphere of aesthet-
ics." Through some atavistic classical inheritance, Sohm took an interest in theater.

"I was going to be an actor. I was involved in community theater as
a kid and high school productions. When I was 15 and still in high school,
the local junior college did a summer drama festival that was open to
everyone, not just college students. I auditioned.

"The festival presented about five productions, but the directors stuck
me in this hysterical musical called *Your Own Thing*—it was a rock adaptation of Shakespeare's *Twelfth Night*. I was cast as a dancer although I'd
never had dancing lessons.

"The choreographer, Tricia Kaye, ran a dance school in the area.
After working with me in the musical, she invited me to come to her studio to take class. I took ballet class—very basic, simple stuff—and thought,
'This is great.' I just loved it. I decided that's what I wanted to do so started
taking three classes a day to get myself up to speed.

"This was around 1970, '71, when men oftentimes started technique
training at a later age. Things have changed. I was lucky that Tricia was
an excellent teacher. The interesting part is that she trained in Salt Lake
City under Willam Christensen." Christensen was ballet master, choreographer, co-director, and artistic director emeritus of San Francisco
Ballet during his long history with the Company, and founder of Utah
Ballet, now called Ballet West.

Tricia Kaye was dancing with Ronn Guidi's Oakland Ballet as a
principal ballerina at the time Sohm trained with her. After just two years
with her in Fremont, he won a Ford Foundation scholarship to study for
a summer at the School of American Ballet in New York. When he
returned, Kaye introduced him to Ronn Guidi who invited him to join
Oakland Ballet.

Guidi had trained in Nuremberg, Germany, and danced with the
Nuremberg Opera Company. He came back to California in 1961 to
establish his own troupe, which in 1965 officially became Oakland Ballet and Oakland Ballet Academy.

His policy for the School was not to follow any one specific syllabus,
but to give attention to individual student's needs and capabilities from
preballet through the professional level. He also believed that dancers

Jim Sohm as Romeo in a 1978 San Francisco Ballet *Romeo and Juliet* performance. (Photograph by Marty Sohl, 1978.)

must be involved in the creative process in class work, while building strong technique. His goal was to produce artists, not just technicians.

He exposed his dancers to a broad range of repertoire to sharpen their artistry, including revivals from the Diaghilev era, works by Eugene Loring, Agnes DeMille, Kurt Jooss, et al., and original ballets ranging in style from classical to jazz. He did not overstep the bounds of his dancers' development, however. Performances were clean and gave the dancers the opportunity to work in both classic and dramatic roles.

Sohm entered this rich mix of creativity, internationalism, and synthesis when he joined Oakland Ballet in 1973. His mentor Tricia Kaye looked after him to guide his development into the professional world. He smiles, "My teacher was standing next to me at the barre, so I had two lessons instead of one."

Oakland Ballet provided its dancers with shoes and a few amenities, but at the time could not afford to pay them salaries, just $25 a performance. To make ends meet, Sohm lived at home and worked a variety of jobs. "I worked in a label printing factory mornings for a couple of months," he says. "I worked in a pie shop during strawberry season; went to buy the strawberries at six in the morning, and made strawberry pies when I got back. I sat in a polling station during elections and crossed off people's names when they voted—I got 25 bucks a day for that. I would do anything, but I saved up a lot of money."

Fortunately he finished high school before joining Oakland Ballet. "When I wanted to go to SAB my parents told me, 'Get yourself together and graduate with proper grades or you're not going to New York. Period.'" He laughs, "I never had any trouble making grades, I just had trouble making an appearance! I was spending all my time at the ballet."

Sally Streets, formerly a member of New York City Ballet, joined Oakland Ballet in 1974; Streets also taught company class at San Francisco Ballet. One day she pulled Sohm aside and said, "How much longer do you want to do this?" She believed in his potential and urged him to give serious thought to joining San Francisco Ballet.

By 1975, Sohm had had enough of dancing for pittance with Oakland Ballet, working odd jobs at all hours, and living at home. He was 19 years old and thought, "This just can't continue. I have to go to San Francisco."

When Sohm entered San Francisco Ballet, Michael Smuin was associate director with Lew Christensen, and the Company's principal choreographer. Smuin had trained with the Christensen brothers (Willam, Harold, and Lew) in Utah and at San Francisco Ballet, and danced with San Francisco Ballet from 1957–62. In 1962 he went East to freelance, dancing on Broadway and television and in his own night-club act with his wife Paula Tracy. He moved to American Ballet Theatre in 1969 as principal dancer and choreographer.

Lew Christensen, San Francisco Ballet's Artistic Director since 1951, invited Smuin to become his associate director in 1973. Smuin was named co-director with Christensen in 1976, and sole director in 1984.

Wrote Arlene Croce in *The New Yorker* November 3, 1980, "As a choreographer, Smuin is all the places he's been as a dancer; his strength is to have grasped what was 'American' in ballet and what was 'classical' in popular dance. Eclecticism flows naturally in his choreography." San Francisco Ballet's 65th Anniversary book describes Smuin's impact on the Company from the late '70s into the early '80s: "During this period San Francisco Ballet's image was shaped by Smuin, who brought in new audiences attracted by his pop sensibility, his whiz-bang choreography, and extravagant story ballets."

This culture of show-biz and classicism was the perfect Petri dish for nurturing Sohm's acting and dancing. "When I went into the Company," he says, "I was so skinny I couldn't lift my dance bag. Michael decided that I was going to be a partner, so he made me a partner."

Smuin saw a partner-in-the-rough in this fledgling *corps de ballet* boy and mentored him in partnering over the next three years.

"A kind of fortunate thing happened in the late 70s," says Sohm. "The premier danseur of the Company, a very tall, handsome man, had snapped his Achilles. Michael partnered *me* with all of the ballerinas." Smuin grasped this opportunity to groom tall, handsome Sohm for principal partner roles.

The ballerinas also helped me," continues Sohm. "*They* made it work. *They* taught me to partner. *That's* how you learn to partner: you need a ballerina to teach you. A good ballerina will tell you, 'This is what

I need here; this is what I need there—' But you have to have the talent for partnering; not everyone has it. I was lucky that I had it. And I was lucky to be mentored by Michael."

Sohm's whole career evolved by the lucky presence of mentors at crucial points in his development. "To be a dancer, that's what it takes," he says. "You're mentored, hopefully, first by a teacher, then by a choreographer, then by a director, then—" He pauses to view the full canvas of his career. "Isn't that what our whole outcome is based on, the passing on of information? Ultimately that's what this business is: ballet relies on people putting their faith in you and you putting your trust in them."

From 1975 into the early '80s Sohm's star rose as San Francisco Ballet danced in two successful New York engagements at the Brooklyn Academy of Music, on tours of South America, Mexico, the Southwest, Italy, Israel, and Greece, and at the Edinburgh International Festival for its first appearance in western Europe. Often he was invited to be a guest artist with leading ballerinas, most memorably with the daughter of his former mentor Sally Streets, New York City Ballet's Kyra Nichols, as Cavalier to her Sugar Plum Fairy in *The Nutcracker* with the Detroit Symphony.

Sohm became renowned for his interpretation of Romeo in Smuin's *Romeo and Juliet*. With his flair for showmanship, Smuin emphasized the spectacle, violence, and pathos of Shakespeare's drama. Wrote Croce in the November 20, 1978 *New Yorker*, "Michael Smuin's staging—simple, broad, nailing down the meaning of every scene—gets at the reasons for the ballet's popularity and capitalizes on them. Prokofiev's *Romeo* is the mass-audience version of Shakespeare." Smuin saw actor-dancer Sohm as a natural for the part and Sohm fulfilled his expectations. Acting and dancing were not for him separate phases of the role.

San Francisco Ballet was the first West Coast company to be featured on PBS' "Great Performances" Dance in America series, and *Romeo and Juliet* was the first full-length ballet to be presented—by WNET-TV on June 7, 1978. (*Romeo and Juliet* was one of four Smuin ballets to be televised by PBS between 1978 and 1985.) *Dance Magazine*'s review of the June 7 telecast called Sohm's Romeo "artfully realized."

San Francisco Ballet's 65th Anniversary book reports that in "August, 1984, a dispute between Smuin and the board could not be resolved, and Smuin's association with San Francisco Ballet came to an end. A search committee was created to find a replacement, with Lew Christensen remaining on. Christensen, who was in poor health, placed a call to Helgi Tomasson and invited him to come to San Francisco to take a look at the Company. It was Christensen's express wish that Tomasson would replace him as Artistic Director," believing that he was the "right man for the job."

Helgi Tomasson took over the Company on July 1, 1985. In less than a decade, he led San Francisco Ballet to "unprecedented prosperity and new heights of artistic achievement."

Before Smuin left, choreography was done almost exclusively in-house. "I started to see that I was being used the same all the time," says Sohm, "as the silk-sleeve, lyrical, romantic partner type. Everyone saw me the same way, because all of the choreography was being done by Company people. I had been dancing in SFB for almost 10 years, had lived in the San Francisco area my whole life, and felt I needed a change."

Sohm had a friend in San Francisco, Janet Sassoon, who had danced with SFB many years ago and also with the Deutsche Oper Berlin in Germany. She was a good friend of the director, Gert Reinholm.

"She and I had talked many times about Reinholm's company and her experiences there," says Sohm. "One day I approached her and said, 'I'm interested in making a change and I'd like to try dancing in Berlin for a bit.' She called Gert Reinholm, and he offered me a position." Sohm took a leave of absence from SFB and flew to Germany to dance Deutsche Oper Berlin's winter-spring, 1984-85 season.

"Reinholm saw me completely differently," he says. "He saw me as a character dancer. I danced some very interesting repertoire, like the Husband in *The Invitation* [1960, Kenneth MacMillan ballet] who rapes the innocent girl, and The Man in *Las Hermanas* [1963, Kenneth MacMillan] who rapes a girl who then hangs herself. These are dark, dark ballets; it was a great, great experience."

Sohm returned to San Francisco to work with Helgi Tomasson, who had been named Artistic Director while Sohm was in Germany. Sohm reflects back, "When I joined San Francisco Ballet in 1975, it was an old, wonderful Company but did not have that much notoriety. We were all working forward together, building toward something, in those early years with Michael. But companies change. They go in cycles."

Temin wrote in her April 2, 2000, *Boston Sunday Globe* article, "Tomasson, Icelandic-born, quiet, the personification of dignity, was chosen by the board because he was the opposite of his flashy predecessor, Michael Smuin, whose brand of show-biz glitz ... was closer to Andrew Lloyd Weber than to George Balanchine, Tomasson's idol."

Tomasson had a vision for San Francisco Ballet and the ability to realize it. In an October 1999 issue of London's *The Evening Standard* during the Company's first appearance in the British capital, Anne Saeks predicted that SFB could become "America's premier company for depth of talent, good taste, creativity, diversity, and leadership."

Tomasson invited Sohm back into the Company in 1985. Says Sohm, "I told him later in my career, 'Helgi, you did wonderful things for me, because the best time to be in a company is when the director is new and everyone is focused and working together to push the product, to get it forward. I had that under Michael when I was young, and now I'm having it again under you. Who has that *twice* in their life? Most people don't even get it *once*, that kind of opportunity to be in a company that's on the push.'"

During the 1991-92 season, when Sohm was 37, he developed severe pain in what he thought was his back. He had to stop dancing for two weeks, during which time the doctor diagnosed the trauma as left hip damage. "I got myself back and finished the season," says Sohm, "which became *increasingly* hard to do.

"One night I had danced a *pas de deux* of Helgi's, and after the performance I took him aside and said, 'Helgi, do you have a minute?' He said, 'What's up?' I said, 'I just got myself back here, and it didn't feel right. I think the work is outweighing the reward. I've spent so much time in physical therapy, icing, cross-training, and for what? On the stage—it just doesn't make *sense* any more.'"

Sohm danced the 1992-93 season, but in a limited repertoire. "Because of my height and my acting ability, I had a good kind of rep, like Head Wrangler in *Rodeo*, Carabosse in *The Sleeping Beauty*, that kind of thing. At the end of the '91-92 season, David Bintley made a ballet for me called *Job* in which I had not one step."

Reviewer Janice Ross in the September 1992 *Dance Magazine* called Sohm's non-dancing Job "the strongest dramatic role of his seventeen years with SFB." She described the ending: "Sohm stoically confronts Satan and the miseries he brings. Job triumphs, his faith unshaken, and walks slowly upstage in the final moments of the ballet, his body aging visibly with every step."

Tomasson's faith in Sohm was unshaken, in spite of the dancer's increasing physical disability. His exemplary class attendance, whether he was hurting or not, and perceptive management of *Nutcracker* rehearsals impressed Tomasson. When an abrupt change in administrative staff occurred, Tomasson asked Sohm if he could do the rehearsal schedule. Sohm responded, "Well, *yeah*." He says, "I went into the office and figured it out."

Tomasson entrusted this weighty job to Sohm as his first administrative challenge, and Sohm succeeded admirably. His integrity about the seriousness of the task and its importance to Tomasson's artistic vision created schedules that were infinitely better than previous ones.

"It's a nightmare job," says Sohm, "because you can't please anyone; someone is always mad at you. People would say, 'I thought because *you* were doing it now it would be better.' I'd say, 'Well, it *is* better. It might not be better for *you*, but it's better for the Company.'" Tomasson saw Sohm's administrative worth.

Doing schedules for two years brought Sohm into frequent contact with senior management, and Executive Director Joyce Moffatt became interested in him for higher-level administrative positions. "It was clear to me that I needed to make some decisions about what I wanted to do," he says. "Helgi sensed that I wasn't going to do schedules my whole life."

In 1993, Moffatt accepted the position of Managing Director with Houston Ballet and invited Sohm to be her assistant. She thought he had a good mind for administration and a broader understanding of the business side of ballet than do most dancers. "Dancers tend to get a very narrow view of what goes on in a company," he says, "and she saw that I didn't have that narrowness. Helgi had been mentoring me with the schedules, and I had a long talk with him about it. He completely understood where I was coming from and gave his okay for me to go. His approval was important to me, because he was my director.

"Helgi had given me so many opportunities when I was dancing, then opportunities *beyond* the dancing. He was very kind to me when my technique had gone ka-fluey, and he was very respectful and very helpful in my administrative work. I would talk to him often about, 'Helgi, when did you know it was time—?'

Sohm made plans to go to Houston, then—"an interesting thing happened during one of my last shows that was kind of a point of validation."

As Head Wrangler in *Rodeo*, Sohm still had what it took to make the ballet work. In the *Saturday Night Waltz*, the boys and girls form a circle and slowly change partners to the sweet, lyrical music. The grace with which Sohm offered his hand or followed a departing partner with his eyes made the dream-like scene unaccountably moving; he showed the value and beauty of what some would consider an ordinary moment. What he didn't show was the revelation this moment gave him.

"When I looked at that group of people I was dancing with, and at each girl who passed by me, I thought, 'I am old enough to be each one of their fathers. It's time to rethink this.' I remember that *distinctly*."

On stage, in mid-performance, Sohm decided to stop dancing at the end of the season.

"I had made the decision, but that was the moment that validated it," he says. "We all need that moment of validation. You are looking for it for a while, then something happens to confirm your decision. That moment told me, 'This is over, Jim. Let's *go*.'

"Also, Helgi needed my spot. He was building his Company with a lot of young dancers, and that was a contract for him. He needed to fill my spot with someone maybe 22, in their prime."

Sohm knew that because of his background and career in the Company, he had the potential to be a ballet master. "I could have been trained to do that," he says, "because you don't just take your shoes off and you're a ballet master. You have to train, and it takes years to learn to really do it right.

"I had been watching what happened to people who left the organization and the choices they made. I started to think, 'If I take that time to train to be a ballet master, that's an investment. But here I am, a single guy, no one takes care of me, and maybe I want more options in my life than that. If that's what I choose to do, then that's what I can do. I can only work in a ballet company, and that would limit my options.'

"I also thought, 'What if there's a change in the guard here?', because those positions typically are filled from within. Helgi would build me into a ballet master, but if he decided to step down for any reason and a new director came in, that person is going to want his own people. So where do I go? There's not really an open market for a ballet master, because everyone's building their own team.'

"So I thought long and hard and thought, 'Maybe administration is the way for me to go. These are practical, transferable skills, because administration is administration. You can learn it in a ballet company, but I could work for an opera company, a museum, or whatever. Even move into the world of business if I wanted to go that way.' So I made the choice to go into administration."

Sohm prepared to go to Houston to work with Moffatt. He bought some khakis and ironed his shirts thinking, "I can't just show up there in ratty jeans—." As a dancer he'd put on whatever, because he'd change into his "work clothes" as soon as he got to the studio.

He polished his external appearance but inside, his confidence was shattered. "I had developed a limp," he says, "that was very damaging to my self-image. Limping on the street is a horrible thing, because you're not sure if you can make the light. And you're so careful about every little thing. 'Oh no, I can't do this because I might throw my back out.' 'No, sorry, I can't sit through a movie,' 'Oh my *god*, I can't play tennis.' It's just ridiculous."

Sohm saw himself as a limping ex-dancer who did rehearsal schedules for a living. "When I was leaving to go to Houston, I told my friend Glenn [McCoy, who later became SFB Executive Director], I said, 'Glenn, I need to *accomplish* something other than this. This is the next part of my life. I don't want to live my life, when I'm walking down the street, having people say, 'You see that man? That used to be Jim Sohm.'"

In Houston with Moffatt, "I sat at her right arm, and I learned everything. She made me do everything, which was incredible. I'd say, 'What do I do?' and she'd say, 'Well, honey, open the file, read it, and write a contract.' Then she'd go over it with me, what was wrong—it was amazing. She gave me a lot of room to do projects on my own, and I learned a tremendous amount."

Moffatt's mentoring helped him to shape a new self-image and establish a détente between his ballet and administrative careers. She genuinely believed in his capability, backing up her hands-on guidance with comments that bolstered his administrative confidence.

He recalls, "She said, 'You know, Jim, you will be a real asset, because this business is becoming flooded with people who have come out of a university program with a Master's in arts management, and they know nothing about the business. You can sit at a negotiating table or whatever, in a meeting with dancers who are airing their grievances and you can say, 'No, I *know* what it takes to do your job; I know.'"

Sohm remained in Houston for a year-and-a-half as Moffatt's assistant. "Then, for varied reasons, she left," he says, "I just felt it was inappropriate of me to stay if she wasn't there. I wanted to come back to San Francisco, but I didn't have a job anymore. I had had this schedule job, but obviously someone else was doing it now; I had actually trained that person to do it before I left."

Tomasson was in Houston at the time observing Houston Ballet, for the company was going to perform one of his ballets later in the season. Sohm says, "He asked me, 'What are you going to do, Jim?' I said, 'Well, I don't know. There's a job open in Pittsburgh for a company manager, and I'll go to interview for that. But I really don't know.' He said, 'Would you consider coming back to work with me?' meaning, 'Would you consider coming back to San Francisco Ballet?' I said, 'I would *love* that. I would absolutely love that.' He said, 'You're the kind of person I like to have working there.'"

A few months passed and a job was arranged. "I came back to San Francisco in 1995 in a little marketing job with the idea that if something else opened up, they'd put me there. I was here a month and the position of Administrative Manager of the School came open. Helgi called me in and said, 'What do you think about it?' I said, 'Give me a couple days.'"

Sohm talked to a friend about the position saying, "This whole time that I've been trying to figure out what to do—you know how you can see yourself sitting in somewhere?—this was never one of the scenarios, that I would end up in the School. I had never even thought about it. My friend looked at me and said, 'That's why you should take it.' He was right."

Who fills a position is life. How it is filled is art. Judging from the administrative aptitude Sohm had shown with the schedules and in Houston, Tomasson sensed that he would bring the same depth, integrity, and intelligence to the Administrative Manager job that he had brought to his dancing.

"Working in the School was a huge learning curve," says Sohm. "In the first year, I never left the office. I was here till 8:00 at night. My theory was to go through everything and learn what everything was before changing anything. How can you change something you haven't experienced yet? Maybe it doesn't need to be changed. How do you know what you need—until you know what you need? Maybe you need something different from what you thought you needed. It's better to delay a project for a few months and let needs come to the surface, *then* do the project, rather than making a lot of assumptions. You waste a lot of time acting on assumptions."

Gradually Sohm changed everything, from administrative staff to paperwork. "We can do our billing now with the stroke of a key," he says; "we're all computerized. I hired a registrar, and we worked with the old system for a year while planning and developing a new system. We worked with computer services to customize existing software to our requirements."

Sohm was an adept manager, focusing on getting jobs done, taking responsibility for finding creative answers, and encouraging teamwork. J. Donald Walters wrote in *The Art of Leadership* (see RESOURCES) that his hope with the book was to "help people in positions of leadership see their roles as artists whose medium is the dynamics of human cooperation." Sohm mastered the art of leadership.

Walters says that a true leader has deep concern for the welfare of others while he thinks of what is needed to get the job done well, putting his personal wishes, not first, but last. "That was an adjustment for me," says Sohm. "When you're a dancer, you spend your whole day thinking about yourself—my shoes, my performance, my career, my variation, my name cut, my massage appointment, my physical therapy appointment. That's how it should be, because that's what it takes to get it on the stage for my performance, for my curtain call.

"But when you go into administration, suddenly you have to think about everyone else. That's your job: to think about everyone else. You become the last person you think about. I immerse myself in that because I'm that kind of person.

"It took me a few years to even that out and say, 'Now, wait a minute, Jim. You need to take care of *yourself* here a little bit. You can't go at this pace. I know you want to do a good job. Well, you *are* doing a good job, Jim. It's okay. Take a week off.'"

In 1996, two important things happened: fifteen-year-old Gonzalo Garcia entered his second year at the San Francisco Ballet School, and Sohm had hip replacement surgery.

Sohm went to physical therapy while Garcia went to class. As he watched the promising young Spanish student advance—Garcia had been the youngest dancer to win the gold medal at the Prix de Lausanne competition—Sohm's heart ached as much as his recovering body. He profoundly missed dancing himself.

"There are no two ways about it," he says sadly. "I miss it EVERY DAY of my life. The fact that I'm School manager and can't even take ballet classes with this plastic hip is the ultimate irony. I can go to the gym and read on the bicycle or do the Stairmaster, but those are solitary activities. There's something so nice about the group activity of taking class, moving to music with your friends in the room, with a structure that you know is making you in shape and making you feel better. I don't have that now."

He does have opportunities to be on stage with the Company, however, in character roles such as Drosselmeyer in *The Nutcracker*, Prince of Verona in *Romeo and Juliet*, the Duke of Corland in *Giselle*. Tomasson's first dance teachers in his native Iceland were a couple who performed during the summer at the Pantomime Theatre in Copenhagen's Tivoli Gardens. Beginning when he was 15, Tomasson spent four years dancing at the Pantomime Theatre. Wrote Christine Temin in her *Globe* article, "So committed to acting and mime is Tomasson that San Francisco has an unusual job category called 'principal character dancer.'"

Sohm fulfills his need for collaborative creative work primarily through his initiatives for the School, where he and his staff work as a team and make decisions together. His initiatives, which include health and nutrition seminars, instructional social events, and opportunities with top local and touring talent, enrich the students' education beyond their ballet training and make SFBS one of the finest ballet schools in the country.

Writer, university lecturer, and physical therapist Suzanne Martin, MA, MPT conducts the exemplary nutrition seminars that Sohm and his staff established in 1999 for Levels 7 and 8 students (the two top levels). The nutrition series includes two one-hour classes for boys and girls on basic nutrition and exercise physiology, and one one-hour class for girls separately to address their unique concerns. Ms. Martin also conducts a cooking class to instruct the students on simple, affordable, nutritious food preparation techniques.

Parents and guardians of students in Boys III, Levels 5 through 8 Girls, and Levels 7 and 8 Boys are invited to attend a seminar to help them understand the nutritional needs of students participating in a rigorous ballet training program.

On September 18, 2002, Levels 7 and 8 students joined several thousand local high school students at Macy's Passport 2002 Microsoft Teen Night. The social event included a reception, fashion show, prizes, live entertainment, and gift bags all geared to teens, and booths equipped with games that instructed the students about HIV transmission and prevention.

To tap into touring talent that comes to San Francisco, Sohm established a close relationship with Cal Performances, a presenting organization sponsored by the University of California Berkeley. "When Cal Performances presents a big ballet event," he says, "typically they will send comp tickets to the students, but I looked for other ways for the students to benefit. When New York City Ballet was here in the fall of '98, Peter Martins gave us permission to come to a dress rehearsal. I invited Merrill Ashley over to teach a pointe class." In the fall of 2001 Cal Performances invited Levels 7 and 8 students to attend National Ballet of Cuba's *Coppélia* dress rehearsal, and American Ballet Theatre invited the same group to attend a *Giselle* dress rehearsal. Eight students also served as supernumeraries in *Giselle* performances.

"You make a package around these appearances, so they're not just spectator events for the kids," says Sohm. "The students get a point of reference."

He also saw opportunities for students in San Francisco's Words on Dance presentations, which are conversations with leading dance personalities. Words on Dance provided tickets for Levels 7 and 8 to attend dance critic Octavio Roca's presentation in 2001, and for Levels 6, 7, and 8 to attend Violette Verdy's interview of Helgi Tomasson in 2000. Ms. Verdy taught a master class to Levels 7 and 8 Girls.

The San Francisco Opera invited Levels 7 and 8 to SFO's High School Night to see a dress rehearsal of *Falstaff*; the minimal $7.00 charge per student was subsidized by the San Francisco Ballet School. SFO staff members presented an informative one-hour workshop about the opera prior to the event to enhance the students' understanding of the production.

Sohm extended the School's annual audition tour to 15 cities, arranges all the logistics for the tours with travel agents, and accompanies the tour team to each city. His initiatives for the School's Summer Program include the addition of Pilates mat classes, fencing for the boys, and nutrition seminars similar to those of the full-year curriculum.

He also mentors students who come to him with questions about their careers such as, "What company should I go into?," "When do I audition?," "Do you think I should go for a competition?," "What about college?" He says, "I don't counsel for problems. We have professionals deal with those issues."

Bob Nelson writes in his book *1001 Ways to Take Initiative at Work* [see Resources], "Creativity requires initiative. Outstanding customer service requires initiative. High quality requires initiative. Organizations continue to thrive only if initiative continues." The San Francisco Ballet School thrives because Sohm is always looking for ways to take initiative for the benefit of the students. He says, "It's all about helping these kids to succeed."

He continues with deep feeling in his voice, "What you do in a School is a very beautiful and delicate thing. We're not a high school or university but a school of *ballet*, a school of the arts. The people who choose the arts are impassioned, and we give them something to *love* the rest of their lives.

"If they get a job in company, not all of them do, we give them a chance at a career. They get to do what they wanted to do the most in their whole life. How many people have that opportunity? They're going to make friends that they're going to have the rest of their lives. They're going to meet people, travel to places, and be exposed to things they never would have had the chance to experience had they gone, as we as dancers always say, into 'the normal world, the real world.' If you were a bank teller, would you

Jim Sohm as Administrative Manager of the San Francisco Ballet School. (Photograph by David Allen, David Allen Photography.)

have been able to go to a reception with the Crown Prince of Japan in Tokyo? You get *incredible* experiences. And we set them up for that. It's a beautiful, beautiful thing to do.

"The greatest reward is when a student has found a job and is leaving. But that's a very sad reward, personally. Sometimes it makes me cry—not in front of them—because I'm so proud of them. But that's what makes us a success: when the kids get jobs as professional dancers." San Francisco Ballet promoted Gonzalo Garcia from soloist to principal dancer in 2002. Says Sohm, "He is one of our *glowing* successes."

He also considers the training a success when a student who has been in the School for many years decides that a career as a professional dancer is not for him or her and pursues a college education. He says, "Our mission is to provide a quality experience that passes on a strong ethic."

Sohm considers dancers at the other end of their careers—those who are ready to retire from dancing and deciding their next steps in life. He advises, "It's important to keep moving forward while remembering what you've learned from your whole career. Of course there were good times, but remember the bad times, too, because *they* will become the good times, eventually, when you see the value of them.

"It would be very easy for me to say, 'Those last performances were a nightmare. I looked around the room, and I was old enough to be everyone's father.' But I don't choose to look at that as a negative. I chose to take that as a positive. It told me that my dancing days were over and it was time to go.

"I didn't set foot on the stage for a few years after that, I went to Houston, but that letting go was what allowed me to be the Duke now because I'm not stuck in, 'I was Romeo. Why am I doing Prince of Verona?' By letting go, now I can get the value of *that* and the reward of *that*.

"If you've had some kind of traumatic injury and that's it, you've got a whole other set of problems, but if you're processing yourself out gradually, the real danger in that is you lose sight of what you did before. Two years ago you were doing Cavalier in *Nutcracker* and now you're doing Drosselmeyer. If you've gone the distance in this career, like a principal dancer would, towards the end it becomes very difficult, because your whole self-image is threatened. You're adjusting your repertoire, everything is harder, and you start to lose your confidence as a person. I know I did.

"When people ask me now, 'What do you do?' I always introduce myself as Administrative Manager of the San Francisco Ballet School and tell them exactly what I do. I don't reveal the fact that I was a dancer unless it comes up in the conversation. Because I want to be known for *this* now. I *did* that.

"I know dancers who have retired that start out apologetically with, 'Well, I used to be a principal dancer in the company, and now I'm the ballet master.' I find that very interesting, because I feel that being a ballet master is not less than being a principal dancer. You're saying something about yourself. I think that what I'm doing now is not less than being a principal dancer. It's a way to participate in this organization at the level of a principal, but with a different kind of work."

Sohm is learning that he changed people's lives as a dancer as he is changing lives now as an administrator and mentor. "It comes to you later," he says, feeling that people aren't as intimidated about approaching him as they were when he was a famous dancer. "Someone came up to me and said, 'You were my hero.' People will say, 'I started taking ballet because I saw you do *Romeo and Juliet pas de deux* in 1978.' It's interesting, how it comes back to you." His leadership, integrity, and vision as School manager brings equally gratifying returns, personally, for students, and for the Company.

Of his steadfast commitment to San Francisco Ballet since 1975 he says, "I think I'm supposed to be here. A company needs people who have an historical perspective of the organization. I believe that continuity is important."

The Latin phrase *Sapere aude* means "To learn, listen." Sohm listened to his body when his dancing skills were waning, to his mind when reasoning through decisions, and to his mentors throughout his life. Successes resulted at each choice point in his commendable career.

ROBIN HOFFMAN
Stage to Page to Worldwide Web

Time magazine featured a special four-page Business Report in their July 20, 1998, issue entitled "Brushing Up on Your Education." There is Robin Hoffman on page three of the Report, in a stunning color photograph that perfectly illustrates her career transition. Hoffman sits highlighted in the foreground with a portable computer poised on her knee. Members of the Paul Taylor Dance Company—Patrick Corbin, Francie Huber, Andrew Asnes, Rachel Berman, and Caryn Heilman—dance behind her, silhouetted against a royal blue backdrop.

Author Laura Koss-Feder begins her Report, "From the boardroom to the back office, Americans are returning to school for quick, practical courses that allow them to keep up with the competition—and with the rapid changes in technology and business." She continues on page three, "Robin Hoffman, 32, a dance notator who records choreography for the Paul Taylor Dance Company in New York City, knows the importance of timing. The former ballet dancer paid $3,400 in February to take a one-semester course at N.Y.U. in multimedia technique. She needed it to keep up with the competition, since computers are slowly replacing graph paper and pencil for dance notation."

Hoffman's enrollment was driven by more than a desire to "keep up with the competition." It was driven by her passion to preserve dances and her vision of becoming a leader in advancing dance documentation from paper-and-pencil notation to multimedia technology. "Slowly I'm pushing the envelope with the technology," she says, "because I really do *care* about saving dances. Sometimes I wish I didn't care so much."

Six years ago when she was learning traditional Labanotation at the

Dance Notation Bureau (DNB) in New York, the thought of becoming a multimedia whiz didn't even occur to her. When Paul Taylor hired her in 1997 to be his staff Notator, and the Internet boom swept the country in 1998, Hoffman knew where she wanted to be: leading dance notation into the future. "Notation is so important," she says, "and so little promoted. It's a matter of education and a matter of visibility. I tend to be visible whenever I can, to make waves and make news." Her outgoing personality and analytical mind, cultivated by her itinerant childhood and complex career, makes her a natural at notation, technology, and promoting them both.

Her leapfrog life began January 26, 1966, in Kalamazoo, Michigan. Her father worked for Ralston Purina, a growing pet product company that promoted him every two years and transferred him to a new city. The family had already moved twice by the time Hoffman started pre-ballet at age six in Arvada, Colorado.

Pre-ballet included tumbling, creative movement, and the five basic ballet positions, but once Hoffman saw real ballet dancers in the Arvada studio, she much preferred imitating them than doing her pre-ballet exercises. She began serious ballet training in Dunkirk, New York, when she was eight. "I just never wanted anything more, from then, on" she says.

Hoffman has a younger brother and a younger sister, both adept at drawing and painting, but neither one a dancer. "My sister started ballet lessons, then decided it wasn't for her and quit. I'm lucky that I didn't have to compete with my little sister."

The family moved to Flagstaff, Arizona when Hoffman was nine. Mrs. Hoffman took her to watch a ballet class in what was reputed to be one of the city's best studios. She quickly saw, however, that

Robin Hoffman as soloist in Choo San Goh's ballet *Variations Serieuses.* (Photograph by David Talbot, 1989, courtesy of Louisville Ballet.)

neither the teacher nor the training was good. She kept her daughter out of ballet, knowing that Robin would be able to resume in a new city soon.

She didn't have to wait until the family moved, however. Six months later two *very* good teachers moved into Flagstaff, established a studio, and welcomed 10-year-old Robin into their classes. "I got really good basic training, beginning and intermediate, from them," she says." In 1977 the Hoffman's moved to Oklahoma City where Robin insisted on continuing ballet. Mothers are often the ones urging their daughters on, "but I was the one demanding," she says. "A demander, definitely." They moved to Carlisle, Pennsylvania, in the summer of 1978, where her interest in ballet intensified.

Hoffman got her first taste of New York City in the summer of 1980 at age 14, via the School of American Ballet's summer course. "I felt as if I was being given tests at SAB," she recalls, "and was supposed to answer in the right way." Psychologically, she didn't fit.

Moving every two years during her first 14 had made Hoffman a perceptive, analytical thinker. She could assess situations rapidly and pick up concepts quickly both in school and ballet class. She had also learned that there are many different correct ways of teaching and learning, depending upon what is being taught or learned.

"I didn't conform to the SAB 'type,'" she says. "Also, I was also put into a level lower than my level of dancing. The classes were neither mentally nor physically challenging."

Two years after Hoffman returned from SAB, she earned a scholarship to the Joffrey School. She returned to New York in 1982 at 16, lived with roommates, and finished high school by correspondence.

"I liked the training in the Joffrey School," she says. "My teacher, Meredith Baylis, explained steps and talked about muscles, tendons, and bones. There was intellectual discussion of how you do things and artistic discussion of why you do them, which suited me very well. I felt I got amazing training there."

The Joffrey Company had established a second home in Los Angeles in 1982, and in 1984 gave a series of lecture-demonstrations in the Dorothy Chandler Pavilion (then the site of the Oscar presentations). Joffrey II, the second company, was on tour, so six dancers from the school were chosen to do the lecture-demonstrations and apprentice with the Joffrey Company for the Los Angeles season.

"I was one of the first Joffrey dancers to perform there," she says. "It was incredible. After the lecture-demonstrations we stayed on to understudy the main company as Joffrey II would have done if they had been available."

When the company returned to New York, Robert Joffrey promoted Hoffman into the second company. Maria Grandy, a dance Notator who had been one of her teachers in Los Angeles, was Associate Artistic Director of Joffrey II. Grandy's fluency with Labanotation intrigued Hoffman, as did her ability to restage ballets from notated scores. "One day when we were on tour, Maria described dance notation and gave us a little lesson in it. I thought it was interesting—it was so logical."

The following summer, Joffrey hand-picked a few young members of the main company and Joffrey II to participate the annual three-week intensive workshop he conducted in San Antonio, Texas, to hone the technique and artistry of his new dancers. "I took class with Robert Joffrey for three hours every morning," says Hoffman, "and learned so much from him."

Back in New York as a Joffrey II understudy for the main company, Hoffman's interest in dance notation deepened. "I became more and more impressed by the reverence the Joffrey Company gave to anyone from an older generation who came to stage a ballet created in an earlier time. I was fascinated by the reconstruction of 'lost ballets' and works from the Diaghilev era, and by the care and respect with which they were researched, mounted, and presented. I came to really appreciate the dances of another era, and how wonderful they could be when carefully and lovingly restaged from notation."

Notation had appealed to Hoffman's analytical mind, and now she saw how it could preserve the time-honored dances she had come to love. Thoughts of becoming a professional Notator herself stirred in her mind.

After two years of dancing in Joffrey II and understudying with hope in her heart, Hoffman realized that she was never going to get into the main company. "Mr. Joffrey liked me and seemed to like my dancing and talent, he just didn't like my body. I'm a tall girl, 5' 6½", but I look taller. I have broad shoulders and wide hips, and he just couldn't get past that. Too womanly or something. Nice, nice legs and feet, which was a plus, but the wide hips he did not like. That was a horrible thing to deal with at 18. It was pretty distressing."

A Joffrey staff member whom Hoffman had befriended was also on the staff of Milwaukee Ballet. He encouraged her to take Milwaukee's summer session. "I was 19 and needed a job, so I decided to go out there, meet the people, and see what came of it. Sure enough, I was chosen to be a trainee, then an apprentice, then got a *corps* contract. I danced with Milwaukee Ballet for two years, 1985–87."

Hoffman had inherited a talent for graphic arts, like her brother and sister. "I have always loved to draw and paint," she says, "and have always done that. I met an artist named Schomer Lichtner at Milwaukee Ballet, who would often sit in on rehearsals to sketch. He offered to look at my drawings and give me advice.

"He told me about the open life drawing class at the University of Milwaukee, where for a few dollars I could draw from a live model for three hours. There was no teacher—the class was organized to give artists practice at drawing the figure. Schomer was the first person to impress upon me the importance of drawing from life rather than photographs, and not to be afraid to make marks on expensive paper! I began to draw and paint almost every night, in the class and on my own."

Early in 1987, Milwaukee Ballet and Pennsylvania Ballet decided to form a "joint venture" under the leadership Pennsylvania Ballet's artistic director. The two companies were to pool their finances and facilities, and make them available for use by both troupes.

"Of course, that meant that almost all the Milwaukee Ballet people were going to lose their jobs," says Hoffman. "I was promised an apprenticeship with the 'new company,' but I didn't *want* an apprenticeship at that point, I wanted a *corps* contract, and I didn't think Pennsylvania Ballet was the company for me.

"When I asked the directors about a contract, they said, 'Well, we don't know yet. We can't tell you what the pay will be, or if there will be pay, but you'll be dancing with the companies for sure.' I thought, 'Oh yeah, *sure*.' So I started going to auditions.

"One of the places I went was Louisville Ballet. Most of my family lived in Louisville at the time, and I had met the directors when I'd been home visiting my parents. The directors had also been up to Milwaukee to see a performance in which I happened to have a critical role, so I got to meet them there, too."

When Louisville Ballet offered Hoffman a *corps* contract, she stopped auditioning. "I had six good seasons with Louisville Ballet," she says, "and I finally came to terms with my shape and who I was as a dancer. Not that everything was ideal or there weren't problems, but in general, it was the healthiest place that I've ever been."

In Louisville she met promising young choreographer Patricia Olalde, who at 21 had already created works for major regional companies including Louisville Ballet, Cincinnati Ballet, and Houston Ballet. The resonance between the two deepened when Olalde choreographed a ballet on Hoffman, *The Edge*, which became one of Hoffman's favorites.

"She was a friend that I dearly valued," says Hoffman. "I could always talk to her about art and dance, and we did things together, went to museums and performances."

In the summer of 1988 when Hoffman was 22, Patricia Olalde was killed in a plane crash. "I was shocked. I just couldn't believe that she was gone, and that all of her dances were going to be gone. Patricia dying was what really pushed me to learn notation. It was like the match that lit the gasoline."

Hoffman had stayed in touch with Maria Grandy and called her to ask where she could learn to read Labanotation. Fortuitously that summer Grandy was going to be one of the instructors in the Dance Notation Bureau's two-week intensive course, Page to Stage, and invited Hoffman to join the class. "Maria Grandy is probably the strongest mentor of my whole career," she says. "Physically, she's the one who taught me how to jump, and she was definitely a mentor in my notation career. She thought I had a good mind for it."

Hoffman intuitively agreed. "I always had a very easy time reversing combinations, picking up steps, flip-flopping roles, and remembering things exactly," she says. "And I noticed things other people didn't. I'm sure I developed that insight moving around so much from teacher to teacher, because I had to learn the details of how each one wanted me to dance."

She went to New York for Page to Stage and immersed herself in Labanotation for two weeks. She emerged from the course a fluent reader.

"The bug had bit me at that point," she says, "and I decided I wanted to be able to write as well as read. *That* took me four years of study, because as with any language, learning to write eloquently takes a lot longer than learning to read or understand."

Hoffman asked for a leave of absence from Louisville Ballet's 1992-93 season to do a full year of notator training at the Dance Notation Bureau. "It was a great year," she says. "I was 10 years into my dance career at that point and stopped performing to study notation. My training involved a couple of lessons a week and some homework. The rest of the time I went all over town taking different ballet classes—and modern classes, *real* modern dance classes, for the first time. I went to the Graham School, I went to the Limón School, and I took classes regularly with Finis Jhung.

"As a professional ballet dancer I was always expected to pick up many different styles immediately, and now modern, which I hadn't formally studied at all, came pretty easily. If I hadn't become analytical enough to learn quickly, or had not developed the awareness that there are lots of correct ways to do things depending on what's required at the moment, I might have had a harder time."

That year also captured Hoffman on videotape as one of the dancers demonstrating in the 1993 Basic Ballet series. "Finis Jhung asked me to be a demonstrator, and that's how I met Dennis Diamond, owner of the Video D Studios which produced the series. Video D was one of the first dance video businesses around, and I have worked for Dennis on many projects over the years, mostly as a dancer." When Hoffman mastered multimedia technology in the late '90s, working for Video D became her "day job" as one of Diamond's multimedia specialists.

Hoffman returned to Louisville Ballet in 1993 to complete her sixth season, 1987–1992, 1993-1994. "At the end of the '93-'94 season it was time to move on," she says. "I had been in an abusive marriage for three years and finally got a divorce—probably one of the smartest things I've ever done. There was just nothing holding me in Louisville anymore it seemed, and I wanted to go back to New York. My certification score was going before the DNB's Board of Examiners, so I moved to New York and stayed with a friend, figuring I could get a foothold there.

"To become a Notator, you have to complete a certification score," she explains, "which is like a dissertation. You have to notate an entire dance, have it checked, and submit it to the Board of Examiners who decide whether or not your analytical skills are developed enough, your conceptualization of movement is good enough, and you are notating at a professional level. Then they either pass you or they don't."

Hoffman notated Bruce Marks' *Lark Ascending* for her certification score. "I still love that piece," she says, "it was my first 'real' notating experience at Louisville Ballet. The rehearsal atmosphere at Louisville was very positive—which is one reason I danced there longer than anywhere else—and Bruce was completely cooperative.

She explains the notation process. "I took my initial notes sitting in the studio writing as fast as I could while Ballet Master Vincent Falardo set *Lark Ascending* on the dancers. When Bruce came to Louisville Ballet in 1993 to coach *Lark,* I observed and refined my notes as he worked, just like the dancers were refining their performance. Afterwards I put my rough rehearsal notes into the computer, perfecting them, printing and reprinting as I found mistakes or thought of a better way to write something. That computer work took a *long* time.

"Putting a score on the computer *always* takes a long time, probably as much time as writing it up by hand, except that if you want to change anything, which you inevitably do, you don't have to start over. You just have to correct or delete or put in what you want, so it saves a heck of a lot of time and trouble.

"We have a software program on the Macintosh for Labanotation, developed by dancer Lucy Venable and programmer Scott Sutherland at Ohio State University. It's a symbol system sort of like a word processor and a drawing program combined. We can set up the staffs, like a music score, and divide them into measures and beats. We have symbols representing directions, body parts, and measurement symbols already drawn for us, and we just have to make them the right size and put them in the right order.

"To really complete a score and make it workable in the future is a *lot* of work, though," she says, "and there's no doing it half way. Something that is incomplete is useless. To fully notate a 30-minute dance with a number of people in it takes a couple of years.

"There is a lot of difficult partnering in *Lark Ascending,* which was an additional challenge, but it was interesting to break down and figure out. My best notating experiences—*Lark* was one of them—are similar to my best dancing experiences: when I like a piece and like what the choreographer has to say; when there are great parts in it that speak to my imagination. Notating a great role carries a thrill similar to dancing one."

Slowly, bar by bar, Hoffman completed *Lark Ascending* to her satisfaction and submitted her score to the Board of Examiners in May 1994.

Shortly thereafter she met Gerald Arpino at a Dance Notation Bureau function and they struck up a conversation. Arpino had become director of the Joffrey Ballet after Robert Joffrey's death in 1988, and he voiced interest in having more of his and Joffrey's works notated. Hoffman returned that she would like to dance in a company where she could notate one work a year. Arpino invited her to come to company class.

She joined the class on this informal invitation, although company administration questioned her presence there. "He would *never* come to watch the class," she says, "but I didn't give up. I kept pursuing it. I asked him again about dancing and notating for the company.

"On July 7, 1994, the very day the Board of Examiners met and passed me as a Notator, Mr. Arpino took me into the company. After all those years, I joined the main company." Recall her 1984 Joffrey apprenticeship, short stint in Joffrey II, and admiration of Joffrey's reverence for dance preservation. "I became a professional Notator and got into Joffrey Ballet on the same day."

Hoffman remained with Joffrey Ballet until 1995, when financial crises forced the company to relocate in Chicago. "The management stopped paying us," she says, "and stopped our health insurance. One by one they called dancers they wanted in the Chicago company, but by the time they got around to deciding they needed me, I had other jobs. I was delighted to say, 'I'm sorry. I'm not free.' I had been through that bit before with Milwaukee Ballet."

Hoffman was in her prime as a dancer and found work easily. Peter Pucci hired her—with a secure contract—for the *Samson and Delilah* he choreographed for Baltimore Opera. "I got extra work with the Metropolitan Opera Ballet and some other freelance things. I pieced together a living from dancing, restaging a couple of things, a little modeling, and god knows what else, for the next two years."

She began to worry about losing her notation skills. "There's not much work for Notators," she explains. "Ballet companies don't have much money so never have enough to pay Notators, which is perfectly silly. Notating so important but is perceived as being very expensive, because a real person has to make a living doing it. It *is* a big expense, but down the road when you have a fully-notated score, it pays for itself. Few dance companies have the money up-front to ever find that out, however."

She accepted a dance position with Berkshire Ballet during the summer of 1997. "That turned out to be a horrible, horrible, horrible summer job," she says. "It was the *worst* I have *ever* been treated as a dancer. I was in so much pain, because the floors were hard, the schedule was packed, I didn't have a bed to sleep on—I slept on an air mattress. Conditions were really, really bad."

Paul Taylor was the only choreographer in the United States to have his own staff Notator to document his work, and Hoffman heard through the grapevine that his Notator was planning to move to Ireland with her husband. "I knew the job would be coming open," she says, "but I didn't think for a minute that I wanted it." She was still a *dancer.* "Then I got a call from the Dance Notation Bureau basically offering me the job, subject to Paul Taylor's approval. Something in my gut suddenly told me to take it, but I didn't. Instead I said, 'Let me think about it for a week.'

"I kept telling myself that eventually the pain of that summer would go away and that I'd want to dance again. But still I thought, 'I can't pass this up. This is an opportunity to sit next to Paul Taylor every day and notate his new work. I have a feeling that there's something in this for me.'

"A week later I called up the DNB and said, 'I *want* this job.' It was a huge decision, because it meant that notating, not dancing, would now be my full-time job. But this gut thing inside me just said, 'Take it. This is important for you. Do it.' So I did." As Edward Villella says, "Life is all about opportunity and missed opportunity."

In November 1997, Hoffman became Paul Taylor's full-time staff Notator, the fourth he had hired over the past twelve years to document his work in Labanotation. "He has choreographed many, many dances over the years," she says, "and has a huge file drawer full of them. If the percentage of those that are notated and those that aren't is not equal, it's catching up fast."

Hoffman sat in the studio observing and writing while Taylor created. When the company went on tour, she worked for hours at her computer transforming her hand-written notes into a formal score via the notation software. "That's when the *really* hard work began," she says.

But the technology fascinated her. Fresh from seeing Taylor's choreography come to life in the studio, she thought, 'Why not develop a way to see the graphic notation and the dance motion on the same screen?' She wanted to learn how to do that.

New York University was offering a continuing education course called Multimedia Technology: Design and Production. Hoffman received a grant from Career Transitions for Dancers that paid for most of her tuition and took the course in February 1998. "I learned all about multi-media software, programming, digitizing video, animation, and all kinds of handy stuff.

"I prototyped a CD-ROM of *Lark Ascending*, with Bruce Marks' permission. The notation is animated and linked with videotape of the same dance, so you can see and compare both at once. When I showed my CD-ROM to Paul, he *got* it right away. He said, 'Oh, of course, both together! What a timesaver!' He understood the value of it, which was very gratifying.

"When I told him I'd be interested in working on some of his work this way, he said, 'You can certainly have access to any of my videos and films. There are a lot of them, and we already have the notation, of course.'" Hoffman was eager to get her first entire score of a Taylor work in his hands, complete with background material, sets, and costume designs right in the score.

She dedicated herself to her job. "I stopped taking ballet class and went to the gym instead. I'd notate all day in the studio, work at my computer, go to the gym, go out at night, get up late the next morning, notate all day, work at my computer, go to the gym—

"I tried to *not* dance, but it didn't stick. I just didn't feel right, so I started going back to class pretty regularly. I'm still not in any kind of tip-top shape, but I'm in shape enough that I can dance. I *don't* miss being in a company, I *don't* miss the grueling rehearsal schedules, the physical hardship, the stress of being good enough at the right moment so you gain favor or stay in favor. But I *did* miss dancing."

Several budding choreographers took an interested in her, and she began to perform again. In 1999 she danced with a small choreographer's showcase; in 2000 Lynn Parkerson choreographed on her; in 2001 Matthew Brookoff invited her to join his young modern dance company. "Matthew in particular made dances for me that were artistically challenging, fed my creativity, made me grow as an artist.

"Dancing for me is in a much more pleasant spot now," she says. "Whenever I do something it's because I've been invited onto the project, and because the choreographer likes what I can do with his or her work. But I do *not* want to dance full-time anymore. My aspirations are definitely elsewhere."

In addition to performing and rehearsing several times a week, Hoffman began to use spare evening hours for non-dancing jobs to supplement her income. "I felt I should have at least been paid like a soloist as a staff Notator, but I wasn't," she explains, "It wasn't Paul Taylor's fault. The Dance Notation Bureau and the Taylor company each paid a portion of my salary, and the DNB is always struggling for funds."

Eager to continue building her technology skills after her NYU course, to advance toward her ultimate goal of developing dance notation technology, Hoffman started designing websites for friends and relatives and offering people technical support—at $25–$30 an hour. She also worked as art and technical director for the popular Internet dance review *Dance Insider* [http://www.danceinsider.com], which involved designing the review's web pages, helping to choose images, and preparing images for printing on the web.

She worked for the DNB and Paul Taylor as a Notator for two-and-a-half years, November '97 to summer '99, becoming increasingly unhappy with her Taylor-Dance Notation Bureau work. "I was so interested in multimedia dance documentation and just was not getting to do any of it. In fact the Bureau would hire outside people to work on it. I would be included in the planning process, but only to offer my opinions and maybe test the work. It completely tore at me that I wasn't able to do the actual programming.

"A Notator is very much an unsung specialist. You get very little money, very little recognition, and absolutely no respect. For someone used to being on the stage, and at least getting some applause when the show is over, that lack of apperception was very, very hard. I know a Notator who loves her job so much that she doesn't mind working in the background. She is able to get on quite well with the satisfaction she gets from actually doing the work. I just found that I wasn't that way. I need recognition for my work."

The more frustrated Hoffman became with her position at the Dance Notation Bureau, the more she tried to find other things to learn to do, other ways to stretch her mind, other avenues down which she might be able to discover what she really wanted to do.

Between 1999 and 2002 she became "ungodly busy," accepting project after project to appease her thirst for learning. "Things were so crazy in New York with the Internet boom," she says, "there were jobs everywhere. I took a short-term job with a start-up company doing digital editing, and made enough money that I was able to leave the Dance Notation Bureau and the Paul Taylor Company."

The job led to an offer from MTV networks, to work in their Internet division, MTVi. "I was in the marketing group of the e-commerce department, and my job was to design and build Internet banner ads and promotional web pages. It was *SO MUCH FUN*. I had such a good team of people around me. For a while, I worked with senior designer Fred Gurnot, and he was wonderful. He was a real artist and a wonderful teacher.

"For a few months there, I just had an ideal, great, inspiring work situation and really enjoyed it. It was so creative, especially when Fred was there. It was perfect. Unfortunately MTVi had a hiring freeze, and they couldn't hire Fred full-time. They had a round of layoffs, and everything started to fall apart after that. Come October 2001, my entire department and most of my company was laid off."

Hoffman built her own website to showcase the design and production expertise she had gained at MTVi. Her site—http://www.robinandben. com/robin—offers a sampling of animated banners created in Flash and animated GIF [Graphic Image Format].

She had stayed in touch with Dennis Diamond at Video D, whom she had met in 1993 during the Basic Ballet taping. Diamond had become widely known as the number-one videographer in New York, so his studio was busy. He hired Hoffman part-time to do video editing, maintain the Video D web site, and handle other work as needed.

"I love the web," she says, "and love designing for the web. I also like the technical part, the programming part. I love Flash animation and want to learn more about that, and I'm also interested in more high-end animation. I thought about going back to school in an animation department or study—which I may eventually do—but the more I thought about things, and the more I researched things, it seemed like art school was the place to start.

"I have such a large movement background, animation comes quite naturally to me. I need to spend a lot of time drawing, painting, and illustrating to gain security in my technique there. I also need to be able to think conceptually and bring ideas out of myself into a project and onto a page.

"I decided that I want to be a creative lead for a project and not just a worker on the project. You can always learn computer applications. You can always learn the mechanics of things. But you have to develop yourself as an artist to be someone who *has* ideas to be a creative lead. It's like notation: to become a good Notator, you have to be a good dancer first. To become good creative lead, you have to be a good artist first.

Robin Hoffman, multi-talented multimedia specialist and artist. (Photograph by Ellen Crane, 2002.)

"I'd do anything I could to learn to think like Fred," she says of her mentor and role model Fred Gurnot. "Fred was pretty cool."

In June 2001, Hoffman married Ben Zackheim, a writer and cartoonist from a family of artists. Her marriage fueled her decision to go to art school. "Ben's work and marrying into this family sort of made it okay to be a visual artist," she says. "My drawing and painting were a hobby up until now, although I told myself I would like to get serious about it someday. That someday has now arrived. Of course the computer probably will figure heavily in the work I eventually end up doing, but I need to spend a lot of time being an artist now."

Hoffman's two greatest gifts as she goes through transition are knowing what she wants to do and having a keen vision of how to get where she wants to go. "Everything I did seemed to be building in the same direction," she says. First dancing, then notation, then the computer, then the Paul Taylor job, then multimedia and the web, then art school."

Her ultimate goal is to become a creative lead for multimedia dance documentation projects. Her complex career has fed that goal. As New York painter Ellen Phelan says, "Being an artist is about everything you know. Being broadly educated makes you a more complex human being, so that you bring more to the discipline." Hoffman says with a smile, "I've seen it all, and what I haven't seen, I'm pretty *ready* to see."

She still has Paul Taylor scores to finish, but what valuable scores those will be when empowered with her deep artistic knowledge and technological expertise. "When I was sitting in archives of the Dance Notation Bureau notating a score, sometimes it was hard to remember why I was doing it. All I had to do was look up at the walls of original scores—those hundreds of dances that I love—then I'd remember why I was doing it. The ones that I danced in, restaged, or watched being restaged are *especially* dear to me. Each one is like the dance was freeze-dried. I can take it off the shelf, reconstitute it, and put it back on stage anytime. Those dances will continue to live long after the lifetime of the artist. One day my notation will be used to stage Paul Taylor works, I hope."

Hoffman blazed a trail away from pure notation into the brilliant new field of multimedia dance documentation. "I still love notation," she says. "Although I tried to make it work for me as a career, I just could not be happy with it. I'm still involved with the DNB, however, as a member of their advisory committee."

Hoffman sees an exciting future in the many ways technology can be applied to dance, and she is one of the dance-tech pioneers in the area of dance documentation. "That's why I got into all of this," she says. "I want to develop ways to make notation easier and more efficient using the computer, with motion-capture and animation enhancing the notation. I've been very active in pushing multimedia dance documentation forward, and the Dance Notation Bureau has supported me—at least given their moral support."

In the spring of 2002, Hoffman's days were packed managing the *Dance Insider* website, working full time at Video D, applying to art schools, moving into a new apartment with her husband Ben, dancing every day, and performing nights. "Nutso," she says of her busy schedule. "But this is may be the last time I dance, so I am trying to savor it as such."

She reflects on her career transition into multimedia technology. "I feel like I had a good career as a dancer, a really good career. I was never a star, and we all hope to be stars when we grow up, but I did a lot of good stuff. I did solos and principal roles, worked with a lot of great choreographers, and worked with a lot of great dancers. I had wonderful moments on stage that I wouldn't trade for anything.

"This next thing that I'm doing is building upon my experience as a dancer. It's like the next act beyond, and I mean that in a good way. It's *exciting*, and who knows, maybe I'll be a star at this."

CHRISTOPHER NELSON
Reverse Transition

Christopher Nelson is an exception to the theme of this book: he was not a ballet dancer. Broadway and modern dance launched his career. His transition message speaks to everyone, however, dancers and non-dancers alike, so his presence is welcome in a book that reveals how identities change as careers change.

Christopher Nelson was born April 29, 1944, in Duluth, Minnesota, where his dancing began through a neighbor's diet plan. "My mother had a friend whose 10-year-old son was overweight. This kid thought that maybe if he took tap dancing, he'd lose some weight. I don't know how he ever got that idea, but his mother called my mother to ask if I would go along. I was seven years old, and lo and behold, I was a dancer. It was just there: the ability, the talent."

Tap dancing was all a talented child could study in Duluth at the time, but movies and television soon changed that. "People started to see movie musicals, variety shows, and commercial dance," says Nelson, "and began to realize the possibilities." Duluth is now home to Minnesota Ballet, and the University of Minnesota Duluth offers a minor in dance with a wide range of courses including world dance, modern, tap, jazz, ballet, dance history, and dance composition.

"I learned about dance from the movies when I was five years old," he says, "because my mother took me to movies after school three or four times a week. My father was a severe alcoholic and always came home drunk, so going to the movies was a way to get away from him. I loved westerns and movie musicals—they helped me escape from my life and made me dream of being a dancer."

Christopher Nelson in a scene from *Cabaret* (circa 1968) in which Melissa Hart (as Sally Bowles) and Nelson (as German sailor) dance at the engagement party of Fraulein Schneider and Herr Schulz. At left in the background is Gene Rupert (now deceased). (Photograph by Friedman-Abeles, reprinted with permission of Billy Rose Theatre Collection, The New York Public Library for the Performing Arts, Astor, Lenox and Tilden Foundations.)

The Nelsons bought a TV when Christopher was 10. That and tap class brought dancing into his home and his body and intensified his dreams.

He performed in a few operettas in high school, but his dreams became reality during his two years at UM Duluth. "I took two modern dance classes at UMD from Nancy Johnson, but she wanted me to study with men so encouraged me to go to New York to study with Paul Taylor or Merce Cunningham, the two leading male modern dancers. Then a man who designed sets and costumes for Equity summer stock companies started doing some musicals in Duluth. He brought in Equity talent to give them a chance to do roles they wouldn't be able to do in New York. By working in *The King and I* and *Showboat* with these people, I saw that I was a dancer and the opportunities available. I decided to take Nancy Johnson's advice and go to New York."

Nelson's decision was an escape as much as an excitement. His life was miserable with "a falling-down drunk" for a father, and as an only child, he had to bear the brunt of the family's problems. His mother worked hard against formidable odds to raise him, but "there are certain socializing things that I just missed the boat on, *completely*," he says. "I had no idea how to get along with people. None. And I didn't know how to talk to people—I just didn't know how to do it."

The confidence of television dancers, the heady applause of his summer stock stint, the promise of personal growth—all emboldened him to leave home. He imagined winning fame, fortune, and friends when he left Duluth. His father didn't understand. New York was just not in his reality, let alone having a son go there to be a dancer.

"I broke through my fears," says Nelson, "and when I was 20, I packed up and came to New York to build a life for myself. Things were so bad at home, it just felt like something I had to do."

In New York, he started to study jazz and ballet. "I was certainly never going to be a ballet dancer at age 20," he says, "but I studied it for the technique it gave me." He also went to the International Dance Studio, where he met Larry Ross, a friend and eventual roommate whom he would meet again in a completely different context decades later.

As Nelson acculturated himself to the New York dance scene, he considered doing concert work as a modern dancer. He studied with modern dancer Jean Erdman, who had performed with Martha Graham, and danced in her company. He also danced in the company of Graham dancer Sophie Maslow. He gained valuable experience performing in summer stock musicals, and dancing in a European night club revue that toured to Québec and Montréal.

When Nelson returned from Canada in 1966, he enrolled at the Martha Graham studio. His career changed direction there in class one day in 1967.

"Someone came up to me to ask if I wanted to be in a Shakespeare in the Park production at The Public Theater. Gerald Friedman was directing *Titus Andronicus* and wanted to use some dancers." Nelson joined the troupe. "We were basically glorified spear carriers, but Joyce Trisler, who is pretty well known in the modern dance world, choreographed, and Olympia Dukakis and Raul Julia were in the cast. I got a taste of working with some very talented people—and I got my Equity card out of that."

Nelson could now audition for Equity shows on Broadway. He saw a notice for *Half a Sixpence* and, terrified, headed for his first audition with little idea of what to expect. "I thought everybody there was going to be a phenomenal dancer, like soloist in a ballet company or something. That's how out-of-touch I was. When I arrived, I saw that there was a wide variety of talent and sensed that I was at least in the running. They only took two of us from the audition, and I was one of them."

During the run of *Half a Sixpence* at New Jersey's Paper Mill Playhouse, Nelson successfully auditioned for the national company of *Cabaret*. "All of a sudden, I was off on a new tack in my life," he says. "When I finished the national tour after seven months, I came back to New York and went into *Cabaret* on Broadway."

Equity card, successful first audition, national tour, and Broadway—all within four years of arriving in New York. These were huge growth experiences for Nelson, personally and professionally, that made him more self-assured and happy to be a dancer.

His talent took him from *Cabaret* into a production of *Oklahoma* at Lincoln Center that used the original Agnes DeMille choreography, then into *Promises, Promises, Follies*, and *No, No Nanette* which showcased his tap dancing.

"What was totally amazing," he says, "is that once I started working, my parents were really supportive. They came to see me in a few Broadway shows and were very proud, especially my father, who always acknowledged me for what I did in the business. I think that was remarkable, because he was totally lost as an addict and therefore as a human being, yet at the same time he accepted me. It's one of the contradictions of being human—all of the things that we are. He was *so lost*, but he absolutely loved me."

Nelson's dancing brought him some of the money and personal growth he had hoped for, but the pleasure his work gave him at 23 began to pall at 26. "The more shows I did," he says, "the more I saw that as a dancer, you weren't treated very well or respected very much. The *actors*, though, *they* were the ones to get the attention and respect. So I thought, 'If I'm a dancer, that's not who I should be. I should be an actor.'"

"I learned a lot growing up about not accepting myself, so I had this crazy idea that if I were an actor, somehow I would transcend who I was. That was *never* true, much to my surprise."

Harboring the misconception of self-transcendence as an actor, he started studying acting and voice in 1971 at age 26 and stopped seriously studying dance. "I thought that by the time I was 30, I was going to be finished as a dancer," he says, "but then I asked myself, 'What am I going to do? I don't want to teach. I don't want to choreograph. So why am I doing this?' In my mind, I stopped being a dancer."

Nelson had started taking courses at Hunter College in 1969 to explore career options, dancing to pay the bills. "Doing Broadway became like having a job," he says. "I was dancing, but I had given up being a dancer. To be a dancer, you have to keep creating possibilities. I was working, I went from one show to another, but I was a dancer who, in a certain way, wasn't dancing. It was like having a typing job or something."

He rarely went to dance class, focusing instead on acting and voice lessons. He landed three acting parts in *Follies* in addition to dancing in the show: Kevin, a waiter, who had a small scene with Alexis Smith, and understudied the two younger versions of the leading men.

In 1977, he played an actor-singer-dancer role in the national company of *Bubbling Brown Sugar*, then repeated that role for a week on Broadway while the featured actor was out of the show. *Bubbling Brown Sugar* proved to be his last Broadway show. "I just didn't get another until I left the business in 1982," he explains.

In 1979, stymied in his career and losing confidence, Nelson turned to est training. Est, which stands for Erhard Seminar Training, is a large group awareness program launched by Werner Erhard in 1971. Est personal development seminars were enormously popular in the 1970s and designed to teach hundreds of people at a time what keeps them from achieving their full potential and living more satisfied lives.

By 1991, the seminars had evolved into Landmark Education Corporation which offers Landmark Forum training and a variety of other programs emphasizing self-discovery, communication, and productivity.

Est training empowered Nelson to pursue more lucrative markets for his acting and dancing. "I had been trying to do commercials, and all of a sudden I was doing commercials. I signed with a very good commercial agency [Don Buchwald and Associates, see www.buchwald.com], and soon I was doing commercials, industrial shows, and was in a production of *Whose Life is it Anyway?*.

"The acting breakthroughs were *huge* growth experiences. I had been so stopped in my life, and it was a big change for me to be able to do something like that, to see myself in such a different way. I was doing things I hadn't been able to accomplish on my own, and the est training made me realize that I am capable of so much more than I think I am.

"The breakthroughs actually became more than I could deal with, personally. Acting was tremendously competitive, and I was used to being part of a group, and not used to self-promoting. I was learning a lot about myself, and it was hard—then my mother died."

In December 1981, Nelson flew to Duluth. "It was *very* painful," he says. "Not only did I have to cope with my mother's death, I had to deal with my father. I ended up spending over a month out there going through an alcoholism program with him where the family was involved, and I was the only family member. It didn't do him any good, but it did me a lot of good. It became part of the process of learning about myself and forced me to take a hard look at my life.

"I thought about becoming an alcoholism counselor, because I wanted to create something that had some stability and meaning in my life. I thought, 'Maybe I'll get a Ph.D. in clinical psychology and become a therapist,' Finally I realized that that was not appropriate for me, that I was running away from my life. But the program with my father made me see the possibility of doing something that would make a contribution, and motivated me to work on expanding who I was."

When Nelson returned to New York in early 1982, he did one live industrial show, choreographed by Susan Strohman, for the floor tile company Kentile. That show marked the end of his career as an actor-singer-dancer.

At age 37, he enrolled in the Gallatin Division of New York University, now called the Gallatin School of Individualized Study. Gallatin is a small, innovative college within NYU that gives students the opportunity to design their own programs of study tailored to their individual needs and interests (see www.nyu.edu/gallatin/). Nelson had stopped going to Hunter in the early '70s during his acting breakthroughs, but his education was paramount now. He designed a curriculum that concentrated on psychology and graduated from NYU in 1986 with a BA in Liberal Arts.

In 1983, someone told him he had beautiful hands and should be a hand model. "I didn't know what that was," he says, "and the agency couldn't help me with how to do it. I needed ways to earn money, so I started talking to people and learned that you could make a lot per hour for print work, less for TV commercials. One thing led to another, and I built up a good business as a hand model.

"My hands were what they call 'executive' hands, and I did every product imaginable—pharmaceuticals, lots of credit cards, the more upscale products—never tools or things that workmen would use. It was just a way of making money, but it was actually wonderful because it taught me how to create a business.

"I worked through a number of print agencies, but like anything, you still have to be in charge of your career, because nobody's going to do it for you. They'll help you, especially when they see you're successful and I was very successful, but I really took charge, took responsibility, and worked hard at it. I did well and learned a lot.

"Then at one point, I started getting bored with hand modeling, because the work wasn't satisfying. The *money* was satisfying, but then even that started to go." Nelson still hand modeled occasionally for the extra paycheck.

After graduating from NYU, still trying to find a stable, meaningful livelihood that made a contribution to society, he enrolled in self-help courses at Landmark Education. "I had those big breakthroughs in my career from doing the est training," he says, "so I have done many of their courses through the years." EST and the Landmark Forum have their proponents and detractors, but they have been extremely helpful for Nelson. "The workshops and seminars basically expand who you are as a human being," he says, "and help you to consciously create your life the way you truly want it to be."

One of the courses he took was an advanced seminar called the Self-Expression and Leadership Program, which inspired him to return to modern dance class at the New Dance Group. Early in 1993 at age 48, he took the Self-Expression and Leadership seminar a second time. The course built on the knowledge he had gained from the first seminar and led to an epiphany.

The curriculum required each student to create a project that expressed himself or herself fully, developed leadership skills, involved the cooperation and partnership of others, and made a significant difference in a community by opening new possibilities for its people. "The dance community was the obvious one for me," says Nelson, "since I was taking dance classes."

The dialogue and exercises of The Self-Expression and Leadership Programs reversed the diminished perception of himself as a dancer that he had harbored in his mind for the past 25 years. "I saw myself as a dancer," he explains, "but I didn't see myself in the dance world in the same way I had, *that* I had given up in my 20s. I'm so sorry that it was so. I didn't know who I was then—I think one of the problems when you're young is that you're trying to discover who you are. It's so hard to find your identity, and that's where the opportunities are, when you're young. I got into acting when I did *Follies* and I liked some of it and didn't like some of it, but I'm not an actor the way that I'm a dancer. I can act, some, but that's not me in my BONES.

"I was so off the track about myself, it took me until I was 48 to get back in touch with as the fact that I am a dancer, that that's who I came to New York, to be, and that I should be *dancing*. You're *always* a dancer;

it isn't just about being young and having that physicality. You're always a dancer in your soul.

"Understanding that about myself," he says, "coming back to who I am after being so off the track for so long, is one of the things that really drives me in my life now." That revelation drove Nelson in 1993 as he contemplated his community project for the Self-Expression and Leadership course.

The course urged students to change the environment in which they express themselves so it welcomes and furthers their contribution. Nelson thought, "I'll take more classes and that will be enough. Who knows, maybe there'll be something I can do. Maybe there's somebody who does performance art or something who could use an older dancer."

He went to Dance Space, one of Manhattan's largest, most respected dance training centers, which offers classes, workshops, and performance programs to over 2,000 dancers a week from beginners through professionals. Founded in 1984 by Lynn Simonson, Charles Wright, Laurie DeVito, Danny Pepitone, and Michael Geiger, Dance Space was celebrating its fifteenth year when Nelson entered the studio. Immediately he felt at home.

The five founders sought to create a place for "the whole dancer," where students from all over the world could condition their bodies, minds, and spirits in a very natural way. "Dance Space is about the process of dancing," says Nelson, "the internal work, the whole being. It isn't at all about competition or externals. The classes are *long*, some go two-and-a-quarter, two-and-a-half hours. They spend easily an hour-and-fifteen to an hour-and-twenty minutes warming you up, so the technique is very safe. That slow, thorough warm-up is exactly what you need when you're an older dancer.

"Dance Space is so completely supportive of the dance community," he continues, "it's really a treasure to be able to go there and study in an environment like that—a wonderful place to be."

Taking class with a reborn sense of himself as a dancer was profoundly exhilarating. "But then I began to realize that just taking class wasn't going to be enough for me. I saw these younger dancers go off and do auditions, and there was nothing available for *me* that I could see." Suddenly Nelson had an idea for his Self-Expression and Leadership project: to create an organization that offered support and performance opportunities to older dancers. He began to network among his friends.

"I heard that Eileen Casey, a dancer with whom I had actually worked on Broadway a long time ago, was interviewing older dancers with the idea of doing a book or something. We got together and started talking.

"She interested John Mineo in the idea—he's a dancer who had been doing *Chicago* on Broadway for the past few years and has done many,

many Broadway shows during his career—and Zoya Leporska. Zoya embodied the history of dance. She came from Russia, danced in San Francisco Ballet and Ballet Society, Balanchine's precursor to New York City Ballet, then went on to a successful career on Broadway. I brought on Frank Pietri—a multi-talented dancer, teacher, choreographer, and director whose career began in the '50s. So there were five of us altogether."

On April 25, 1994, Nelson, Casey, Mineo, Pietri, and Leporska assembled a group of about 30 dancers ranging from age 40 to 85 in a studio at the New Dance Group. They discussed the possibility of establishing an organization that would address the needs and concerns of older dancers. By the fall of '94 Dancers Over 40 was born, soon to become Dancers Over 40, Inc.

Nelson had realized the community project he conceived in the Self-Expression and Leadership course. "One of the things they talk about at Landmark Education" he says, " is having a context for our lives. Something that isn't just about us personally but is about making a contribution in the world. That's part of what drove me in starting Dancers Over 40: first, my own personal agenda, and there's nothing wrong with that, but at the same time making a contribution. I think we all want to do that, and I think it becomes more important to do that as we get older— or maybe we just become more *aware* of the importance of doing that. If you just have your own personal agenda, life isn't as satisfying."

The value of his contribution to the dance world is evident from Dancers Over 40's mission:

• Provide a community of interest and support for maturing artists.
• Increase the visibility of the age group as valuable, employable performers and advocate for their continuing employment.
• Offer a stimulating environment where artists can continue to grow, create, and share their work with the public as they age.
• Demonstrate to the public and the cultural community that age and changing physicality are resources, not limitations.

Within two years, DO40 had grown from five founding members to over 500 dancers, choreographers, and related artists who had passed their 40th birthdays. Nelson became another Landmark success story. "They had no idea that this project would become a not-for-profit organization with many members."

In the fall of 1996, Dance Theater Workshop produced a week-long performance series by Dancers Over 40 members called "Prime Time." A narrator wove together all varieties of dance, including modern, ethnic, Broadway-style choreography, and the Latin Quarter Showgirls. The series attracted sell-out crowds and won critical acclaim.

Such achievements led DO40 to expand its mission to:

• Examine the societal issues related to age discrimination and create new perspectives on age in our society.
• Educate the public and individual artists about the physical, intellectual, and psychological issues all people face as they mature.
• Address the many concerns surrounding artists' creative development as they grow into middle age and old age.

To fulfill its mission, Dancers Over 40 publishes a monthly newsletter, sponsors social gatherings, offers workshops and panel discussions with choreographers, teachers, dancers, medical professionals, and arts leaders, gives career and emotional support, and provides "a safe, stimulating space in which to fail/test/try new things" [June 1998 Dancers Over 40, Inc. newsletter].

The May 1998 *Dance Magazine* featured an article on page 58 entitled "Bodies of Knowledge" in which Nelson says, "This organization reflects something that's happening in the world. We're becoming aware that it's ridiculous to squander the valuable resource that older people represent, whether you're a dancer or not. It's very exciting to be a part of that."

The same article quotes Jiří Kylián, artistic director of Netherlands Dance Theater, its junior ensemble NDT2, and NDT3, a chamber company of dancers over 40 who all enjoyed illustrious careers in both ballet and contemporary dance. Says Kylián of older dancers, "I think it's foolish if we as choreographers are not able to use this fantastic experience. These dancers have worked with some 40 or 50 choreographers in their lives, so you can imagine the information that is stocked in their bodies. It is a little history of dance that is inside them, and I think that choreographers can easily page this library, find out things that interest them, and produce wonderful things for dancers between 40—and death."

What former United States Poet Laureate Billy Collins said of poetry can be applied to dancers as well: "past, present, and future cannot be kept in separate canisters like salt, sugar, and flour. In poetry's [dance's] traditional mix of constant and variant, there is more variant today than constant." Like good poets, older dancers bring layers of subtlety to a work. Says choreographer Christopher d'Amboise, "They know how to phrase and articulate the choreographer's utterance."

Nelson talked with DO40 members about their experiences in the organization, including Larry Ross, his former roommate, whom he met by surprise at the December 12, 2000 Holiday Party. "Everybody felt that one of the most gratifying things with Dancers Over 40 is when someone has something wonderful happen from an opportunity the group created—they meet someone they haven't seen for decades or something changes in their life. That is *so satisfying* to me, personally," says Nelson, "it makes all the work worthwhile. Most wonderful of all, though, is to create performing possibilities for older dancers and to see them get joy out of that. That is *so* rich."

In the fall of 1994, 44-year-old Kitty Lunn came to a Dancers Over 40 meeting in a wheelchair. Her story filled the group with horror, compassion, and excitement. Horror and compassion, because in 1987 this former ballet dancer and actress was preparing for her first Broadway show when she slipped on a piece of ice, fell down a flight of stairs, and broke her back. She has not been able to use her legs since, despite four spinal surgeries and years of physical therapy.

While rehabilitating, she learned through a friend that Actors Equity Association had a committee for actors with disabilities, and that there were disabled professional actors who were *working*. Inspired, but terrified, she returned to an acting class she had joined before the accident. "Instantly I knew I was doing the right thing," she says. "I learned that my ability had nothing to do with my disability or the fact that I use a wheelchair."

What excited the Dancers Over 40 group that evening were Lunn's goals: she wanted to return to dancing and start her own company. Her determination and passion struck vibrant cords in Nelson. He helped her to create Infinity Dance Theater and became the first company member. In harmony with the mission of Dancers Over 40, Infinity includes both able and disabled dancers with no limit on age. (The current company is comprised of dancers ranging in age from mid–20s to mid–60s).

The Kennedy Center's October 19, 2000, Millennium Stage Performance Archive describes Infinity Dance Theater as "a non-traditional dance company committed to expanding the boundaries of dance and broadening the world's perception of what a dancer is. The company performs works that include a variety of disciplines not traditionally associated with concert dance performances such as on-stage singers, actors, theatrical techniques."

Lunn keeps her company busy with national and international concerts, lecture demonstrations, and inclusive dance classes. Beyond performing, she has developed a curriculum for documenting and teaching her wheelchair dance technique based on the principles of classical ballet, jazz, and modern dance.

Says Nelson, "Kitty is a very focused professional committed to artistic excellence. She isn't sort of playing at this because she happens to be disabled. She demands and gets professional standards from her dancers."

Rave reviews confirm Infinity's artistic merit. In the November 2001 *New York Fax: Performing Arts Magazine of New York*, Teresa Kaye lauded a performance citing the dancers' expressiveness, originality, clean line and technique, and potent dramatic communication. She concluded, "They were wonderful!"

Wrote Phyllis Goldman in the August 31, 2001, *Back Stage: The Performing Arts Weekly*, "Kitty Lunn is a marvelous creature, an exquisite dancer with an upper body of seamless fluidity, a touching emotional tone in her movement quality, and a complete mastery of her instrument. ... Infinity Dance Theater gave three performances at [New York's] Kaye Playhouse in July and everyone who attended was blown away."

Nelson has co-starred with Lunn in *The Last Night in the World* since 1996, when choreographers S.D. Christopher and Roxanna Young created the work on them. Wrote Theresa Kaye of a 2001 performance of the work, "*The Last Night of the World* was a searing, passionate duet between Lunn and Christopher Nelson. Both performed with physical and emotional vigor, like a pair of flaming teenage lovers." When Lunn and Nelson dance together, they transcend themselves and catch fire.

Says Nelson, "Obviously I can't do the physical things that somebody young can do. An inner life, that's what I have to offer. And the ability to push the boundaries of physicality, which I really like to do. Pushing the boundaries is one of the things I love about Infinity."

Nelson's inner spark, his dancer's soul, brought him success on Broadway, and he still radiates that dancer's inner fire on stage. His message is deeper, however, as a mature dancer. "It took me a long time to see that my *real* contribution is as a dancer, and that I could bring the community of older dancers together in some way by dancing.

"Performing with Infinity to me is a political statement, a personal statement, and an artistic statement. I hope that older dancers see that physically, you can do a lot more than you think you can do, you don't have to give up. People think that you're a dancer because of your physicality, and that is *not true*. You're a dancer because of your *being*. *That's* what makes the dancer, and that does not go away. The physicality changes, absolutely—it's certainly changed for me dramatically—but the being, the inner life, does not change. You always have that. *My* inner life becomes richer and richer every year."

Nelson worked days and nights for Dancers Over 40, unpaid, and for Infinity with minimal rehearsal and performance pay. He was forced to get a "B" job to make ends meet. "A B job is a money job; your A job is your art," he explains. "Your B job is just a way of earning money while you do your art."

In 1995 he started to do word processing as a temporary employee at Segal Advisors, a pension plan consulting group. Nelson's temp job and occasional hand modeling provided a living income while he performed and rehearsed with Infinity, served as President of Dancers Over 40, and took class at Dance Space; he worked out at the gym on the days he didn't dance.

He also made time for his personal life, "because you have to have some sort of a balance," he says. "I realize that life is never going to be perfect, but I strive for balance. There's always something that's out of balance for me, though, always. No matter what. I don't do any of it perfectly.

"I think you almost have to be driven to do all of what it takes—the dance classes, rehearsing, weight training, cardiovascular, things to earn a living, things to have a personal life—to create some sort of balance. It's very hard sometimes. Sometimes I want to stop and say, 'Wait a minute. I just can't do all of this. There's gotta be a better way here.'"

To try to find a better way, Nelson sought help from Career Transition For Dancers in 1998. CTFD arranged for him to take the Myers-Briggs Type Indicator, a widely-used personality inventory that assesses preferences, abilities, and interests, and guides people to integrate their self-understanding into their lives.

Nelson learned from the Myers-Briggs that of greatest importance to him are: being involved in work that contributes to his own personal growth and inner development, and contributing to growth and development of others. He didn't quite know what to do with that self-understanding at the time, however, so pressed was he then to earn a living while managing Dancers Over 40 and dancing.

In 1999 he took a proofreading course to supplement his income with editing jobs. He thought, "I won't be able to do hand modeling forever, so I'd better start looking at other possibilities. But I'm older, what else am I going to do?" His quandary was that of many dancers: how to earn a good living at what they love to do. Nelson hoped that Dancers Over 40 might work into something so considered taking arts management courses, but he really didn't have answers to his career dilemma. He thought. "I'll try to do whatever I can day-to-day but it's *hard*, it's so hard to be doing all of these things."

One thing he was clear about. "I know that whatever, I have to keep dancing. I use the most of myself when I'm dancing, it's the place where I feel the most complete. Stopping that is just not an option. If I give up dancing, my life is finished in a way."

Segal had continued to call Nelson back since 1995 whenever they needed extra help. His good work won him a permanent part-time position there in 1999, and in the summer of 2001, Segal invited him to work full time. "I'm not a full-time employee," he says, "because there's reorganization going on in our division. But I'm learning some of the duties of the analysts beyond the secretarial work I do."

Nelson served on DO40's Board of Directors through the spring of 2001, but when he started working full time at Segal he had to relinquish his Board position to someone else. Doing both, plus dancing, was too much.

"The only downside of leaving," he says, "is giving up a feeling of control and turning the organization over to other people. That was hard, but I had to do it. I couldn't keep living my life like that. I started Dancers Over 40 when I should have, and I think I gave it up when I should have. Other people—fresh blood—these need to happen. But occasionally I get pangs of giving up the control."

By the end of end 2001, Nelson had to give up Infinity, too. The ailing American economy brought more and more companies to Segal for help with their pension plans, and Nelson's hours were extended to cover the increased business. At first he liked the feeling of being needed and the extra income. Segal was a good company, and he enjoyed the people there.

"I talked to the head of Segal Advisors and told him that I wanted to be a full-time employee, have more responsibility, learn more. Then all of a sudden my B job was the only thing I was doing. I realized after a while that that was not satisfying enough for me, and that I needed to explore possibilities of a career that expresses *me*." His life had veered way out of balance.

Nelson went to the midtown library on 5th Avenue and 40th Street to explore resources on careers and career transitions. He came home with a number of books and website addresses.

Curious about what his temperament and career penchants were at this point in his development, he re-took the Myers-Briggs Type Indicator online. This time the results hit home. "Taking that again was one of the best $30 I've ever spent," he says. "It showed me that the most important things in my life are personal growth and helping other people"— the same results the MBTI had produced in 1998.

Nelson became excited about building a career for himself that would create new opportunities for people as they age. "A career that will confront stereotypes of age and expand possibilities for people, so they are seen as complete, unique human beings at what*ever* age in life they are," he says. "With all the Baby Boomers coming along, I think there are probably many, many jobs and possibilities for older people that haven't been created yet. I'm not interested in a political agenda or advocating that way, but in working one-to-one and with groups. My plan is to do something that isn't a B job, where I can make good money, and that really expresses *me* in the world—and hopefully to be able to perform again as a dancer."

His career-building project was a microcosm of his career goal, for by applying the knowledge he gained from his own career enrichment to others, he could help them to have richer lives, too. "This project is important to me in both ways," he says. "It's loving the process myself, and wanting to use that to help other people, especially as they age.

Nelson went back to the library to study books on aging. One book that made a big impression on him was Betty Friedan's 1993 *The Fountain of Age*. "What she talks about is exactly what I'm interested in," he says. "She points out that for the first time in history more and more people are living to be over a hundred years old. She says traditionally people have looked at age as the absence of youth, and it *isn't*. Age is an *adventure*, and the more we grow and learn, the more we develop into unique, distinctive human beings."

Anthropologist Ashley Montague asks in his 1981 classic *Growing Young*, "What, precisely, are those traits of childhood that are so valuable and that tend to disappear gradually as human beings grow older? Curiosity is the most important; imaginativeness; playfulness; open-mindedness; willingness to experiment; flexibility; humor; energy; receptiveness to new ideas; honesty; eagerness to learn; and perhaps the most pervasive and the most valuable of all, the need to love.

"How many adults retain these qualities into middle [and old] age?" he asks. "Few." He counters, however, that those who cultivate the qualities of childhood into their adult lives grow young.

"The unique and outstanding trait of human beings is that we remain in an unending state of development," he says. "Growing young into what others call 'old age' is an achievement, a work of art. It takes time to grow young. We begin to see that the goal of life is to die young—as late as possible."

A group of people that is cultivating youth's valuable qualities is the membership of Dancers Over 40.

"One of the things Betty Friedan talks about," says Nelson, "and the psychologist Erik Erikson [1902–1994] in his Eight Stages of Psychological Development, is issue of generativity versus stagnation in middle adulthood." Generativity refers to the adult's ability to care for another person, such as by parenting, or in the broader sense of supporting or passing on to other people in some way unique to you.

"I think that's really exciting, and I think that's one of the things that Dancers Over 40 can offer: supporting younger dancers as well as encouraging older dancers. I went into a Board meeting in October [2002] and talked about how we could use our age, experience, and creativity as a generative force to take the *roof* off of creativity, and also how we could use our generativity to support younger dancers. Hopefully some possible ways of doing that will develop out of that meeting.

Nelson went to a Dancers Over 40 Works in Progress evening in

Christopher Nelson, right, in *After All*, a choreographic work by Robert Koval commissioned for the 1996 Olympic Arts Festival. On the left is Kitty Lunn, founder and artistic director of Infinity Dance Theater; in the center is Robert Koval. (Photograph by Robert Koval, 1996.)

March 2002. "It was absolutely wonderful—an *exciting* two-and-a-half hours of works in progress by mature dancers. That's one of the things that Dancers Over 40 should be doing: supporting members to be creative and live their vision—not just in dancing, but supporting them in *any* form of creativity."

Friedan quotes Carl Kane in *The Fountain of Age* who speaks about reversing the shrinking world of the elderly into an expanding one. He describes septuagenarians at Harvard's Institute for Learning in Retirement. "Suddenly you're with people *alive*, people with imagination, [and] your world is growing again instead of shrinking. You are surprised at how many new things open up, and you make them your own." Dancers Over 40 similarly expands each member's world of imagination and growth.

Nelson's primary creative outlet now is his project to build a career. "Absolutely, that's creative," he says, "but nothing could ever take the place of dancing and performing. *Nothing.* I know that no matter how wonderful the career is, it will never be dancing."

He still takes class at Dance Space once or twice a week, does 40 minutes of stretching before work nearly every day, and goes to the gym for cardio and weight workouts. Regarding his return to performing he says, "I don't have plans at this point. Somebody asked me to perform in a concert they were doing in the Joyce SoHo, but I had to turn them down. I knew I didn't have the time, energy, or focus to do that right now. Not while I'm working *more* than full time at Segal.

"Definitely at some point I want to perform again, though. I'm not sure how it will be, but I can't give that up completely. One of the wonderful things about taking class is that it's a chance for me to get in touch with being an artist. In those two hours and fifteen minutes, when we do a combination I can be that artist and bring something to it I don't get to do in the rest of my life."

His career odyssey and class provide a way to satisfy his creative needs until he can return to the stage. He says, "I actually get real enjoyment and excitement out of the idea of creating the next thing to expand possibilities for people, and I'm willing to be responsible for that. Assuming that responsibility is the hard part, I think. I have to keep forging ahead without answers about what that next thing will be, take a day at a time, and do what I can."

A Sanskrit proverb says, "Where there is right action, there is victory." Nelson is doing the right actions to succeed, actions he recommends to other dancers in transition as well:

- research areas of interest,
- talk to lots of people,
- use the services of Career Transition For Dancers and other support groups,
- set short-term and long-term goals,
- try different things and learn from their outcomes,
- concentrate on the next step you can take to keep moving toward the career you want,
- be kind to yourself, understanding that building a new career is a long, continuous process,
- be willing to "not know" and to "not have answers" while you keep taking the next step in your creative process of growing.

"I used to think it was creative people, artists, who had to keep reinventing themselves," he says, "but now I see that many, many people these days have to keep reinventing themselves. The rules keep changing, the technology keeps changing, and you never know what you're going to be doing next.

"In a certain way, my life has prepared me for this project. I've always asked myself, 'Am I being big enough in the world in my life?' It was the same thing that came up for me when I had those breakthroughs in the est training, when I went to NYU, with Dancers Over 40, and when I performed with Infinity. Looking back, some huge accomplishments for me were when I broke through fears because I thought, 'I'm not being big enough.'"

Nelson achieved the breakthroughs not only because he broke through his fears psychologically, but also because he took responsibility to make them happen. As psychiatrist Thomas Szasz says, "The issue is not whether or not we have found ourselves, but whether or not we have taken responsibility for creating ourselves."

A motivator as powerful for Nelson as his need to be a bigger person is his need to make a contribution. Friedan speaks of the "empowerment of age," and this is exactly what Nelson wants to do with his life: empower himself to be able to empower others as they age.

"What would be wonderful," he says, "is that somewhere down the line Dancers Over 40 would be transformed so it would no longer be necessary to have Dancers Over 40; that there wouldn't be this division or cutoff time because of age, physicality, or whatever. I hope that some day the dance world will accept all dancers as dancers, and I want to be a part making that happen."

The November 1998 Dancers Over 40 newsletter printed at the end of its mission statement: "Dancers Over 40 envisions a time when age discrimination and viewing age as a limitation will be socially and culturally unacceptable in the workplace, in the home, and in the mind of all Americans."

This is how Nelson's story speaks to all of us, as does the life of every dancer in this book: its affirmation of our ability to recreate ourselves as our lives change.

"I think it will take a long time to eliminate barriers of age," he says. "But it's something thing to work for, and it's my goal to help bring that about. I think it's what I'm meant to do in my life."

APPENDIX A:
MAP OF INNOVATION
AND TRANSITION

When a business effects a major innovation in company culture, operations, or products, organizational energy swings between optimism and pessimism as the innovation proceeds, in the pattern of the following graph.

A dancer's emotional energy rises and falls similarly as he or she goes through the process of transition. As the statement on the page opposite the graph reads, "The way innovation [or career transition] is handled is critical in retaining enthusiasm and commitment, and in overcoming the inevitable problems that arise." Dancers need to develop a good support system of friends, colleagues, counselors, or career transition specialists, to rise to levels of optimism and confidence where they can build new identities and lives.

This map reinforces the theme that dancers' career transitions are metaphors for the universal process of transition that individuals, organizations, and cycles of nature undergo repeatedly over time.

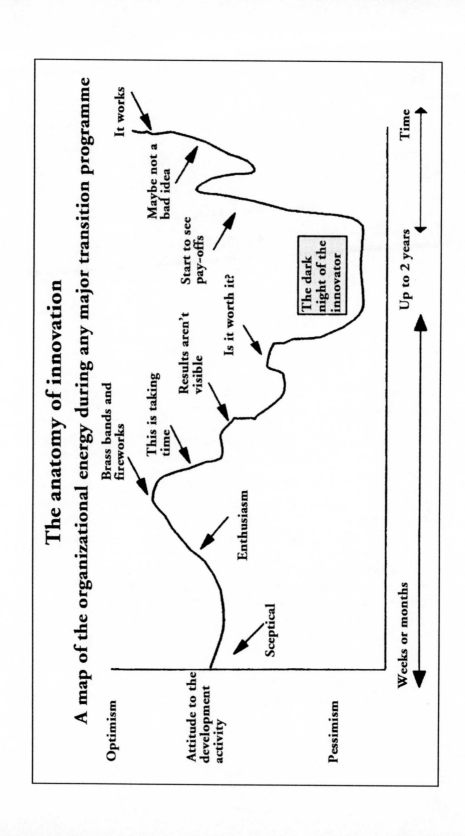

The way innovation is handled
is critical in retaining enthusiasm and commitment,
and in overcoming the inevitable problems that arise.

From the book *Innovation and Creativity*
by Jonne Ceserani and Peter Greatwood of Synectics
Kogan Page Limited, Publishers, 1995
Published in association with AMED
(Association for Management Education and Development)
ISBN 0 7494 1593 2

APPENDIX B:
TRANSITION TIPS

Fear not—dancing is the hardest job in the world. If you can do that, you can tackle anything and succeed!
—Anonymous dancer quoted in Ellen Wallach's article "Life After Performing" in Dance/USA's February 1988 *Update*, page 10.

Each dancer offers helpful advice, inspirational words, or a personal philosophy about career change. The page numbers indicate where each dancers' chapter begins, guiding you to the life story surrounding each quote.

Jean Pierre Bonnefoux
(See story beginning on page 30)
When you're not looking for teachers anymore, you're not looking for learning, or you stop wanting to grow—your life stops. As long as you say, "I'm going to find a teacher, I'm going to find some great people whom I can look up to, great masters—that's what's going to guide my life." As long as you do that, then your life goes on in an exciting way.

Michael Byars
(See story beginning on page 103)
Each dancer's experience with transition will be different, but generally:

1) Get the best academic education you can—before, during, and after your performing career.

2) Prepare financially as early as possible—set aside some of your earnings, advocate for transition benefits in your dance company's contract, help raise money for transition organizations—to allow you time to experiment with other professional pursuits and acquire necessary skills after you stop dancing professionally.

3) Develop friendships and interests outside the theater or ballet school (including through supporters of your dance company)—these may lead to activities and contacts that will play a part in your transition.

4) Most of all, enjoy your dance career, and realize that few people are as fortunate to have a profession that they feel so passionate about. Having felt that passion, you'll know when the right next step comes along. Be patient and confident!

Max Fuqua
(See story beginning on page 138)

It's kind of fun to think of yourself as *anything*. Whatever you want to be. Realize that being a dancer teaches you so many skills, so many practical ways of living life, that you *are* able to do pretty much anything. Actually the choices are overwhelming in a way. So its not really like you've lost your identity and you don't know what you're doing. It's more like, you have so much to choose from, really. And that's great, that's a great position to be in.

Linda Hamilton, Ph.D.
(See story beginning on page 166)

What's important is that you find meaning. The dancer is still inside of you, and it takes time to get on the right path for a lot of people. Probably the utmost difficulty is fear. So I would always recommend that dancers have enough time to prepare financially and psychologically before they leave. The more information you can find out, the better.

Robin Hoffman
(See story beginning on page 202)

Having interests and ambitions beyond your dance career is a big advantage, but it is only part of the transition battle. My best advice, based on my own experience, is to find a good psychotherapist, someone smart who will ask you the right questions to help you work through the inevitable grief of leaving behind something that you love.

If you have hang-ups about seeing a shrink, I recommend suspending for a little while your disbelief that a successful transition is possible. You're dealing with the psychological issue of your identity as a dancer, and the psychological fallout from your physical separation from dancing and performing. This is all *on top of* the huge decision of what you want to be and do next. Any way you slice it, your transition is going to be a big deal, and recognizing it as such, in my opinion, is wise.

McBride, Patricia
(See story beginning on page 30)
Dancers are such intelligent people, and they've had life experience. Trust yourself and the knowledge that you have, because it may surprise you—the knowledge that is there. Don't be afraid of the future because it has many surprises, and just treat the future like you did when you were dancing: you had hopes and dreams and you can still keep those for your second career. Just find what makes you happy and go for it.

Nelson, Christopher
(See story beginning on page 216)
Talk to people—other dancers who have made successful transitions, people at Career Transition For Dancers (see Resources, page 250), people who may be farther along in the transition process than you are.

Be kind to yourself, take it one day at a time; allow your transition to "be in the moment."

Set short-term goals, because long-term goals can be overwhelming. Then take action, one step at a time. This [career transition] is a big stride to take, so concentrate on breaking it down into small steps toward your short-term goals.

Ose, Amanda
(See story beginning on page 153)
You have to be 100 percent passionate about ballet or it's really hard to do it. Once you lose that and you're asking yourself why you do this eight hours a day, and why you're working on perfecting each little step over and over…. Once you start questioning it, your interest is wandering, or if something else is calling you, go explore. It's time to branch out to do other things. Life is to short to devote yourself to something that you don't absolutely love.

Plourde, Jeff
(See story beginning on page 111)
The hardest part of transition is thinking too far in advance. You get so uptight, so immobilized. Just take one year, one day at a time. Ask yourself, "What's the first step I need to take to get where I want to be?"

Raffa, Nancy
(See story beginning on page 85)
Dance is one of the most beautiful art forms, but it is a courageous thing to do to select that as your lifestyle. Lay stepping stones to becom-

ing an excellent person rather than stepping stones to becoming excellent in a specific career.

Sidimus, Joysanne
(See story beginning on page 177)

In the art world, I believe we have a responsibility to each other. If we collaborate—develop creative ideas by coming together—we can help each other and, ultimately, the condition of artists.

Sohm, Jim
(See story beginning on page 186)

Just keep moving forward. Remember your whole career and see the value of the bad as well as the good.

Stevenson, Ben
(See story beginning on page 65)

I think it's important to find a job you really like doing, something that is going to give you some amount of happiness, something you want to do.

Choose very carefully something that flows off of you easily, as opposed to something you've got to really struggle with, or you're going to be struggling to do it for the rest of your life.

Stiefel Inch, Erin
(See story beginning on page 121)

I hope other dancers realize that, no matter how difficult it is to stop dancing, it's not the end of our lives. Hopefully we can continue to enhance the world in other ways. Living in the past really does no good when there is so much more to give to society. Dancers are bright, gifted, and creative, and the possibilities for us to chose new, fulfilling avenues are endless.

Verdy, Violette
(See story beginning on page 19)

Transition is only that. It's a reconversion of the same, wonderful energies and knowledge. And it's a continuity. Do not see it as a break, as an interruption. See it as a lovely transformation, reconversion, redirecting of energies, a refining process, and a tremendous chance to continue to grow up.

Villella, Edward
(See story beginning on page 11)

Make a list of eight or ten things that you like most to do, then work like crazy to build your life around those.

APPENDIX C:
ADAPTIVE SKILLS AND
PERSONAL QUALITIES

Dance literature, and studies by researchers, psychologists, and participants in projects of the Getty Education Institute for the Arts, Harvard Graduate School of Education, Career Transition For Dancers, Dance/USA, and members of the International Organization for the Transition of Professional Dancers, cite positive behavioral, intellectual, and personal characteristics that dancers develop as a result of their rigorous, progressive training. Dancers notably excel in educational and professional pursuits, and become valuable contributors to the workplace, because they possess these characteristics.

The following table lists a number of these, and ten aspects of ballet training that develop them. Understand that there is not a one-to-one relationship between the aspects of training the resulting attributes. It is the confluence of ballet stimuli over time that creates such disciplined, high-achieving individuals.

Included for comparison after the table is the list of adaptive skills prepared by Suzie Jary, Director of Client Services at Career Transition For Dancers. Her list is reprinted here with the kind permission of Ms. Jary and CTFD Executive Director Alex Dubé. **No copies of this list may be made without requesting permission from Career Transition For Dancers in writing.**

Address requests to:

Alexander J. Dubé, Executive Director
and
Suzie Jary, Director of Client Services
Career Transition For Dancers [with an upper case "F"]
165 West 46th Street
Suite 701
New York, NY 10036-2501

TEN ASPECTS OF BALLET TRAINING	CHARACTERISTICS DANCERS DEVELOP AS A RESULT OF THEIR BALLET TRAINING
1. Each class begins with exercises to promote the body's flexibility and coordination. Dancers use these exercises to warm up and prime both the body and mind for the serious work ahead.	• Concentration • Discipline
2. Dancers are taught to analyze each movement in order to understand exactly which muscle, nuance of body English, or aesthetic component they must master to achieve desired results.	• Keen analytical sense
3. Classes and performances engage physical, mental, and emotional faculties. From their very first class, dancers learn to be fully present and in the moment.	• Focus • Energy • Stamina
4. Choreographers use dancers' bodies as their instruments, thus engaging dancers in the choreographic process.	• Creativity
5. Dancers are corrected and recorrected throughout their entire careers, and are constantly reminded of the ideal they are trying to achieve in physical articulation, emotion, and musicality.	• Ability to take direction • Comfort with criticism • Attention to detail

(TEN ASPECTS OF BALLET TRAINING)

(CHARACTERISTICS DANCERS DEVELOP AS A RESULT OF THEIR BALLET TRAINING)

6. The best students are chosen to demonstrate steps in class and lecture-demonstrations, and are given preferential roles when they mature into - performers.

- Motivation to achieve and excel
- Equanimity toward competition and rejection

7. There are no short-cuts to great dancing. Daily, constant work is the only path to success.

- Aptitude for setting and meeting short-term and long-term goals

8. Classes include very fast, complex combinations of steps which students must perform immediately, repeatedly, and ambidextrously with minimal instructions. Professional dancers perform on stage six days a week, and often in ballets they have learned only that morning.

- Self-confidence
- Acute memory
- Ability to think quickly on feet and under pressure.

9. Dancers learn interpersonally but often practice individually to master a step or perfect a role.

- Cooperation
- Independence

10. Ballet is the only art in which professionals take daily class throughout their careers. They do so not only to keep the body in shape, but to *continue to learn* from each class they take.

- Ability to learn by doing
- Motivation to continuously improve and hone skills

DANCERS ARE A VALUABLE RESOURCE IN
THE WORLD OF WORK

Dancers Develop these Adaptive Skills
(Positive Personal Qualities & Characteristics)

Ability to work independently and as part of a team
Disciplined and dedicated
Ability to take direction
Persistent and able to work and respond under pressure
Trained to think on one's feet and adapt to change
Intelligent and hard working
Vitality, energy and physical stamina
Engaging physical presence

Strive for excellence
Keen motivation to improve and hone one's skills
Individuals who are successful in one career are more
    likely to be successful in another
Learning skills of focus and concentration
Listening and observing skills
Strong sense of commitment and responsibility

Prepared by Suzie Jary, M.S.W., C.S.W
Director of Client Services, Career Transition For Dancers,
New York City
Presented at the First International Symposium of the
International Organization for the Transition of Professional Dancers
Lausanne, Switzerland, May 1995

Reprinted with permission of Career Transitions For Dancers
The Caroline & Theodore Newhouse Center for Dancers

APPENDIX D:
CAREER TRANSITION
RESOURCES

Books

Dance Magazine College Guide. Updated annually, is the preeminent source for information on college and university dance programs. Includes more than 600 listings for undergraduate and graduate programs, a search guide to help you find schools that meet your personal criteria, program profiles, expert advice, student perspectives, and much more. See http://www.dancemagazine.com/cgonline/default.lasso.

Darling, Diane. *The Networking Survival Guide: Get the Success You Want by Tapping Into the People You Know.* New York: McGraw-Hill, 2003. Chock-full of effective networking tips and techniques covering the entire networking process, from reasons we network to ethnic and cultural factors. In between Darling offers help with getting started, networking best practices, guidelines for networking conversations, advice for the shy—a wealth of great information.

Hamilton, Linda, Ph.D. *Advice for Dancers: Emotional Counsel and Practical Strategies.* San Francisco: Jossey-Bass, 1998. Includes chapters on self-acceptance, teaching practices, body shape and appearance, relationships, professional aspirations, performing, injury, and career transition.

Hoff, Ron. *"I Can See You Naked."* Kansas City: Andrews and McMeel, 1992. The best guidebook in the business on how to give successful presentations.

King, Norman. *The First Five Minutes: The Successful Opening Moves in Business, Sales, and Interviews.* New York: Prentice-Hall, 1987. A timeless classic that explains how to create a positive image for lifelong career success.

Leach, Barbara, Editor. *The Dancer's Destiny.* Lausanne, Switzerland: International Organization for the Transition of Professional Dancers, 1997. Essays on dance and dancers, dance education, careers in dance, and dancers in transition, based on proceedings of the First International Symposium of the IOTPD, Lausanne, May 1995.

Nelson, Bob. *1001 Ways to Take Initiative at Work.* New York: Workman, 1999. This book is an invaluable guide for self-development both on and off the job. A must for anyone who wants to learn, grow, and raise his or her visibility in an organization; or receive pay raises, bonuses, and advancement for good performance.

Occupational Outlook Handbook. A nationally recognized source of career information, designed to provide valuable assistance to individuals making decisions about their future work lives. Revised every two years, the *Handbook* describes what workers do on the job, working conditions, the training and education needed, earnings, and expected job prospects in a wide range of occupations. See http://www.bls.gov/oco/.

Sidimus, Joysanne. *Exchanges: Life After Dance.* Toronto: Press of Terpsichore Limited, 1988. Comments from ten artistic directors are interspersed among interviews with twenty former dancers.

Tullier, L. Michelle, Ph.D. *Networking for Everyone!: Connecting with People for Career and Job Success.* Indianapolis: Jist Works, Inc., 1998. One of the best networking books on the market. Gives you skills you can use for a lifetime.

Walters, J. Donald. *The Art of Leadership.* New York: MJF Books, 1987. Principles drawn from Walters's successful leadership experience fill this classic book with practical techniques for tapping into your own potential and bringing out the best in others. The book's concise chapters are perfect for people with busy schedules, and the numbered summary lists that conclude each chapter can serve quick refreshers.

Wendleton, Kate. *Building a Great Résumé.* Franklin Lakes, NJ: Career Press, 1999. This and the three works following are all superb job-search books recommended by Career Transitions For Dancers, as is The Five O'Clock Club (see Organizations, New York).

_____. *Interviewing and Salary Negotiation.* Franklin Lakes, NJ: Career Press, 1999.

_____. *Job-Search Secrets.* New York: Five O'Clock Books, 1997.

_____. *Targeting the Job You Want.* New York: Five O'Clock Books, 1997.

Organizations

CANADA

Dancer Transition Resource Centre (DTRC)
66 Gerrard Street East, Suite 202
Toronto, Ontario M5B 1G3
Canada Phone: 416–595–5655
Toll-free: 1–800–667–0851
E-mail: info@dtrc.ca
http://www.dtrc.ca

GREAT BRITAIN

Dancers Career Development
Rooms 222–227 Africa House
64 Kingsway
London WC2B 6BG
England
Phone: + 44 20 7404 6141
E-mail: linda@thedcd.org.uk
http://www.thedcd.org.uk/

NETHERLANDS

Netherlands Dancers Transition Programme
Kunst en Cultuur Pensioen en verzekering
Postbus 85806
2508 CM Den Haag
Phone: + 31 (0) 70 306 56 78
E-mail: pbh@kunst-cultuur.nl

SWITZERLAND

International Organization for the Transition of Professional Dancers
(IOTPD)
Avenue des Bergieres 6
CH - 1004 Lausanne

Switzerland
Phone: + 41 21 643 24 05
http://www.dtol.ndirect.co.uk/iotpd.htm

Swiss Association for the Dancers' Career Transition
9 rue Chabrey
1202 Genève
Switzerland
Phone: + 41 22 734 3244
E-mail: s.jaillet@bluewin.ch

UNITED STATES

American Dance Therapy Association (If you wish to become a dance therapist.)
2000 Century Plaza, Suite 108
10632 Little Patuxent Parkway
Columbia, MD 21044
Phone: 410–997–4040
E-mail: info@adta.org
http://www.adta.org

Career Transition For Dancers (CTFD)

New York office
The Caroline & Theodore Newhouse Center for Dancers
165 West 46th Street, Suite 701
The Actors' Equity Building
New York, NY 10036-2501
Phone: 212–764–0172
E-mail:

California office
5757 Wilshire Boulevard
Suite 902
Los Angeles, CA 90036-3635
Phone: 323–549–6660
E-mail: info-la@careertransition.org
http://www.careertransition.org

Career Transition For Dancers offers scholarships, career counseling, seminars, support groups, a career resource library, a national tool-free hotline [800–581–2833], and financial assistance. Its years of support to dancers and the dance community earned CTFD the 2001 Capezio Dance Award.

Dancers Over 40, Inc. (DO40)
PO Box 237098
New York, NY 10023

or

Scarlett Antonia
PO Box 2211
Peekskill, NY 10566
Phone: 800–799–5831
E-mail: AntoniArts@aol.ccom
http://www.achorusline.org/DO40/Intro.html

Dance/USA
1156 15th Street, NW
Suite 820
Washington, DC 20005-1726
Phone: 202–833–1717
E-mail: asnyder@danceusa.org
http://www.danceusa.org/

Two of Dance/USA's publications include articles on career transition: February 1988 *Update* and Summer 1995 *Journal.*

International Association for Dance Medicine & Science (IADMS)
Department of Dance
1214 University of Oregon
Eugene, OR 97403-1214
Phone: / Fax 541–465–1763
http://www.iadms.org

The Five O'Clock Club (5OCC)
300 East 40th Street, Suite 6L
New York, NY 10016
Phone: 212–286–4500 or 800–538–6645
E-mail: Info@FiveO'ClockClub.com
http://www.fiveoclockclub.com

"America's premier career counseling network." The Five O'Clock Club and its proven job-search methodology have been praised on The Today Show, CNN, NPR, Larry King, CNBC, in *Fortune Magazine, The New York Times, The Chicago Tribune, The Wall Street Journal,* and *The Economist.*

Websites

Answers 4 Dancers
http://www.answers4dancers.com

    Award-winning dancer, choreographer and journalist Grover Dale has created a straight-talking, animated website chock-full of "real questions, real answers, and real possibilities" for dancers and the fitness-involved of all ages and stages of career development or career transition. Menu items include Q&As of the Month, Ask Grover, subscription information for *Dance & Fitness Magazine* which Dale edits, Success Secrets, Agent Alert, Audition Workshop, Auditions4Dancers, Employment Survey, and much, *much* more.

Ballet Alert! Online
http://www.balletalert.com

    Created by Alexandra Tomalonis, editor of *DanceView*, a quarterly review of dance founded in 1979 as *Washington DanceView*, and *Ballet Alert!*, a bimonthly newsletter devoted to classical and neoclassical ballet founded in 1996. An extension of her print publications, Ballet Alert! Online offers information on ballet dancers, companies, and choreographic works; an interactive message board; news, reviews, and more.

Dance Dance Dance
http://www.dancedancedance.com/

    An award-winning dance site dedicated to inspire the art of swing dancing and all forms of couples dancing. Created for dancers by world dance champions Jamie & Gail Ariasother. Includes instructional dance videos in Lindy, Lindy Hop, East Coast Swing, West Coast Swing, Hustle, Latin, Tango, Salsa, and more.

Dance Insider
http://www.danceinsider.com/

    Received a Best of the Net award in the spring of 2001. Includes Flash Reviews of performances, posted the day after the show; Advice for Grown-Up Dancers; Hot Classifieds; Interviews; instructions for ordering back issues of *The Dance Insider* magazine; and more.

Dance Links
http://www.dancer.com/dance-links/

    Dance Links was begun by dance videographer Amy Reusch on behalf of the newsgroup alt.arts.ballet and is now the work of three people: James White, Jon Wright, and Amy Reusch. Information categories include ballet companies, modern/contemporary/other dance companies (e.g., flamenco, tap, jazz, world), dance presenters and performance listings, newsgroups, dance publications, dance frequently-asked questions (FAQs), dance organizations, funding resources, university dance, dance schools, dancers, and dance web indices.

Dance Magazine
http://www.dancemagazine.com/
   Includes feature articles, articles on dance education, resources for young dancers, dance news and reviews, editorial columns, advice for dancers, international performance calendar, information on *Dance Magazine College Guide* and *Dance Annual* (formerly Sterns Directory), classified ads, dance school directory, index to advertisers, and more. June 1993 issue featured the article "Careers in transition: building on experience" by Richard Dean Jenkins (pp. 42–45).

New York Foundation for the Arts
http://www.nyfa.org/
   Offers a huge array of resources, including NYFA's National Directory of Programs for Artists. Search by discipline for grants, residencies, apprenticeships, space, equipment, health and safety, insurance, business, legal resources, jobs, and more.

New York Public Library for the Performing Arts dance catalog
http://www.nypl.org
   This is only a catalog. You must go to the Performing Arts Library at Lincoln Center in New York City to access materials listed in the catalog. Nothing circulates. NYPL Web search procedure: type in the URL **http://www.nypl.org** > click on **Catalogs** under Online Resources > click on **CATNYP** > click on **Dance Collection**. You may search The Dance Catalog by author, author/title, title, subject, journal/periodical title, words in titles, names or subjects, call numbers, and rlin numbers— or click the Help option.

Business

   The following websites provide valuable information on career development, specific industries, and companies. Wendy Alfus Rothman, one of the nation's leading authorities on job-search research, advises on searching these sites:
   "If you want to use the Internet as an effective tool to advance your job search, it is vital to have a goal and remain focused: 'I'm going online for forty-five minutes, and this is what I need to know when I get off.'"
   (Quoted from her excellent article, "Getting the Most Out of the Internet: Research Pointers from Wendy Alfus Rothman," in Vol. 13, No. 7,

September 1999 issue of *The Five O'Clock News*, a publication of The Five O'Clock Club; see Organizations, above).

Directory on the Alta Vista home page
http://www.altavista.com
Click on Directory, then on Business for dozens of categories, listings, and links to jobs, services, company information, and much more.

Hoovers
http://www.Hoovers.com
Searching on news articles and companies from the home page yields a wealth of business information and links. Some links require a fee, but there is a lot you don't have to pay for.

Vault
http://www.vault.com
Gives inside information on major industries and thousands of companies. Includes industry guides, career guides, company profiles, a free newsletter, and much more. Heavy on advertising, but definitely worth exploring. Membership is required, but free. Simply go to the site, click on Join, fill out the short membership form, and your user name and password will be e-mailed to you.

Wet Feet!
http://www.Wetfeet.com
Although geared toward college students, this site offers career development, industry, and company information for job-seekers of all ages and levels.

APPENDIX E:
DANCER MASTER LIST

Bonnefoux, Jean-Pierre
CAREER LOCATIONS: Paris Opera, New York City Ballet
CURRENT LOCATION: Charlotte NC, North Carolina Dance Theatre,
Artistic Director and Executive Director

Byars, Michael
CAREER LOCATION: New York City Ballet
CURRENT LOCATION: New York City, Coudert Brothers LLP
Attorney

Fuqua, Max
CAREER LOCATIONS: San Francisco Ballet, Zurich Ballet
CURRENT LOCATION: Dallas TX, Plaza Health Foods, Inc., owner;
International Health Food Entrepreneur

Hamilton, Linda
CAREER LOCATION: New York City Ballet
CURRENT LOCATION: New York City, Clinical Psychologist, Fordham
University Associate Professor

Hoffman, Robin
CAREER LOCATIONS: Milwaukee Ballet, Louisville Ballet
CURRENT LOCATION: New York City, Art School Student, Labonotator,
Multimedia Specialist

McBride, Patricia
CAREER LOCATION: New York City Ballet
CURRENT LOCATION: Charlotte NC, North Carolina Dance Theatre,
Associate Artistic Director, Master Teacher

Nelson, Christopher
CAREER LOCATION: Broadway dancer
CURRENT LOCATION: New York City, Co-founder of Dancers Over 40, Inc.; Segal Advisors

Ose, Amanda
CAREER LOCATION: Pacific Northwest Ballet School
CURRENT LOCATION: Stanford CA, Stanford University, Student

Plourde, Jeff
CAREER LOCATIONS: Fort Worth Ballet, Ballet Dallas, Ballet West, Ballet Austin, Southern Ballet Theatre
CURRENT LOCATION: Litchfield CT, Deloitte & Touche, Senior Accountant

Raffa, Nancy
CAREER LOCATIONS: American Ballet Theatre, Miami City Ballet
CURRENT LOCATION: Miami FL, Miami City Ballet School, Teacher, Performance Outreach Coordinator

Sidimus, Joysanne
CAREER LOCATIONS: New York City Ballet, London Festival Ballet, National Ballet of Canada
CURRENT LOCATION: Toronto, Canada, Dancer Transition Resource Center, Founder, Executive Director

Sohm, Jim
CAREER LOCATION: San Francisco Ballet
CURRENT LOCATION: San Francisco CA, San Francisco Ballet School, Administrative Manager

Stevenson, Ben
CAREER LOCATION: London Festival Ballet
CURRENT LOCATIONS: Houston TX, Houston Ballet, Artistic Director Emeritus, Fort Worth Dallas Ballet, Artistic Director

Stiefel Inch, Erin
CAREER LOCATION: Zurich Ballet
CURRENT LOCATION: Selinsgrove PA, Student, mother

Verdy, Violette
CAREER LOCATIONS: Paris Opera Ballet, New York City Ballet, International Guest Star
CURRENT LOCATION: Bloomington IN, Indiana University Ballet Department, Tenured Professor of Dance

Villella, Edward
CAREER LOCATION: New York City Ballet
CURRENT LOCATION: Miami FL, Miami City Ballet, Artistic Director

INDEX